Tamburlaine, as pictured by André Thevet in *Les Vrais Pourtraits et Vies des Hommes Illustres* (Paris, 1584).

MARLOWE'S

Tamburlaine

A Study in
Renaissance Moral Philosophy

ROY W. BATTENHOUSE

Vanderbilt   *Nashville*

MANUFACTURED IN THE UNITED STATES OF AMERICA
SECOND PRINTING, WITH CORRECTIONS, 1964

To my father

Henry Martin Battenhouse

PREFACE

T HE following pages offer a reinterpretation of the play which is generally reckoned the earliest great tragedy in English. Recent events have lent this play an ironic modernity, for its hero is a fourteenth-century Dictator and world conqueror. The ways of *realpolitik* are boldly displayed in *Tamburlaine*. It is of more than academic interest, therefore, to inquire how an earlier century regarded such a phenomenon. Did men then view Tamburlaine, as certain modern interpreters have done, in a Carlylean spirit of hero worship? How did the dramatist himself analyze his hero? Did Marlowe have a perspective for evaluating the span of history which he exhibited—or is his play mere haphazard chronicle? If we are intent enough, perhaps we can discriminate a meaning insinuated in the drama. This is the delicate task of interpretation. Since Marlowe's art and learning have long commanded applause, no apology need be made for attempting thus to enlarge our appreciation of his mind and method.

But since the interpretation of *Tamburlaine* has important interconnections with various subsidiary interests, a few words of further prefatory comment are in order.

I was first aroused to the study of *Tamburlaine* during the course of a seminar with Professor Tucker Brooke in 1936 while I was mulling over the vexing problem of Marlowe's "atheism." It seemed to me that, actually, Marlowe's religious views are much more baffling than is generally acknowledged. Modern biographers, fascinated by what is most colorful, incline readily to equate Marlowe's views with the scandalous testimonies given of him by Kyd and Baines. But the blasphemous and desperate character pictured in those testimonies is most difficult to reconcile with the Marlowe who studied Divinity at Cambridge and whose loyalty to her Majesty's religion was vouched for by the Privy Council. When we hunt for a solution to the puzzle, the best clue we have is that Marlowe seems to have been a government spy. But if this was so, have we not two suppositions to choose between? Either we can interpret the Kyd-Baines evidence as meaning that Marlowe had been deceiving the Queen and other good Protestants such as Walsingham, Chapman, Sidney, and Raleigh, with whom he seems to have been in familiar company; or, alternatively, we can conjecture that Marlowe had attempted, as part of his espionage work, to incite into some compromising act or statement the people who were suspected of sedition—men such as Kyd, Baines, and Cholmley. If we accept the latter inference—which seems to me quite as likely as the former—then the famous testimonies to the dramatist's "atheism" have value mainly as records of Marlowe's zeal in laying down camouflage. In that case what are we to suppose that the Marlowe behind the camouflage really thought?

This was the question that fascinated me, and I saw no hope of answering it by arguing simply from the evidence of existing biographical documents. If Marlowe was in real life an actor in the disguise drama of Elizabethan underground politics, then words reported of him—particularly when reported by witnesses themselves politically suspect—must be regarded as dramatic talk. Furthermore, is it reasonable to suppose that, in the chief characters of his plays, Marlowe dared to reveal his own political and religious beliefs? Perhaps we have no hope at all of resolving the riddle. And yet Marlowe's plays do bear the unmistakable stamp of earnest and passionate thought. Provided we read them cautiously and comprehensively, can they not give us some evidence for judging Marlowe's mind? If *Tamburlaine*—the play which exhibits most centrally the theme of "atheism"—is examined systematically for its meaning and method, may we not gather from it certain insights which can contribute to Marlowe biography? In any case, the effort at a proper interpretation of *Tamburlaine* has value in its own right; and whether it has value incidentally to the clarification of Marlowe biography I must leave to the biographers to decide. The present study is rather strictly limited to the area of literary criticism, with only a hope that its conclusions may have significant bearing on problems of Marlowe biography.

A second subsidiary concern has been my interest in Elizabethan thought. Quite irrespective of Marlowe problems, this area seems to me to need more discriminating investigation than scholars have yet given it. It is particularly desirable to have a map of the intellectual situation before one attempts Marlowe criticism. Marlowe spent six years at the university, and his mind was extraordinarily active. To trace his art to its sources is not easy: he has not, like Coleridge, left letters and notebooks and marginalia to guide us; and we have therefore to pick our way much more slowly than on the road to Xanadu. Source clues which I have been able to spot in *Tamburlaine,* when added to those noted by critics before me, lead in many directions. A particular passage in *Tamburlaine* may have several apparent "sources"—an episode in some history, an echo of Spenser, a touch of Seneca, a reflection of Machiavelli, perhaps even a distant analogy to something in Scripture. Tracing episodes of the play to these buried origins is a manifold task.

However, Marlowe has one great advantage over Coleridge as a subject for study. Much more than Coleridge, Marlowe writes within a tradition. Whereas Coleridge's use of imagery and situation is guided often by the mere associationism of dream psychology, Marlowe's use of artistic materials everywhere reflects the impress of a well-formulated point of view. Marlowe's work has articulated design. We exclaim with Goethe, "How greatly it is all planned!" The parts and the whole of *Tamburlaine* have pattern demonstrably in accord with certain formulas and chief doctrines of Elizabethan Humanism. No piece of the play is haphazard. Even more important therefore than the tracking down of "sources" atomically considered is the delineating of that organic body of Elizabethan thought which gives to particular source materials their meaning and interpretation. Comprehensive criticism must interpret art in terms of an intellectual milieu. This is the method which Mr. Panofsky has used so fruitfully in his recent *Studies in Iconology,* where he has surveyed the doctrines of Neoplatonism in order to put in proper framework the interpretation of Michelangelo's art. Since Marlowe's art in its attention to colossal figures bears obvious likeness to Michelangelo's, a somewhat similar approach cannot, certainly, be inappropriate.

Fully half my study, therefore, is devoted to intellectual background. First I have attempted to give perspective on the Elizabethan meaning of "religion," "atheism," and "Machiavellianism." Then I have boldly undertaken to chart Renaissance theory regarding Fortune, Fate, Providence, God, history, sin, and the function of poetry—matters which directly concern the interpretation of tragedy. Here I have drawn extensively from the views of Nashe, Greville, Sidney, Mornay, and La Primaudaye. I have sketched separately the thinking of Raleigh and of Chapman, whose minds, deserving of more detailed critical treatment in their own right, are important here because presumably closest to Marlowe. In the six background chapters my aim has been to provide a discriminating map of the great tradition of Reformation Humanism, somewhere within which Marlowe seems to me to belong.

The precise character of Reformation Humanism is, I venture to say, too little understood by literary critics. By some it is considered to be practically identical with the medieval background; by others, as somehow equivalent to modern Liberalism, Progress, and Enlightenment. Actually it is neither. One acquainted with the Humanism of St. Thomas will find himself ill at ease in the Humanism of Chapman, and so will the follower of John Dewey. Reformation Humanism is thought which stands free of the Church but has a mortal horror at the thought of breaking free of God. It is both anti-Scholastic and deeply religious. Centrally, it is the tradition of Elizabethan Protestantism; but the Catholic Erasmus, the Anglican Nashe, and the Puritan Milton all belong to it. Shakespeare, I must add, does not seem to me to belong to it. Perhaps in a deeper sense than we have yet appreciated, Shakespeare is "the rival poet."

My final concern, however, has been, not *Tamburlaine's* background, but the drama itself. To the general reader I should like to say that my discussion of the play is fairly complete without the background chapters. Those chapters, intended to be sufficiently detailed to satisfy the historian of ideas, can be skipped by anyone whose interests are more purely literary. I should regret greatly if any genuine enthusiast for *Tamburlaine* became bogged down by my prefaces and preambles.

I am happy to acknowledge, especially, the personal interest and encouragement shown by Professor Tucker Brooke, who has twice read my chapters—once in the version which I submitted, under his direction, to Yale University in 1938 in partial fulfilment of requirements for the Doctor of Philosophy degree. To Professor Roland H. Bainton of Yale University, and to Professor George Thomas of Princeton University, I am indebted for the critical reading of several of the background chapters. Lately, the entire manuscript has been very carefully read by Professor William R. Parker of Ohio State University, whose friendly disagreements and apt suggestions have aided me considerably in the final touches of revision. Professors Walter Clyde Curry and Claude Lee Finney of Vanderbilt University, and my father, Professor Henry M. Battenhouse of Albion College, have also commented helpfully on the manuscript. The editors of *P. M. L. A.* have kindly granted me permission to incorporate sections from my article "Tamburlaine, Scourge of God," appearing in the June, 1941, issue.

Quotations made in this study have not been modernized in spelling; but abbreviations have been expanded. All quotations from *Tamburlaine* and all references to the text of the play are to the edition of C. F. Tucker Brooke in *The Works of Christopher Marlowe* (Oxford, 1910).

It is appropriate that this book should be bound in the colors which its hero loved—blood red, black, and gold.

Vanderbilt University   Roy W. Battenhouse
September, 1941

PREFACE
TO A SECOND PRINTING

A reissue of this book, out of print now for some years, is appropriate to the Marlowe and Shakespeare Quatercentenary. For in recent studies of both of these dramatists, the relevance of their inherited religious and moral tradition has become increasingly evident. In Marlowe's case, this development is requiring a radical readjustment in critical perspective. Some twenty years ago when my book first appeared, its contention that *Tamburlaine* should be read as a two-part play consistently shaped within a broadly Christian moral tradition struck many readers, predictably, as a thesis scarcely credible. Today, however, the once popular vogue for identifying Marlowe's rebel heroes with a supposed unorthodoxy in the playwright's own creed is under heavy attack and plainly on the wane. In retrospect, Leo Kirschbaum characterized it recently as "probably, the worst and most continuous example of the so-called personal heresy in English literature" (*The Plays of Christopher Marlowe;* Cleveland: World Publishing Co., 1962).

Contributing to the emergence of a changed critical climate have been the numerous essays that, from many sides lately, have demonstrated the traditional morality and Protestant theology implicit in the artistic shaping of the tragedy of *Dr. Faustus.* But besides these, M. M. Mahood's *Poetry and Humanism* (London: Jonathan Cape, 1950) and Douglas Cole's *Suffering and Evil in the Plays of Christopher Marlowe* (Princeton: Princeton University Press, 1962) have argued forcibly that, in all of Marlowe's heroes, we are being shown the disastrous effects of human fancy and misdirected desire. Miss Mahood sees Marlowe, from *Tamburlaine* onwards, as tracing with objective sympathy but with a critical eye the downfall of men's aspiring claims to self-sufficiency in disregard of divine grace. Mr. Cole, similarly, finds in Marlowe a predominantly Christian conception of tragic fate, in which human self-will is revealed as the principal cause of catastrophe. "In Marlovian tragedy it is not the universe that is destructive, but the heart of man." With such readings I am in general agreement and am gratified to find in them corroboration for my own pioneering view.

On the single play *Tamburlaine,* the present study offers fuller interpretation of the play's many details, along with a systematic review of the drama's symbolism in relation to Marlowe's sources. The most significant part of my study I believe to be its middle chapters, especially the last two of the "Background" chapters and the first two in the "Anatomy" of the play itself. In these the reader will find, in nucleus, the basic esthetic and moral considerations which, in my judgment, shaped Marlowe's writing. In particular, I would urge attention to the full meaning of the "Scourge of God" concept. Its pattern-implications are crucial, I think, to any total reading of *Tamburlaine.* They may be crucial also for Shakespeare's *Hamlet,* as Fredson Bowers has recently indicated ("Hamlet as Minister and Scourge," *PMLA,* 1955), although Bowers perhaps stops too soon in his application of the pattern. The concept of a "Scourge of God," as formulated long ago by Isaiah, and as applied to Tamburlaine by Fortescue and Whetstone, Marlowe's principal sources for his story, involves the paradox of heroic virtues tragically hell-bent; of human aspirations magnificently splendid but cruelly tyrannous; and of an idealism misdirected into unwitting parody of divine majesty. The wicked actions exhibited in a Scourge's career remain governed by a higher providence, which both uses and overrules man's ambition and folly. In such paradox a basic paradigm is provided for a Christian reader or writer of tragedy. Other paradigms, both classical and Christian, can be assimilated to it.

The complete text of my original study is here reprinted without alteration, except for the correction of typographical errors and of a few inapt sentences.

R. W. B.

London, Canada
February 1964

TABLE OF CONTENTS
꙰ ꙰

INTRODUCTION

THE PROBLEM OF INTERPRETATION

李 李

A LTHOUGH *Tamburlaine* was published anonymously, Marlowe's authorship of the drama has not in recent times been doubted. Critics have easily recognized that the spirit which animates the hero Tamburlaine, however variously we may describe it, is fundamentally the same spirit which lives in Faustus, Barabas, the Guise, and Mortimer. These tragic heroes are all of the same stock. The interpretation of any one of them has a significance beyond itself for the interpretation of the others. *Tamburlaine,* acknowledged as Marlowe's earliest play, can therefore be regarded as a pattern-example in which to discover the dramatist's general tragic method and theory.

But most modern interpretations of *Tamburlaine* have been markedly romantic. Critics such as F. S. Boas, John Ingram, Miss Una Ellis-Fermor, and lately Philip Henderson have proceeded virtually to abolish the distinction between drama and autobiography. Professor Boas may be said to have stated the point of view of these critics when in 1896 he wrote of Tamburlaine:

> But this figure is not, in the strictest sense, dramatic, with an objective and independent individuality; it is rather, in its highest aspects, an embodiment of its author, and of the epoch which he supremely represents.[1]

And for their notions of that epoch, unfortunately, these critics seem to follow Symonds' glowingly pagan interpreta-

---

[1] F. S. Boas, *Shakspere and His Predecessors,* p. 41. Compare John H. Ingram, *Christopher Marlowe and His Associates* (London, 1904), p. 108; U. M. Ellis-Fermor, *Christopher Marlowe* (London, 1927), pp. 24 ff.; Philip Henderson, *And Morning in His Eyes: a book about Christopher Marlowe* (London, 1937), p. 233; and the latest book by Boas, *Christopher Marlowe* (Oxford, 1940), pp. 76, 98.

tion. What Symonds saw as the "spirit" of the Renaissance—
men magnificently intoxicated with dreams of the infini-
tudes of power and beauty—this our modern critics see in
Tamburlaine and credit to Marlowe.[2]

On the basis of this method which turns drama into a lyric
confessional, both Miss Ellis-Fermor and Mr. Ingram are
able to emphasize Marlowe's youth and his modernism.
Ingram believes that

> In *Tamburlaine,* written with the freshness of youth, Marlowe not
> only gives untrammelled scope to his imagination, but bares his very
> inmost mind to our gaze, dauntlessly proclaiming by the mouths of
> his dramatic puppets his own opinions.[3]

He refers to Marlowe as

> This youthful ringleader of free thought, this champion of revolu-
> tionary upheaval against countless centuries of mental oppression. . .[4]

Miss Ellis-Fermor, similarly, feels that "to understand Marlowe demands eternal youth"; and midway in her discussion
of *Tamburlaine* she remarks on Marlowe's modernism:

> Marlowe appears to have been on the verge of formulating the idea
> that the spirit and "desire" of man are neither more nor less than
> God in man. . . . The conception . . . is startlingly modern, or at
> least startlingly independent of his contemporaries.[5]

There is a very practical difficulty in the romantic interpretation of *Tamburlaine* as presented to us by Ingram

---

[2] Ellis-Fermor, p. 35, even considers Bajazet's reference to the "superstitious bells" of the Christians as a remark expressive of "the feelings of Marlowe
and not of the Turk." This interpretation of Bajazet's speech originated with
Ingram, p. 111, and is repeated by Henderson, p. 248, who sees in the line Marlowe's "hatred of the Church." See, however, Samuel Chew, *The Crescent and
the Rose* (New York, 1937), p. 197. Chew quotes the line as indication simply
that Marlowe was familiar with the sixteenth-century accounts of European visi-
tors to the Orient, in which a matter almost invariably remarked was the
Moslem prohibition of the use of bells.

[3] *Marlowe,* pp. 110-11.

[4] *Ibid.,* p. 112.

[5] *Marlowe,* pp. 24, 33.

and Miss Ellis-Fermor. The interpretation breaks down exactly at the most critical point in the drama. When Miss Ellis-Fermor comments on Tamburlaine's famous soliloquy in *Tamb*. I. II. vi., she declares her belief that the words represent Marlowe's own view and are "perhaps the noblest lines he ever wrote," but

> And then, at the end, comes the inevitable bathos. To what is all this aspiration and hunger directed? "To the ripest fruit of all," Marlowe tries to persuade us:
>
> > "The sweet fruition of an earthly crowne."
>
> We do not believe him. We go back to the lines about the "faculties" of the soul and take care never again to link them with what follows. For the fact is that Marlowe has suddenly—it may be all unconsciously—broken faith with his idea.[6]

Miss Ellis-Fermor's dilemma has resulted because, unable to stomach the frank worldliness of Tamburlaine's ambition, she nevertheless wants to admire Tamburlaine's "spirit." Her criticism fails, because she has studied the drama not with the eyes of an Elizabethan, to whom ambition was sin, but with the eyes of a modern, to whom upward striving is noble.

A further weakness in the romantic method of interpreting *Tamburlaine* is that it finds it impossible to maintain a meaning for Part II of the drama. Romantic critics, disappointed in the hero of Part II and displeased by the introduction of what they term "irrelevant episodes," easily conclude that in Part II the story degenerates, that its drama is

---

[6] *Ibid.*, p. 29. Miss Ellis-Fermor is evidently merely enlarging upon what Mr. Ingram had said, p. 106: "The bathos of the conclusion, even if it be correctly transcribed and if no connecting lines have fallen out, cannot destroy the grandeur of the poet's aspirations, 'still climbing after knowledge infinite.' "

inferior to Part I.[7] They tell us that Tamburlaine is "a character who can, by the very nature of his being, only have a first part"![8] Admittedly, the patent insanity of Part II is not pretty. Romantic criticism is compelled therefore to postulate a sharp dichotomy between the two parts of the drama:

> The Tamburlaine of the second part of the play is marked by a savageness, an ever-increasing extravagance, a lack at once of inspiration and of balance. The freakish, unrestrained moods of these later scenes have little or nothing to do with the glittering figure of the earlier part who spoke of the destiny of man:

> > . . . To weare our selves and never rest. . . .
> > . . . Still climbing after knowledge infinite.

> . . . He is unbalanced now rather than superhuman. . . . Dignity and clearness of vision all go down before this increasing insanity. . . . The Tamburlaine of the second part has sunk down to an oriental despot, savage, extravagant, half insane; a type of which history furnishes enough records and for the creating of which none of the high instincts are needed that produced the original idea of the play.[9]

Alternative to the interpretation of *Tamburlaine* set forth by the romantic critics, there is a second view offered us in recent interpretations by Mario Praz, T. M. Pearce, and

---

[7] See Ellis-Fermor, pp. 45-6; and her edition of *Tamburlaine the Great* (London, 1930), Introduction, p. 41. The view that Part II is degenerate drama is typically stated by the reviewer of Miss Ellis-Fermor's *Tamburlaine* in the *London Times Litt. Supp.* for Oct. 2, 1930, p. 777. The reviewer speaks reprovingly of the "second part: that straining, unequal, blundering second part, with its plunges into the ridiculous . . . its shocking rant, its woful degradation of the whole idea of Tamburlaine, its almost childish inconsequence about religion." Ingram, p. 120, thinks that the second part "furnishes proof of the haste and want of revision with which it was given to the world." However, it would seem that Elizabethan audiences did not regard Part II as inferior drama; for the most famous contemporary allusions to the play are to Part II. The chariot episode called forth Pistol's parody of it in *Henry* IV, II. iii. iv.; and the blasphemy scene stirred Greene to his denunciation of "atheist Tamburlan."

[8] Ellis-Fermor, *Marlowe*, p. 39.

[9] *Ibid.*, pp. 39-40.

John Bakeless.[10] These commentators attempt to be ruthlessly historical. They analyze rather than sympathize with Marlowe's hero; and, being emancipated from romantic adoration of Tamburlaine, they direct their efforts toward emphasizing the amazing iconoclasm of Tamburlaine's (and Marlowe's) mind.[11] Correctly, it seems to me, they place Tamburlaine in the same ethical class with Marlowe's other titans. Mr. Pearce and Mr. Bakeless find no need to contrast the two parts of the *Tamburlaine* drama, for they recognize in its hero from the beginning not youthful romanticism, but Machiavellianism.[12]

Regarding Tamburlaine's desire for "The sweet fruition of an earthly crown," Pearce has a view directly contrary to Miss Ellis-Fermor's. The words, he says, appropriately punctuate the worldliness of the whole speech—a speech which is based, as Tamburlaine's whole character is based, on the Machiavellian doctrine of a universe in which there is ceaseless warfare, climbing and aspiring without rest, and survival only for those who embody physical and mental force.[13] As for Tamburlaine's love for beauty, Pearce finds it a "nonmoral beauty" of fame, of valour, and of victory.[14] He declares, further, that Tamburlaine's attitude in the famous blasphemy scene (*Tamb.* II. v. i.) is "aggressively rational, man assertive," a bold deviation from the accepted religious dogma of Marlowe's time.[15] Pearce assumes that the blasphemy is the dramatist's uttering of his own views.

[10] Praz, "Christopher Marlowe," *English Studies,* XIII (1931), 209-23; Pearce, "Christopher Marlowe—Figure of the Renaissance," *University of New Mexico Bulletin,* Vol. I, No. 1, March, 1934; Bakeless, *Christopher Marlowe* (New York, 1937), pp. 5, 183.

[11] Bakeless believes that "Marlowe never suspects that his magnificent chieftain is at bottom a bloody and useless brute" (p. 11). But must Bakeless make Marlowe stupid to make himself wise?

[12] Bakeless, p. 5; Pearce, p. 13.

[13] Pearce, p. 15.

[14] *Ibid.,* p. 40.

[15] *Ibid.,* p. 19.

Professor Praz and (in his recent views) Professor Boas seem committed to this same general line of interpretation. Praz concludes of Marlowe that

The serious portions of his table-talk, together with passages in his plays justify the appropriation to Marlowe of the epithet of "atheist," as it was then understood, i.e., a scoffer at institutional religion, a free-thinker. . . .[16]

And Boas reaches the same conclusion, arguing however almost entirely on the basis of manuscript documents relative to Marlowe, rather than on the plays. Apparently reversing his earlier notion of Marlowe's relation to his epoch, Boas now believes that Marlowe was "a propagandist, provocative, explosive force," "a rationalist intelligence beating its destructive way through all that was held in reverential awe by its contemporaries and ruthlessly desecrating the Holy of Holies." [17]

Pearce and Bakeless have avoided one of the pitfalls of the romantic interpretation by tracing the Tamburlaine "spirit" to an historic source in Machiavellianism. They are thus able to take a detached—rather than an admiring—view of Tamburlaine's ethical philosophy. But at the same time, with less judiciousness, they still retain the chief pitfall of the romantic interpretation, the identification of Tamburlaine and Marlowe. Bakeless, fresh from his biographical investigations which have led him to characterize Marlowe as the terror of London's Shoreditch police, makes no apology for using even the most violent of Tamburlaine's speeches as representing Marlowe's thought.[18] Pearce, who likewise draws freely from Marlowe's dramatic works to picture Marlowe's own mind, comes armed also with the lingo of

---

[16] "Marlowe," p. 209.
[17] *Marlowe and His Circle* (Oxford, 1929), pp. 76-78. Boas repeats this view in *Mod. Lang. Rev.*, XXVI (1931), 461.

modern psychology and builds a portrait of Marlowe compounded of three phrases: 1) iconoclastic rationalism; 2) abnormal nervous energy; and 3) unco-ordinated personality factors. Pearce suggests that a pressure upon the pituitary gland, or excessive thyroid tendencies can explain these elements in Marlowe and in Marlowe's Titans. It is a line of investigation which has been developed also by Professor Praz. Handling modern psychology with somewhat more finesse, Praz gives Marlowe the epithet of "molochiste" [19] and adds:

Marlowe was himself a dispersive character, morbid and tormented by the *soif de l'impossible,* briefly, what modern psychologists call a schizoid personality.

Marlowe's thirst for impossible things is a sublimation of his own attitude to sex. If one wants to call things by a smart classical name, one may say that Marlowe laboured under a Ganymede complex.[20]

These critics, by laying aside sentimentalism, have given us a consistent Tamburlaine and a consistent Marlowe. But in identifying Marlowe with his titan they not only employ dramatic material unjustly, but they identify Marlowe with doctrines which were anathema to every Elizabethan moralist.

Somewhere midway between the two schools of interpretation which I have distinguished there lies a conservative third approach, which we may call the common sense view of Tamburlaine. It is represented, for example, in a brief critical note by Professor Grierson. Objecting to Miss

---

[18] Bakeless, p. 8, e.g., declares that Marlowe's own hot-blooded temper can be deduced from a hundred passages in the plays—for example, from the lines

What daring God torments my body thus
And seeks to conquer mighty Tamburlaine?

See also Bakeless, pp. 109-10.
[19] "Marlowe," p. 213.
[20] *Ibid.,* pp. 220, 218.

Ellis-Fermor's treatment of Marlowe's plays, Grierson reminds us that a play is the work of three factors: the author, the subject, and the audience.

> In expressing his own thought and feeling Marlowe has to remember both what his audience will expect or tolerate and the tradition embodied in the story he is dramatising.[21]

Another critic, Willard Thorp, takes a similar attitude. He says:

> We know that Marlowe was in his private life anything but a conformist in matters of religion and morality. It was not possible for him, however, to write himself into his plays and expect the audience to receive and applaud heroes whose ethics were subversive and revolutionary. His problem as an artist became one of accommodation, of finding some means by which he could speak out his *Schmerz* without alienating his audience.[22]

It must be said to the credit of these critics that they use common sense in refraining from attributing unqualifiedly to Marlowe's own view the ethical reflections voiced by Tamburlaine. This is a step in the direction of allowing for dramatic objectivity. However, even with these critics the romantic hypothesis still lingers. Thorp supposes that basically Marlowe's titans speak the dramatist's own sentiments; and Grierson considers Marlowe as "in desire and dream, at any rate" sympathetic with the spirit of Tamburlaine.[23]

---

[21] H. J. C. Grierson, *Cross Currents in English Literature of the XVIIth Century* (London, 1929), p. 120.

[22] "The Ethical Problem in Marlowe's Tamburlaine," *Journal of English and Germanic Philology*, XXIX (1930), 386. See also Thorp's *The Triumph of Realism in Elizabethan Drama, 1558-1612* (Princeton, 1928), pp. 40-49.

[23] Grierson throws out a further remark which the reader wishes might have been developed—the remark that Marlowe was in as close *imaginative* sympathy with his aspiring heroes as on one side of his nature Milton is with the dauntless Satan. Does Grierson mean that Marlowe was no more—and just as much—a free-thinker as Milton? And does Grierson mean to imply that Marlowe is to be identified *ethically* with Tamburlaine no more—and no less—than Milton is to

A fourth type of critical view is represented in the work of Miss Leslie Spence,[24] who alone has pushed the claim for Marlowe's artistic detachment to the point where it includes also ethical detachment. By examining Marlowe's use of historical sources in Perondinus and Mexia for *Tamburlaine* I, Miss Spence argues that the Marlowe-Tamburlaine identification is "purely fanciful," and that Tamburlaine stands in no closer relationship to the mind and spirit of Marlowe than do Julius Caesar and Coriolanus to Shakespeare.[25] "This identification of Tamburlaine and Marlowe," Miss Spence forthrightly declares, "has the effect of magnifying the personality of the dramatist but at the same time it minimizes his ability as a playwright by assuming that he lacked the detachment necessary to create an objective character."

Miss Spence is particularly insistent to argue the point that Tamburlaine's mental qualities of infinite ambition, lust of dominion, and unbounded belief in his own victorious destiny are elements in the sixteenth-century historical accounts of Tamburlaine, not products of Marlowe's invention. Miss Spence's attempt thus to put the whole portrait of Tamburlaine (including moral as well as factual elements) on an objective basis provides, I think, a very timely check, particularly to those critics of the biographical school who, having just come from reading the Kyd and Baines

---

be so identified with Satan? Such a view would seem to me quite tenable. But surely it need not mean that *either* author has as his conscious intention anything other than a *mimesis* of representatively satanic desires and actions. These require to be vicariously imagined in order to depict them; and for this artistic purpose a Marlowe or a Milton may make use of dreams which, at some time or other, he has experienced as temptations. But he does not thereby give his moral approval to these dreams.

[24] "Tamburlaine and Marlowe," *P. M. L. A.*, XLII (1927), 604-22; and "The Influence of Marlowe's Sources on Tamburlaine I," *Modern Philology*, XXIV (1926), 181-99.

[25] "Tamburlaine and Marlowe," p. 604.

libels, find it so very easy to ascribe Tamburlaine's fervors to a ground in Marlowe's private morals. Miss Spence tries to make it possible for us to regard Marlowe as a mature playwright turning history into good actable drama.

However, it seems to me that Miss Spence's attempt falls somewhat short of success. Her study has proved that Marlowe did not distort history. That fact is very important to recognize; solid criticism must begin with the knowledge that Marlowe did not invent the elements of ambition, lust, and self-confidence that characterize Tamburlaine. But going beyond Miss Spence's work, we must evaluate carefully those points at which Marlowe does amplify, emphasize, reconstruct, and (in Part II) conflate,[26] add, and invent. Perondinus and Mexia are not enough to explain, for example, the prominence which Marlowe gives to the concept of the "scourge of God." Or again, they cannot tell us why Marlowe made such conspicuous use of crowns.[27] And finally—and most importantly—these historical sources provide us with no source whatever for the three most promi-

---

[26] This is well illustrated in the subplot of Part II centering in the story of Sigismund and Orcanes. See Ellis-Fermor's *Tamburlaine*, pp. 41 ff. Miss Ellis-Fermor comments that this subplot "all seems a little irrelevant both to the action and to the general sentiment of the play." I regard it, however, as an excellent illustration of Marlowe's desire to introduce morality elements into the historical fabric of his drama.

[27] In her second article, "The Influence of Marlowe's Sources," pp. 195-96, Miss Spence lists Marlowe's use of crowns in Part I of the drama and admits that these episodes, and four other episodes in Part I, have no source in the histories. Whether such additions are, as Miss Spence judges, "trappings rather than meaningful episodes" is a matter for careful consideration. Miss M. C. Bradbrook in *Themes and Conventions of Elizabethan Tragedy* (Cambridge, 1935), pp. 144-45, discusses Tamburlaine's use of crowns and also the non-historical episode in which he discards his shepherd's clothes; she regards these matters as symbolic, significant, and indicative of the formalized character of Marlowe's method. In fact, Miss Bradbrook's emphasis is just the reverse of Miss Spence's. Miss Bradbrook minimizes the historical elements in the play, advances the view that the actual battles are not of great importance, and emphasizes instead the pageantry nature of the action. I would propose that the two points of view are polar and must be harmonized in a comprehensive study. *Tamburlaine* has, certainly, both a solid foundation in history and also the decorative symbolism of extrahistorical action. The two factors combine in the totality of Marlowe's dramatic design.

nent episodes of Part II: the chariot scene, the blasphemy scene, and Tamburlaine's impassionate fury which burns Larissa at the death of Zenocrate. A fourth important episode, the treachery and defeat of Sigismund, involves historical events which happened a generation after the death of the historical Tamburlaine, and most of which did not happen to Sigismund at all, but to Vladislaus.

Extrahistorical factors such as these throughout the two parts of the drama are too important to be ignored. They can be understood, I suggest, only by the discussion of Marlowe's moral philosophy, by a search for the intellectual basis of what Miss Elizabeth Holmes has termed the "metaphysical quality of [Marlowe's] imagination." [28] This metaphysical quality consists not merely in the symbolical way in which Tamburlaine marshals hosts of place names, and numberless numbers—facts to which Miss Holmes has called our attention. The metaphysical quality of the drama, as I shall hope to demonstrate in the course of this study, involves also the metaphysics of the play's design, its ethical problems, its plot.

Most noteworthy is the fact that Marlowe's additions to historical material serve commonly to emphasize the morality aspects of his drama. We must remember that the European histories which brought Marlowe the story of Tamburlaine were already moralized accounts.[29] For example: Tamburlaine's lowly origin, contrary to fact, was emphasized in order to make his ambition and his success on Fortune's wheel the more prominent; Bajazet's fall was made the occasion for a warning against trusting in riches and pomp; and Tamburlaine was made to call himself the "wrath of God." None of these morality suggestions has Marlowe allowed to go unused; instead, he has amplified

---

[28] *Aspects of Elizabethan Imagery* (Oxford, 1929), p. 20.
[29] See Spence, "Tamburlaine and Marlowe," p. 610.

them. Then, in Part II particularly, he has added morality elements of his own gathering or invention.

In both parts of the drama the artistic use of morality themes has served to formalize the action. Extrahistorical episodes enhance the story's import as parable. I believe it can be shown that *Tamburlaine* carries out the effort, made by the author of the earlier *Cambises,* to combine the morality play with the dramatization of history.

To substantiate this thesis, I propose to investigate comprehensively the sources for the drama. Such an investigation will involve a study of the morality literature of Marlowe's day. Marlowe plainly had, in addition to the historical sources on the basis of which Miss Spence has tried to explain the drama, certain sources of another sort—sources in the literature of moral philosophy, literary theory, and religious apologetics. Our study must include close attention to the Elizabethan meaning of such concepts as fortune, fate, scourge of God, providence, religion, atheism, tragedy, and sin; for it is about these concepts that the moral texture of *Tamburlaine* is woven. We have every right to assume that in matters of moral philosophy Marlowe was saturated with the best learning of his day. We know that he studied for six years at Cambridge, and, if we may judge from the terms of the Archbishop Parker scholarship which he held during that time, he was reading in such studies as would have prepared him to take Holy Orders.

We can say with some assurance that the morality element in the Tamburlaine story was what interested thinking men of Marlowe's day. Sir Richard Barckley introduces Tamburlaine's story to illustrate the vanity of men who hunt after worldly glory.[30] He emphasizes Tamburlaine's low birth and high success, then points the moral:

---

[30] *The Felicitie of Man, or His Summum Bonum,* p. 264 (ed. of 1631). First edition in 1598.

And what cause is there to glory in honourable estate . . . when the basest men in the world have attained to the highest dignities?

And when we turn to La Primaudaye, whose account of Tamburlaine is generally listed as one of Marlowe's sources, we find that he has set Tamburlaine's story with other examples in chapters treating "Of Pride" and "Of Fortune." [31] But the most significant evidence is in Fortescue's *The Forest*, a translation from Pedro Mexia which is generally considered Marlowe's principal source. This work leaves no doubt of the moral light in which the conqueror's history is to be regarded. The clue appears in a passage which has gone unobserved by editors of *Tamburlaine,* who have noticed only the account of Tamburlaine given in Part II, Chapter 14. However, Tamburlaine appears as chief example in Part I, Chapter 15, which is entitled "How for the most parte, cruel kings and bloody tirants are the Ministers of God, and how notwithstanding they continually end in state most wretched and extreme misery." Here the author makes the important point that certain wicked idolaters are called "Ministers of God" because (in accord with the prophecy of Isaiah) they "enter at the gates of Babylon" as "executors of Gods iust wil for the punishment of *Babilon*." Cyrus, Darius, Totila—and Tamburlaine—are examples. Having quoted Tamburlaine's boast to be the "Ire of God," Fortescue's history continues:

whence we haue in fine to conclude, that all such cruel and incarnate deuils, are instruments wherwith God chastiseth sin, as also with the same approoueth and tryeth the iust, and yet they not withstanding are not hence held for iust, ne shall they escape the heuy iudgement of God. For necessary is it that example of it happen, but wo be vnto him by whom it happeneth.[32]

---

[31] *The French Academie* (London, 1586), trans. T[homas] B[owes], chaps. 23 and 44.
[32] *The Forest,* p. 35ʳ (second edition, 1576).

Such words ought to make it possible for us to understand the "Scourge of God" title which Marlowe's hero bears.

Furthermore, if we give a little attention to the reception of Marlowe's play by his contemporaries, we discover that they commonly cite the drama for its morality. John Davies of Hereford plainly viewed Tamburlaine as a mighty warning against ambition. In *Wittes Pilgrimage* we read:

> When with my Minds right Eye, I do behold
> (From nought, made nothing lesse) great Tamburlaine
> (Like Phaeton) drawne, encoacht in burnisht Gold,
> Raigning his drawers, who of late did Raigne:
> I deem me blessed in the Womb to be
> Borne as I am, among indiffrent Things.
> No King, nor Slaue, but of the meane degree
> Where I see Kings made Slaues, and Slaues made Kings.
> When, if my Meannesse but one Thought conceaue
> That minds but mounting, this Thought keeps it downe:
> And so I liue, in case, to take or giue,
> For loue, or Meed, or Scepter but a Crowne:
>   Yet Flowres of Crownes, for Poesies expence,
>   Poets might take, and giue no recompense.[33]

Sir Walter Raleigh,[34] and Sir William Alexander[35]—both probably thinking of Marlowe's play—refer to the episode of Bajazet's fall as noteworthy illustration of how God's Providence works. Thomas Dekker calls Tamburlaine "Fortune's best minion" and then pictures the fate of all Fortune's minions in the cry of a king who has suddenly been deposed by his goddess:

> Thou painted strumpet that with honeyed smiles
>   Openest the gates of Heaven and criest, "Come in";

---

[33] Stanza 11, ed. A. B. Grosart, *The Works of John Davies of Hereford* (Edinburgh, 1878), II, 22.
[34] See *History of the World* (1614), Preface, Sig. D^v-D2^r.
[35] See *Doomes-Day* (1614), Fourth Houre, stanza 85.

Whose glories being seen, thou with one frown
In pride, lower than hell tumblest us down.[36]

And Greene, though he may have misunderstood Marlowe's intent, did not neglect to note the play's moral significance—as the well-known reference to "atheist Tamburlan" testifies. What is difficult to understand in Greene's attitude is how he could have condemned Marlowe for "impious instances of intollerable poetrie," when in *Alphonsus of Aragon* Greene himself had simply copied in exaggerated form the themes of pride, violence, and blasphemy exhibited in *Tamburlaine*. Since Greene castigates himself along with Marlowe, perhaps his criticisms should be understood as another instance of the conventional remorse about worldly poetry which we find in Chaucer, Sidney, and Spenser.

That Elizabethan treatments of tragic history were permeated by moral considerations has been very well shown us in recent studies by Miss Campbell and by Professor Farnham.[37] It is now a clearly established point that Englishmen of Marlowe's day thought of history as the record of God's Providence, and of the world as the theatre of His judgments. As Humanism made religious thought increasingly rational, history was rationalized to make every act and event appear in a moral light. Follies began to be considered as sins, for which mundane calamity was evidence of Divine punishment.[38] Farnham tells us that in the narratives of the *Mirror for Magistrates* punishment is visited most commonly on the fault of ambition.

Ambition, plainly, is the central theme of *Tamburlaine*.

---

[36] *Old Fortunatus,* I. i. An echo of the symbolism of *Tamburlaine* appears in Dekker's stage direction: "FORTUNE takes her chair, the kings lying at her feet so that she treads on them as she ascends to her seat." (Cf. *Tamb.* I. iv. ii.)

[37] Lily B. Campbell, *Shakespeare's Tragic Heroes* (Cambridge, 1930); and her Faculty Research Lecture, *Tudor Conceptions of History and Tragedy in "A Mirror for Magistrates"* (Berkeley, 1936). Willard Farnham, *The Medieval Heritage of Elizabethan Tragedy* (Berkeley, 1936).

[38] Farnham, p. 285.

Why, then, may we not regard Marlowe's play as a moralized history after the pattern of the *Mirror for Magistrates?* [39] Does not *Tamburlaine* share the typical concern of Renaissance tragedy: the theme of man's faulty passions and God's just providence? If our answer can be affirmative, then modern interpretations of *Tamburlaine* based on the notion that the play is an autobiographical document of Marlowe's romantic revolt against orthodoxy will have to be sharply reconsidered.

I should like to make it possible for us to decide between two alternative views regarding Marlowe's purpose in writing tragedy. One view, that adopted by our modern critics, makes Marlowe's plays fit a nineteenth-century notion of tragedy, in which heroes are tragic only because their reach exceeds their grasp. Miss Ellis-Fermor thinks Tamburlaine tragic only because "there are certain instincts and desires at work in the mind that are so wholly things of the spirit that to pursue them to realization and fulfilment is not within the power of human thought." [40] And Bakeless writes of Marlowe:

His heroes fall, indeed, as tragic heroes must; but they fall solely because they have sought the unattainable. Except in this one play [*Edward II*], Marlowe neglects Aristotle's doctrine of ἁμαρτία, that the ruin which overtakes the tragic hero must come from some flaw in his own character; and he anticipates the view—popular in our own day—that tragedy results simply enough when man comes into conflict with forces outside himself, forces too great for him, forces

---

[39] The problem I here raise has never been considered, except cursorily by Farnham. And though Professor Farnham is exceedingly well acquainted with the moral bases of tragedy from Boccaccio to the *Mirror for Magistrates,* he applies this knowledge to Marlowe's plays with the most curious results. *Faustus,* he finds, "seems to be written with the desire to widen and extend, instead of rebel against, the authority of medieval doctrine" (pp. 401 ff.). But *Tamburlaine,* which Farnham dates only a year earlier, is "a medieval tragedy reversed, a rebellious violation of all that *De Casibus* tragedy had set out to convey" (p. 369). Farnham offers no explanation for this sudden and total reversal of dramatic method, except to say that "Marlowe outgrew this young man's worship of pomp" (p. 373). The "outgrowing" must have been rapid!

[40] *Marlowe,* p. 39.

that grudge to poor humanity all that mere mortals never shall attain. For Marlowe, warlike conquest, metaphysical skill, vast wealth, political power all end in death because his heroes all reach for things that must elude the grasp even of extraordinary mortals. He is an early Hardy.[41]

The second view, the typical Renaissance notion of tragedy, is that tragedy deals with the fall (not the falling short) of men, and that the tragic fall is both a consequence and a punishment of sin. The art form of drama, in seeking to mirror this tragedy, has a didactic purpose: it seeks to instruct men in self-knowledge and to lead them to moral amendment. William Baldwin states this view in his dedicatory address "To the nobilitye and all other in Office" in the 1559 edition of the *Mirror for Magistrates:*

For here as in a loking glas, you shall see (if any vice be in you) howe the like hath bene punished in other heretofore, whereby admonished, I trust it will be a good occasion to move you to the soner amendment.

---

[41] *Marlowe*, pp. 5-6.

BACKGROUND OF *TAMBURLAINE*

ELIZABETHAN RELIGION
AND ATHEISM

W HEN we speak of Elizabethan religion we are designating a very fluid area of belief. In the broad sense, all Protestant forms of religion in Elizabeth's reign may be called Puritan, since their intent was to "purify" traditional faith of its "superstitions"; but the Established Church soon came to see in its left-wing party—presently denominated as Puritans—a Charybdis as dangerous to religion as was the Scylla of Roman Catholicism. To sail the middle area was a matter of some considerable strategy. Apologists found that the "true religion" was best defined in terms of moderation, decency, order, and practical reason. The need of the hour was for political loyalty and for an ethical idealism to support it. Above all, responsible churchmen were on guard against antinomianism; for they wished in England no repetition of the German Peasants' Revolt, or of the Münster tragedy of Anabaptism, or of the St. Bartholomew's Day massacre.

The Age of Elizabeth, therefore, was predominantly an age of Moral Philosophy. The mysteries of Faith were held in high reverence, but the definition of them was discouraged; for more "necessary to salvation" than dogma were thought to be the fundamental truths of the moral life. Representative Elizabethan authors gave their efforts religiously to the exposition of moral philosophy—in epic poetry, as in the *Faerie Queene;* in tragic poetry, as in *The Mirror for Magistrates;* in didactic verse, as in the poems and translations of Chapman; in prose history, as in the work of Raleigh, Beard, and others. It would seem that the important Protestant doctrines of the "calling" and of the "priesthood of all believers" encouraged poets to think

21

of themselves as *vates* and reformers, and helped historians to regard themselves as called upon to be apologists for divine justice. Morality enlisted the concern of the nation. The views of Sir Philip Sidney—a man in so many ways the ideal of his age—furnish apt illustration of the character of the thinking of Elizabethan Christians. Sidney regards "morall doctrine the chiefe of all knowledges." [1] He defines poetry as essentially Fable—that is, an action contrived to adumbrate moral philosophy. The parables of Jesus he judges to be delightful statements of "morall commonplaces" and therefore to be regarded as poetry—along with the tragedies of Sophocles and the dialogues of Plato. We should note particularly that Sidney thinks well of the human reason. He remarks that the Fall of Man has left us an "erected wit" capable of knowing what perfection is, but an "infected will which keeps us from reaching it." [2] He seems to believe in poetry as offering the practical means for reforming man's Will by appealing to man's Reason.

Sidney's reverence for Reason is nicely illustrated by Fulke Greville's account of the famous death at Zutphen in 1586:

For instantly after prayer, he entreated his quire of divine philosophers about him, to deliver the opinion of the ancient heathen, touching the immortality of the soul: First, to see what true knowledge she retains of her own essence, out of the light of her self; then to parallel with it the most pregnant authorities of the Old, and New Testament, as supernatural revelations, sealed up from our flesh, for the divine light of faith to reveal and work by. [3]

This paralleling of pagan authors and Scripture, later so characteristic of Milton's religious syncretism, was no doubt

---

[1] *Defence of Poesie*, ed. Feuillerat (Cambridge, 1923), p. 9.

[2] *Ibid.*, p. 26. It is worth remarking that Sidney's doctrine at this point seems to agree not with the view of Calvin, that the Fall corrupted man's reason as much as his will, but with that of Calvin's opponent Castellio in the *De Arte Dubitandi*, that the Fall was a calamity to the will only.

[3] *The Works of Fulke Greville* (1870), ed. A. B. Grosart, IV, 137.

encouraged in Sidney by the views of his Huguenot friend Philip Mornay;[4] but the roots of this religious humanism go back to Zwingli and Erasmus and behind them to Florentine Platonism.

English Protestantism, in general, was humanist. Luther, with his disdain of reason, got very little attention from Elizabethans; Melanchthon, the Protestant Scholastic, seems to have had somewhat more influence;[5] but the most considerable religious influence, at least among men of letters, was that of the French Huguenots—Protestants who had inherited the literary humanism and philosophical theology of Ficinus and Marguerite of Navarre together with the *devotio moderna* of the Dutch mystics.[6] A broad culture in the classics together with a liberal piety characterized French Protestantism, which was from the beginning a movement among the nobility rather than of the common folk. Chief among its spokesmen were La Primaudaye, Du Bartas, Mornay, Gentillet, Ramus, and Calvin—all of whom were much read in England and translated in English editions. The circle of their sympathizers includes most prominently Norton, Sidney, Raleigh, Golding, Nashe, Sylvester, and the Countess of Pembroke;[7] and in Scotland, King James and

---

[4] Philippe de Mornay, Seigneur Du Plessis-Marly (1549-1623) was a Huguenot refugee to England at the time of the St. Bartholomew's Day massacre. Regarding Mornay's associations in England, see Sidney Lee, *The French Renaissance in England* (Oxford, 1910).

[5] Henry VIII and Cranmer repeatedly attempted to bring Melanchthon to England; and as early as 1536 the king's injunctions to Cambridge University include the article that the students are to read among others Philip Melanchthon. Raleigh and Burton cite Melanchthon with approval.

[6] See Abel Lefranc, "Marguerite de Navarre," in *Grand Écrivains Francais de la Renaissance* (Paris, 1914), pp. 139-249; and Albert Hyma, *The Christian Renaissance* (Grand Rapids, 1924), Chap. vii.

[7] The Countess, who translated Mornay's *A Discourse of Life and Death*, published it in 1592 in the same volume with her translation of Garnier's *The Tragedy of Antonie*. Sister of Sir Philip and patroness of the academic Senecan dramatists, the Countess seems to have gathered about her the poetry of Elizabethan Protestantism. Also, like Raleigh, she seems to have taken an interest in occult matters; for she employed Sir Walter's half-brother, Adrian Gilbert, in the study of chemistry.

Buchanan. The Lady Margaret Professor of Divinity while Marlowe was at Cambridge was Peter Baro, a Huguenot refugee who had received the appointment in 1574 through Burghley's sponsorship. It is significant to remember that Baro, though he came from Geneva, was not a strict Calvinist. His liberal Protestantism had leanings toward "Arminianism" which involved him in controversy with the Puritan preacher Laurence Chaderton in 1581, the year in which Marlowe entered the university.

The most popular Huguenot in England was Du Bartas. His *La Semaine* (1578), which put Protestant doctrine and Scriptural history in poetry's winsome garb, was everywhere praised—by Harvey, Spenser, Daniel, Drayton, Lodge, Hall, and Jonson.[8] King James of Scotland, enthralled by a manuscript copy of the *Premiere Sepmaine* given him in 1579, published in 1585 a translation of Du Bartas' earlier *L'Urania* (1573), then in 1587 lured the poet to Scotland. James begged him in vain to stay and honored him with a knighthood and considerable gold. Elizabeth's court, likewise, received the poet with acclaim. In 1588 there was licensed (but apparently never printed) a *Translation of Salust du Bartas done by Sir Ph. Sidney.* Sylvester began issuing fragmentary translations of Du Bartas in 1590.

Calvin represents, in Sidney Lee's phrase,[9] the "left wing" of the Huguenot movement. His *Institutes* appeared in 1536; yet it was not until 1555 that Calvinist congregations began to be established in France. England's acceptance of Calvin was even more slow and guarded. The predominant party in Elizabethan Protestantism shied away from the systematic theocracy and the dogmatic Biblicism of Geneva. The Anglican apologists wished by a more liberal humanism to steer the *via media* somewhere between rigid Calvinism and Rome. Their use of Calvin was therefore eclectic. He

---

[8] Lee, pp. 340-55; H. Ashton, *Du Bartas en Angleterre* (Paris, 1908).
[9] Lee, p. 285.

was most likely to be approved at points where his views echo those of Zwingli, or of the classic philosophers. For despite Calvin's claim that his views rest on Scripture only, his theology does not wholly abandon that spirit of humanistic culture in which he had written his commentary on Seneca's *De Clementia.*[10] Calvin had been in the beginning, and was still at bottom, a humanist.

The liberal breadth of Elizabethan Protestantism can be illustrated by calling attention to the work of Arthur Golding. Golding translated many volumes of Calvin's sermons —and seems to have thought it an equally pious work to translate Ovid's *Metamorphoses,* Seneca's *Of Benefits,* and Beza's *Tragedie of Abraham's Sacrifice.* Together with Sidney, he translated also Mornay's *The Trewnesse of the Christian Religion.* Nashe praises Golding both for his Ovid and for his "many exquisite editions of diuinitie turned by him out of the French tongue into our owne."[11] And it must be remembered that Nashe was himself, on occasion, a Protestant apologist for the Queen's religion.

In the intellectual climate of Elizabethan times the humanism of the French Protestants and of their English friends has a far-reaching importance. Men who were constant readers of Cicero, for example, were bound to be impressed not only by that author's excellent rhetoric but also by his praise of reason, his wistful doubts, and his universal deism. The Greek and Latin classics, as Douglas Bush

---

[10] Quirinus Breen, *John Calvin: A Study in French Humanism* (Grand Rapids, Mich., 1931), pp. 146 ff., devotes a chapter to "The Precipitate of Humanism in Calvin the Reformer." He points to the fact that the humanism of Calvin's early years may be seen as influencing Calvin's later theological theory of Common Grace. As expressed in the *Institutes,* this theory declares that despite men's depravity there are sparks of truth in all men, and that the light of truth that is manifest in heathen writers is to be admired.

[11] Nashe's Preface to Green's *Menaphon* (1589), ed. R. B. McKerrow, *The Works of Thomas Nashe* (London, 1904-10), III, 319. For a full list of Golding's translations, see Louis T. Golding, *An Elizabethan Puritan* (New York, 1937), pp. 149 ff.

rightly remarks,[12] "were not a mere innocuous genteel tradition." Seneca and Plutarch were much more than mere "literary" men: they were storehouses of pagan philosophy, displaying the characteristic thinking—aristocratic, didactic, rational, and ethical—of the best secular culture. Renaissance readers, much impressed by the wisdom and virtue of these Ethnic philosophers, found Christians' manners too often vastly inferior; and in the effort to reform these Christians it was easy to adopt the arguments—and hence the philosophy—of the enlightened pagans. Secularism began to interpenetrate orthodoxy.

This tendency was accelerated by the Reformation, which brought with it for the Anglicans a desperate need for rational armament. Combatting papacy, it was difficult to appeal unqualifiedly to the authority of the Church; and fearing sectarianism, it was difficult to rest wholly in the authority of Scripture. The *via media* therefore had to make Reason central to the triad of Church, Reason, and Scripture, which was now invoked as the source of authority in religion.

Under these circumstances Platonic theology came into great favor. Its vogue reflects the desire of the Reformers to amalgamate reason and religion. Liberal Platonizing Christianity (which Paul Shorey says[13] had "always tended to deviate into heresy even in the best intentioned of the liberal Greek Fathers,") had lately been revived by the Florentine humanists. It now became the chief arsenal for Protestant attacks on Scholasticism, Aristotle, and the papacy. Notable among the attackers was Ramus, called by his fellow scholars "the French Plato." Defending in 1536 the proposition that "All that Aristotle has said is false,"

---

[12] *Mythology and the Renaissance Tradition* (Minneapolis, 1932), p. 71.
[13] *Platoni.. n Ancient and Modern* (Berkeley, 1938), p. 81.

Ramus offered, as Perry Miller says,[14] liberation "from
the gloomy cave of scholastic metaphysics into the spacious
meadows of classical literature." More modest humanism
of the Platonic variety is witnessed by William Baldwin's
immensely popular *A Treatise of Morall Phylosophye*
(1547), which includes a series of lives of the pagan philosophers beginning with Trismegistus.[15] Baldwin justifies his book by quoting St. Augustine's statement:

> If they which be called Philosophers, specially of Plato hys secte,
> haue spoken ought that is true, & appertinent to our feith, we ought
> not onli not to feare it, but also to chalenge it as our own, from
> them which are no ryght owners thereof.[16]

Even Calvin generously calls Plato "the most religious and
most sober" of all philosophers.[17] *The French Academie*
of Pierre de La Primaudaye is termed by its translator
Thomas Bowes a "Platonicall Academy and schoole of
Morall Philosophy." And Platonic authorities appear with
overwhelming frequency in Mornay's *Trewnesse of the*

---

[14] *The Puritans* (New York, 1938), ed. Perry Miller and Thomas A. John-
son, Introduction, p. 29. The influence of Ramus is difficult to exaggerate.
William Temple's text edition of Ramus in 1584, dedicated to Sidney, was probably well known to every Cambridge scholar. In the next century Milton wrote
an *Artis Logicae Plenior Institutio* (1672) after the method of Ramus, calling
him "the best writer on the art." Ramus associated logic with poetry. He
recommended certain classic poets not merely for style and eloquence, but as
models of reasoning. He argued that they, by speaking directly from nature
herself, reveal nature's comprehensible logical structure. And he offered as the
proper tool for discovering nature's design and architecture a logic based on
Plato's guiding principle of "dichotomy." In Marlowe's *The Massacre at Paris,*
where Ramus appears as the special victim of the Catholic fury of the Duke of
Guise, the Duke contemptuously calls him a "flat dichotomist."

[15] The *Short Title Catalogue* records 18 editions of Baldwin's *Treatise* before
1640. Baldwin (I. vi.) calls Trismegistus "the most excellent . . . the most
auncient . . . most worthye" of all the philosophers. The mystical writings of
Hermes Trismegistus were immensely popular in Renaissance times: The *Hermetica* in Ficinus' Latin translation (1471) had 8 editions before 1500, and at
least 22 editions by 1641. See *Hermetica* (ed. Walter Scott, Oxford, 1924-36),
Introduction, p. 33.

[16] Prologue.

[17] *Institutes,* I. v. 11.

Christian Religion.[18]   Much of the secret of Plato's appeal can be seen in Sidney's confession in the *Defence* that he thinks Plato of all the philosophers the "most worthie of reverence" because the "most Poeticall." Myth and drama, imagination and reason, piety and ethics—these Plato combined in a way that delighted the Renaissance humanist.[19] The peculiar merit of Platonism—particularly of Neo-Platonism—is in its liberal understanding of Reason. Reason is, on the one hand, logic and discursive reasoning; but at a higher level it is also intuition, resting beyond logic on illumination. Thus the reasoner is both a scientist and a seer. Held with Christianity, Platonic reason gives great scope to natural religion—so great that Ficinus, for example, tried to demonstrate the rationality of the whole Christian creed. Like Raymond of Sebonde, Ficinus has a natural theology which includes nominally the whole dogma of the Church.

Aristotle's thinking offers no such opportunities. As Ramus pointed out, Aristotle has nothing to say about Providence,[20] Divine Justice, the Creation, and the Immortality of the Soul. Protestant apologists, who considered these four doctrines as the indispensable minimum of true religion, were in sympathy with Ramus' contention that

---

[18] See esp. chap. iv. (on our knowledge of God) and chap. vi. (on the Trinity). Plato, Philo, Proclus, Iamblichus, Trismegistus, Porphyry, Dionysius the Areopagite, and Plotinus throng the pages. Mornay gives six full pages (pp. 83-89) to a summary of Plotinus' notion of a divine trinity.

[19] Shorey remarks aptly enough, p. 82, that Platonism encouraged heresy by stimulating free inquiry and mythopoeic imagination. But the Humanists were willing to risk heresy to combat Scholasticism. And what other tradition had they to fall back upon? The Occamist, with its double-truth, and its choice of thoroughgoing skepticism or fideism, made religion too anti-rational to suit the humanist. It is true that beginning with the seventeenth century we see the Occamist position in Bacon's views; but at the same time Donne, who had to defend the Anglican position, fell back upon Platonism. Shorey, p. 12, calls Plato "the chief and best source of ethical and natural religion throughout European literature."

[20] See also Leontine Zanta, *La Renaissance du Stoicisme au XVI° Siècle* (Paris, 1914), pp. 34, 42, where it is pointed out that because Aristotle fails to define a doctrine of Providence, he is therein compared by Bessarion unfavorably with Plato and neglected by Pompanatius in favor of Stoicism.

Aristotle's conception of God was "atheistic." [21]   In the eclectic thinking of the Renaissance, the Stagirite might be valuable for ethics, but he was useless for theology.   Plato was more religious.   The thinking of the Renaissance humanists was perhaps, as Douglas Bush contends,[22] closer to the Middle Ages than to modern times.   Yet historians must not fail to recognize also, especially with the entry of the Reformation, the beginning of a discontinuity with the past, the appearance of a shift in emphasis and hence of perspective.   The religion of the Elizabethan Compromise is marked by at least three tendencies which help to explain why moral philosophy was then so much the literary vogue.   These tendencies, as I note them, are: an increased use of reason rather than dogma in the defense of religion; a liberalizing of the Catholic notion of revelation; and a tendency to define religion in terms of conduct rather than of creed.   Each of these "notes" is significant enough in its bearings on literature to demand some detailed comment.   We need to understand the manner in which these tendencies were working to condition the thinking of Marlowe's audience and the perspective of playwrights who wrote for this audience.

I

Acontius,[23] Castellio,[24] the Sozzini, and others who

---

[21] See Frank P. Graves, *Peter Ramus and the Educational Reformation of the Sixteenth Century* (New York, 1912), p. 174.   Note also the complaint of Erasmus: "And we endeavour ourselves to glue fast together the decrees of this man [Aristotle] and the doctrine of Christ—which is as likely a thing as to mingle fire and water together." *Against War*, ed. J. W. Mackail (Boston, 1907), p. 40.

[22] *The Renaissance and English Humanism* (London, 1939).

[23] Acontius came to England in 1559, was granted naturalization papers in 1561, and became a member of the Dutch Church in London.   He enjoyed the patronage of the Earl of Leicester and was occasionally in the employ of Elizabeth.

[24] Castellio addressed his Latin Bible to Edward VI, and set forth in the preface his characteristic view that Deed is more important than Creed.   A good summary of Castellio's liberalism is by R. H. Bainton, "Sebastian Castellio and the Toleration Controversy of the Sixteenth Century," in *Persecution and Liberty*

sought to remove "idle" and "foolish" controversy by reducing clashing theological systems to a lowest common doctrinal denominator seem to have been not without influence on Elizabethan religion. Though the main party in the Church of England did not go so far as these modern radicals, yet the Church's apologists desired in support of simplified religion some authority other than ecclesiastical; and they appealed therefore, almost as much as these independents, to the authority of Reason, Nature, and Experience. Hooker, Anglicanism's foremost spokesman, held that the certainty of the essential truths of Christianity could be established by Reason. He argued that the greatest moral duties we owe towards God or man "may without any great difficulty be concluded" out of certain self-evident principles universally agreed upon.[25] It was a cardinal tenet of Protestant humanism that Christians ought to conquer not by arms but by the persuasive force of truth.

Yet is was recognized, too, that Reason might need supplementation. Walsingham declared that the Queen's policy against both Catholic and Puritan dissenters rested upon two principles: that conscience must be won by agencies of persuasion and instruction; and that meanwhile, when conscience led to faction, the state was obliged to employ repression.[26] This double strategy explains the twin themes of Elizabethan literature: religious education and patriotism. It also accounts for the close association of "irreligion" and sedition. The Queen's religion being the "true religion," it followed logically that sedition was "atheism." The two crimes are closely equated in the charges against Marlowe—

(New York, 1931), pp. 183-208. The *Short Title Catalogue* lists no English editions of Castellio's theological works but records English editions in 1560 and 1577 of his *Dialogorum sacrorum libri quatuor.* These were dramatizations of Biblical stories in Latin for school use, aimed to teach classical Latinity without the corruption of morals in evidence in Plautus and Terence.

[25] See W. K. Jordan, *The Development of Religious Toleration in England to the death of Elizabeth* (1932), pp. 228-29; and Hooker, *Laws,* I. viii. 3-10.

[26] *Ibid.,* p. 200.

and commonly in charges against Anabaptists and Papists.[27]

Against "atheism" and sedition the proper weapon was thought to be the Liberal Arts. To be a champion of the Queen's religion, one needed to be a gentleman scholar. Thomas Nashe, in calling upon university men to "Arme your selves against nothing but Atheisme," expresses his belief that moral philosophy and natural reason are the only "common ground" on which the enemy can be met. He insists that preachers must be armed with the "Arts of all Nations"—with logic, rhetoric, history, philosophy, music, and poetry. By 1593 when he set forth these stipulations Nashe had had considerable experience in battling the Martinists. His words, therefore, should not be taken lightly. Also, we may very properly speculate as to whether Marlowe, when he was collaborating with Nashe on *Dido* or while he was studying for Holy Orders, may not have imagined himself as preparing to fill the following prescription:

These Atheists (with whom you are to encounter) are speciall men of witte. . . wil you then hope to beate them down with fusty brownbread dorbellisme?

Skyrmishing with Atheists, you must behaue your selues as you were conuerting Gentiles. All antique hystories you must haue at your fingers-end. No Phylosophers confession or opinion of God that you are to be ignorant in. Ethnicks with their own Ethnick weapons you must assayle. Infinite laborinths of bookes he must runne thorough, that will be a compleate Champion in Christs Church. . . Christ when he sayd, *You must forsake all and follow him,* meant not you should forsake all Artes and follow him.[28]

"Our Atheist we haue in hand," Nashe concludes, "with nothing but humaine reasons will be rebutted." It is note-

---

[27] See G. T. Buckley, *Atheism in the English Renaissance* (Chicago, 1932), pp. 49-53; and cf. Friedrich Brie, "Deismus und Atheismus in der Engl. Ren.," *Anglia,* 48 (1924), 163-4.

[28] *Christs Teares* (1593), ed. McKerrow, II, 121 ff. Cf. II, 37 ff.

worthy that Nashe's outlook was the view also of the apologist Philip Mornay, who drew upon

whatsoeuer he found eyther in the common reason of all Nations, or in the peculiar principles of the cheefe Philosophers, or in the misticall doctrine of the Jewish Rabbines, or in the writings of the Historiographers and Poets.[29]

The writings of Mornay are a good example of the rational temper of the times. This valiant champion of Protestant "true religion" against all atheism proposed by the arm of Reason not only to confute the views of the atheists but, even further, to prove to these blind ignorants, out of their own writings, the truth of the Christian Religion. Against the Jews, Mornay undertook to prove his faith on the basis of the Old Testament, "yea even to the verifying of the gospel"; against the Gentiles he would "proove and verify" his own principles on the basis of the writings of Gentile philosophers.[30] In Mornay's view "Atheists offend not through reasoning, but for want of reasoning." The Christian, by using "principles common to both sides," can from the writings of philosophers and historiographers "drawe both the Godhead of Christ, and the truth of our Scriptures: Certesse in like manner as by Arithmetike. . . ." Mornay realizes that so confident a use of reason must meet some criticism from his fellow Christians. He defends himself by assuring his readers that he does not regard reason as the measure of faith, or even as the measure of nature: both faith and nature are mysteries. But mysteries can, by the use of reason, be made allowable and credible. In fact, belief can be shown to be obligatory. For though belief is beyond the measure of reason, yet reason "lifteth

---

[29] Golding's Epistle Dedicatory to his and Sidney's translation of *The Trewnesse of the Christian Religion* (1587).

[30] *Christian Religion*, Preface. Compare Mornay's earlier *A Treatise of the Church*, trans. I[ohn] F[ielde], (London, 1579), p. 68.

us up as it were upon her shoulders" to "make us see" Faith. Mornay's limits for reason are not too clear: he is anxious obviously not to claim too much for reason, and so says that "many things exceede reason"; but he is anxious also to show that regarding the Incarnation, for example, "reason is able both to teach it to us, and to defende it."

Golding, who wrote the Epistle Dedicatory to the English translation of Mornay, was enthusiastic about Mornay's method:

> he hath so effectually brought his purpose to passe; that if any Atheist Infidel or Iew hauing read this his worke with aduisement, shall yet denye the Christian Religion to be the true and only pathway to eternall felicitie, & all other Religions to bee mere vanitie and wickedness; must needes show himself to be either vtterly voyd of humaine sence, or els obstinatly and wilfully bent to impugne the manifest trueth against the continuall testimonie of his owne conscience.

We see here the familiar supposition of Renaissance humanism—the notion that speculative problems can be resolved with common sense and practical reason.

We must take particular note, also, of the skeptical character of a good deal of Elizabethan rationalism. Cornelius Agrippa's *De Incertitudine et Vanitate Scientiarum* (1527) had an English translation in 1569 and a second edition in 1575. This book, written in the Platonic tradition of Reuchlin and Picus, is the work of a learned humanist who is piously contemplating the dangers of his own learning. Adopting the anti-intellectualist stand that true felicity consists not in the knowledge of goodness but in a good life, Agrippa argues that Arts and Sciences are vain because they cannot bring that felicity. They can, it is true, teach us the wisdom of the Serpent—the negative good of a knowledge of good and evil. But by this learning Adam lost Paradise. Seeking this blessedness, the philosophers are tormented in hell. A good will avails more than a good understanding.[31]

Like Agrippa, most Elizabethan Protestants gave first place in religion to the will and the moral life. And they used Agrippa's skepticism as basis for a curiously double view of learning, by which learning is seen to be at the same time both exceedingly valuable and exceedingly dangerous. Thus Sidney, for example, had a moral end in view when he labored in his *Arcadia,* as Greville says, "to turn barren Philosophy into pregnant Images of life"; yet he discovered when he regarded his work from a "purer Horizon" the "vanity of these shadowes, how daintily soever limned" and so bequeathed his unfinished *Arcadia* to the fire. Greville, balancing the two viewpoints, decided to withhold the burning "untill the world hath purged away all her more gross corruptions."[32] Apparently he considered the Arcadia's moralities, at least during the world's present sick period, a medicine too valuable to lose.

When we examine Greville's own writings we find this double perspective constantly in evidence: exhibits of wicked Machiavellianism claim attention side by side with appeals to Christian pietism. Humane learning, it is held, cannot give us the truth that "refines our fleshly humor"; but still it can display our error and thus point us to the divine Wisdom, in which the salvation of the soul lies.[33] In other words, the arts cannot give salvation and hence are vain; but they can give knowledge of our sinful selves and hence are valuable. To the reader of Marlowe's plays, certainly,

[31] *Of the Vanitie and Vncertaintie of Artes and Sciences,* trans. Ja[mes] San[ford], (London, 1575), p. 3.
[32] Greville's *Life of Sidney,* ed. Nowell Smith (Clarendon Press, 1907), pp. 15-17.
[33] See *Poems and Dramas of Fulke Greville,* ed. Geoffrey Bullough (Edinburgh, 1939), Introduction, I, 55 ff.

this antithesis must be illuminating. I think there can be no doubt that the first half of the paradox states the ostensible moral of *Faustus* and *Tamburlaine;* and that the second half of the paradox furnishes a justification for their composition.

The thinking of Nashe too exhibits the dual view. On the one hand, he proclaims learning as dangerous: it is impious to wish to "ransack God's closet"; "superaboundance of witte" makes men atheists; Aristotle was justly punished for his wit-pride;[34] Socrates and certain poets illustrate a "humor of monarchizing" which is to be associated with atheism.[35] Nashe's very phrases could be taken as a catalogue of the sins of Faustus. But, on the other hand, Nashe is equally outspoken in urging that learning is to be encouraged, for it has practical value in combatting atheism. The man who would be a successful champion of God's Church must be trained in all the arts and sciences.

A point to be observed here is that the skepticism of these Elizabethans is not thoroughgoing. Nashe rejects the philosophy of Pyrrhonism as being atheistic, at the same time that he is borrowing heavily from Sextus Empiricus and Agrippa.[36] The inconsistency does not disturb him—apparently because he regards reason simply as a tool or weapon. Its usefulness is its justification. In so far as Nashe's methods and views were those of Elizabethan apologists generally, the resulting religious philosophy may best

---

[34] *Christs Teares*, ed. McKerrow, II, 118-19, 124. Nashe warns that Aristotle, unable to solve the mystery of the Nile river, plunged himself into it and was drowned. This legend, which is told also by Gregory Nazianzen, was used by Lorenzo Valla in his *De Libero Arbitrio* to attack philosophy presuming to solve the mysteries of God. See Arpad Steiner, "The Faust Legend in the Christian Tradition," *P. M. L. A.*, LIV (1939), 402-3. Valla's book was put on the *Index*.

[35] *The Terrors of the Night* (1594), ed. McKerrow, I, 351.

[36] McKerrow, II, 116, and "Nashe's Reading," V, 110 ff.

be described as pietism. Its antecedents go back to Cusa's *De Docta Ignorantia.*[37]

II

The liberalizing of the notion of revelation we can describe more briefly. The general tendency of Elizabethans to elevate poetry, symbol, fable, allegory, and ideal truth was accompanied by a loosening of adherence to historic Christianity, the visible Church, and the sacramental system. The poet was honored as a *vates*. He was thought of as a channel of revelation—for does not the poet Ovid in his fable of Deucalion and Pirrha reveal the story of Noah's flood? Nashe, who thought this was Ovid's intention, remarks on the "deeper diuinitie" of poets' inventions and claims for poetry "a more hidden & diuine kinde of Philosophy."[38] It is true, of course, that similar views can be found in the Middle Ages; but it must be said that with the Renaissance the "divinity" of poetry becomes less peripheral and more central to religion. Comes and Landinus, Italian Neo-Platonists, discovered in the fables of literature not only philosophy but also theology. Elizabethans following in this school of thought looked to the "doctrine" of poets (and especially of those divine poets, the Scripture writers) to provide sufficient revelation to make it possible to dispense with the "external" authority of dogma.

This glorification of poetry results, of course, directly from the great scope allowed to natural religion. If, as not a few Elizabethans believed, human reason can demonstrate all the truths essential to salvation, then it follows logically that a poet can exercise all the functions essential to a priest, that universal history can show all the essential truths of

---

[37] See Rudolf Stadelmann's discussion of "Die Skeptische Wurzel des Cusanischen Transrationalismus," in *Vom Geist der Ausgehenden Mittelalters* (Halle, 1929), pp. 44 ff.

[38] *Anatomie of Absurditie* (1589), ed. McKerrow, I, 25 and 29.

Scripture, and that Nature is essentially as much the garment of God as is the Church. Thus Poetry, History, and Nature take on a religious significance as parts of a broad sacramental system. All things become symbols or signs (cf. the Platonic notion that the body is a "tomb" and a "sign"). All action becomes important as "memorial"—hence Zwingli's interpretation of the Lord's Supper. Zwingli was equally broad in his theory of the church: it was the assembly of the saved and might include, besides Christians, certain religious pagans quite independent of Christian revelation. The liberal viewpoint has its source pretty certainly in Neo-Platonism, which regards all nature and all history (not merely Christian history) in a religious light as being a divinely provided means for the revelation of transcendental truths. The emphasis thus given to Natural Religion was welcomed by Elizabethans, because it helped rationalize the practical need for tolerance.

Reformed apologists argued, generally, that Christian Faith far transcends pagan wisdom; but yet they made much of the fact that the partial revelations of the pagans served well to witness to certain fundamental truths of religion. The philosophers could turn attention to "the school of Nature," which *The French Academie* (1594) plainly declared is "the schoole of God." [39] Cicero appears in "The Religious Treat" offered by Erasmus; and when the author comes to Socrates he exclaims:

What a wonderful elevation of Mind was this in a man that only Acted by the light of Nature! I can hardly read a story of this Worthy without a *Sancte Socrates Ora pro Nobis*. [40]

---

[39] Second Part, p. 61.
[40] *Twenty Select Colloquies*, trans. R. L'Estrange (1680), ed. Charles Whibley (London, 1923), p. 97.

Zwingli declared he would rather see Socrates and Seneca among the elect than the Roman pontiff.[41]

Thomas Bowes, English translator of *The French Academie,* goes so far as to suggest that the great Last Judgment will be conducted by the pagan philosophers and that Christians will do well to prepare for that terrible day by learning ethics from the wise ethnics:

it is to be feared, that those selfe same men shall rise vp in iudgement against vs that professe Christianitie, and condemn vs in that great and terrible day. For how many of vs want that knowledge of the eternal power, diuinitie, and prouidence of God, which was in *Parmenides, Plato, Aristotle,* and others, indued onely with the light of nature, whereby they were led from the view of the creatures, to the consideration of the inuisible things of God? And if we looke into the liues of men in these daies, and consider what neglect there is of those mutuall duties which God commandeth vs to exhibite one to another, we shall soone see, that many a million of carnall Gospellers come farre short euen of those ciuill apparant and halfe vertues of the Heathen, and may therefore be sent backe to learne holiness of *Socrates,* iustice and innocencie of *Aristides,* charitie of *Cymon,* vpright dealing of *Phocion,* fidelitie in performing promises of *Regulus,* moderation of *Camillus,* parsimonie of *Curius,* grauitie of *Cato,* and what not of Heathen men, whose sight in these thinges was better at midnight, than ours is at midday.[42]

This strongly humanistic emphasis has importance for our study of Marlowe, because we shall find that the dramatist's treatment of Christian perjury in *Tamburlaine* II, for example, reflects the ethical background we are here describing.

We should note also that the Elizabethans, in reducing the emphasis on institution and dogma in religion, elevate

---

[41] See Zanta, p. 60.
[42] The Epistle Dedicatorie. My text is that of the first English edition, 1586.

the importance of experience. Experience proves to Faustus, for example, the truth of the Scripture text "The wages of sin are death." It is experience that makes Orpheus a better guide than Aristotle: "ther is a by Prouerb, ORPHEVS can describe Hell, better than ARISTOTLE: raised vpon a Fable, that he fetched his Wife from thence." [43] Poetry is preferable to philosophy, according to Sidney, because poetry presents doctrine in a more lively experience. Questions of truth are commonly referred to the court of experience rather than to the authority of dogma. "Come," says Faustus, "I think hell's a fable." "Ay," replies the wise Mephistophilis, "think so still, till experience change thy mind." [44]

III

Thirdly, there is the emphasis on conduct. Grounded on the skepticism and pietism we have already spoken of is the familiar Elizabethan conclusion that virtue is of more importance than speculation. Nashe goes indeed so far as to say that questions touching the origin, nature, and immortality of the soul are "unnecessary questions." "What do al these things auaile vnto vertue?" he asks. The "onely ende of knowledge ought to be to learne to liue well." [45] Nashe's view is no isolated example. Greville, faced by the multiplicity of religions in his day, proposed as the method

---

[43] George Whetstone, *A Mirour for Magestrates of Cyties* (1584), Dedication.

[44] Borrowing from a tradition which goes back to Erigena and Platonic philosophy, Renaissance writers such as Sebastian Franck, Valentine Weigel, Boehme, and Whichcote adopt a revised eschatology in which Heaven and Hell are inward conditions or states of the soul, not terminal places. See Rufus M. Jones, *Spiritual Reformers in the Sixteenth and Seventeenth Centuries* (London, 1928). Compare also Greville, *Caelica*, C-CI.

[45] *Anatomie of Absurditie*, ed. McKerrow, I, 47-48. Nashe's sentiments are thus remarkably similar to those of Castellio in the preface to his Latin Bible of 1551. Castellio declared that no agreement has been reached and none is necessary on such obscure matters as the nature of Christ and the Trinity or of Heaven and Hell. God is veiled in *obscurity* but his commandments are *clear*. See J. W. Allen, *A History of Political Thought in the Sixteenth Century* (London, 1928), p. 91.

for finding the good one: "Good life should find a good
RELIGION out." [46] And Ramus defined theology simply
as "the science of living well." [47]

The centrality of conduct means that "blasphemy" is now
more dreaded than "heresy." Castellio, for example, will
not allow the persecution of heretics, but he recommends
the punishment of blasphemers. [48] Offense against God's
honor is the great crime. The humanist critic La Noue can
point out that the Jews had enough religion to punish
blasphemy by stoning, and the Turks and Saracens enough
fear of God to abstain from blasphemy.

Surely all these nations shall in the last day rise against vs Christians
. . . who endued with more knowledge than those blind people, doe
offend tenne tymes more then they. [49]

The humanists also reinterpret certain Biblical texts in a
broad nonecclesiastical sense. Christ's seamless robe, a traditional proof text against schism or sectarianism, is now
interpreted: "As *Christs* coate was without wemme: so his
life was without crime." [50]

The humanist's view of sin, also, is broad—is, in fact, almost more secular than specifically Christian. Sin comes to
mean simply fault or flaw or crime. The author of *Willobie
His Avisa* can set the fall of Adam side by side with the
downfalls of Helen and Cressida—and attribute the tragedy
in each case to the fault of Discontent. The offense is essentially against order. The offenders need to be reminded

---

[46] *A Treatise of Religion*, stanza 15, ed. Grosart, I, 244.
[47] Graves, p. 185.
[48] See Bainton, "Castellio and the Toleration Controversy," p. 201. Castellio
goes on to say that "the great blasphemers are those who confess God with the
mouth but deny him in fact." The description, certainly, fits Tamburlaine.
[49] *The Politicke and Militarie Discourses of La Noue*, trans. E[dward]
A[ggas], (London, 1587), p. 5.
[50] Francis Meres, *Palladis Tamia* (1598), p. 11ʳ, ed. D. C. Allen (1938).

by the architecture of the world "That every creature keepes his course, his compasse and his place." [51] The implication is that rebellion against the social order and sin against God are identical. This interpretation is furthered by such representative works as *The Mirror for Magistrates,* where the chief cause adduced for tragedy is the fault of Ambition. In other words, popular literature has come to regard the traditional Deadly Sin of "pride" as simply interchangeable with or coextensive with the broad vice called "ambition." And we hear Raleigh crying out against Ambition as a crime "without hope of redemption." [52]

But in that case: what hope of redemption can there be for Tamburlaine—in whom Discontent, Ambition, and Blasphemy are his proudest display? Is he not, to use Calvinist terminology, an example of the "non-elect," reprobated to damnation?

IV

We are now prepared to understand what the Elizabethans meant by atheism. Atheism was for them a very loose term, defined—as religion was defined—largely in terms of conduct. [53] Nicholas Breton gives us the Character of "An Atheist or most badde man" and describes him as a dare-

---

[51] Ed. G. B. Harrison (London, 1926), pp. 177 ff.

[52] *History of the World* (1614), II. xii. 7, p. 432.

[53] In general, it may be said that the humanists built on Plato's attacks on atheism defined as the denial of cosmic moral law. (See *Laws* X, 885; *Repub.* 364B-365E.) But it must be admitted that the philosophic meaning of the term "atheism" gets very confused, because while *all* Renaissance humanists would hurl the term atheist at Epicurean doctrine and the denial of Providence, *some* Renaissance Christians insisted on using the term also to characterize people who seemed to them to hold Christian dogma too loosely—men such as Bodin and Raleigh—tolerant Christians of a more or less deistic tendency. The result is that Bodin, who himself considered atheism as the one thing intolerable because it makes nonsense of the universe, was frequently denounced as an atheist both before and after his death.

devil figure of desperation." [54]   In sum, it can be said that the
Elizabethan atheist was one whose impious, unmannerly,
or dissolute life gave testimony convincing to his fellow
men that he evidently took no stock in the minimal essential
of Elizabethan religion: a God who rewards and punishes.[55]
Charges of atheism were recklessly tossed about; for when
a man's faith was read by his conduct it was not difficult to
see "atheism" everywhere. "There is no Sect now in England so scattered as Atheisme," Nashe wrote,[56] and he vig-
orously entered himself as a champion against it. Yet Harvey repeatedly hurled the charge of atheism against Nashe.
Thomas Beard, who hurls the charge at Marlowe, very apparently uses "atheism" as that denial of minimal doctrine
that is to be inferred wherever there are reports of wicked
living. In the chapter where he tells the Marlowe story,
Beard's opening words direct the attack against

Epicures and cursed Atheists, that denieth the prouidence of God,
beleeue not the immortality of the soule, thinke there is no such
thing as life to come, and consequently impugne all diuinity, liuing
in this world like brute beasts.

In the course of the chapter Beard applies the term Atheist
to Pope Leo X and Pope Julius II.[57]
To the Elizabethan the term atheism was, by a sort of
Platonic dichotomy, simply the opposite of "true religion."
Henry Smith entitles his book *Gods Arrow Against Atheists*
(1593), when actually his attack is not merely against
atheists in the strict sense, but also against Gentiles, Mahom-

[54] *The Good and the Badde* (1616), ed. Grosart, *Works of Breton* (Edinburgh, 1879), II, 10.
[55] See, e.g., Nashe, *Christs Teares*, ed. McKerrow, II, 115-6.
[56] *Ibid.*, II, 121-2.
[57] Cf. Burton, *Anatomy of Melancholy*, III. IV. 1. 2, ed. A. R. Shilleto (London, 1893), III, 382. He calls Leo X, Alexander VI, and Julius II "mere
atheists," alleging that "they hold there is no God."

etans, the Church of Rome, and the Sectaries. These are the same lines of warfare which Mornay laid down when he undertook his apologetics against "Atheists, Epicureans, Paynims, Iewes, Mahumetists, and other Infidels." The point seems to be that the Protestant apologists, confident of the power of reason to "prove" the true religion, are ready to take on *all* opponents as atheists.

The arch-atheist was thought to be Machiavelli. And so the Pope was considered to be not only an atheist but also a Machiavellian. Thus Thomas Bowes, in dedicating to Sir John Puckering (the same Sir John to whom Kyd submitted his libel of Marlowe) a translation of the Second Part of *The French Academie* (1594), writes:[58]

A third reason that moueth mee to become an humble petitioner, that this booke may be gathered vnder the wings of your Honours safe defence, is the constant report of your great care, that none be entertained into your retinue and familie, whose hearts are possessed with a liking of that Antichrist of Rome, within the compasse of whose iurisdiction, this dangerous infection of Atheisme beganne first in this latter age of the worlde to breake foorth . . . where that monster *Machiauel* first beganne to budde, who hath now spredde abroad his deadly branches of Atheisme ouer the most countries in Christendome. . . . And yet Machiauel beeing Secretarie to that Florentine estate, and employed altogether in ciuill affayres, may seeme in some sort inexcusable [sic] if hee bee compared with manie of those vnholy Fathers of Rome, who making open profession to bee the Ring-leaders (forsooth) of the whole worlde to bring them vnto GOD, were plunged irrecouerably in this bottomlesse gulfe of Atheisme.

We may compare Marlowe's *The Jew of Malta,* where Machiavelli is made to say:

---

[58] Cf. Brie, pp. 162-3, where John Dove, *Confutation of Atheism* (1605), cites Leo X as an example of Machiavellian atheism; and see also Burton, *Anat.,* "To the Reader," ed. Shilleto, I, 57, where Papists and Jesuits are termed "a *Machiavellian* rout."

> Though some speake openly against my bookes,
> Yet will they reade me, and thereby attaine
> To *Peters Chayre* . . .[59]

The reason for this confusion and even identification of Papism and Machiavellianism is not difficult to explain. Both were charged with the *misuse* of religion—therefore of "atheism." Such are the confusions which arise when ideas are defined in moral rather than in intellectual terms. It is scarcely to be wondered at that Nashe found

almost as much confusion of Religion in euery Quarter, as there was of tongues at the building of the Tower of Babell.[60]

A *via media* rooted in moral considerations could be made intelligible only by making much of classical ethics. This is what Spenser does in the *Faerie Queene*. The Red-Crosse Knight, before he can defeat the Dragon, must acquire the virtue of Holiness—a virtue displayed principally within Aristotelian and Platonic categories. The way to Holiness is the path of the golden mean, midway between the defective spiritual state of Sansjoy and the excessive of Abessa or Corcecca; the final attainment is in an act of contemplation largely Platonic. The line of Spenser's thinking is duplicated later in Burton.[61] Though Burton is com-

---

[59] Prologue, 10-13. Likewise, the Elizabethans associated Ignatius Loyola and Machiavelli: the two appear together in Lucifer's court in Donne's *Ignatius his Conclave;* and the Jesuit Parsons is termed by W. Watson "this most Atheall Polypragmon [i.e. "polypragmatic" or Machiavellian] Parsons." See Mario Praz, "Machiavelli and the Elizabethans," *Proceedings of the British Academy,* XIV (1928), esp. pp. 83 ff.

[60] *Pierce Penilesse* (1592), ed. McKerrow, I, 172.

[61] See Merritt Y. Hughes, "Burton on Spenser," *P. M. L. A.,* XLI (1926), 545-67. Hughes comments that "in a very real sense Spenser's Legend of Holiness was a great tapestry illustrating the best liberal religious thought of the English Reformation" (p. 553); and he remarks, very aptly, that this liberal thought begins with Erasmus and culminates in seventeenth century Latitudinarianism. I note that Burton, in elaborating his theory of love, quotes Plotinus and Ficinus repeatedly. He uses Plotinus' definition of religion, and quotes approvingly Cardan's view that Plotinus is one of the *triumviri terrarum* (ed. Shilleto, I, 85; III, 414).

pelled to admit that the Aristotelian categories are not strictly applicable, because there can be no excess in the love of God, yet he uses the terms "excess" and "defect" to indicate alternative forms of error in men's love and worship of God. Thus, like Spenser, he judges religion with a philosopher's measuring rod rather than by ecclesiastical canons. In the category of "excessive" religion Burton places "all superstitious Idolaters, Ethnicks, Mahometans, Jews, Hereticks, Enthusiasts, Divinators, Prophets, Sectaries, and Schismaticks." Burton's other category equally ignores ecclesiastical distinctions in order to include broadly all enemies of common sense. "Defective" religion apparently means simply a dull conscience:

> In the other extreme or in defect, march those impious Epicures, Libertines, Atheists, Hypocrites, Infidels, worldly, secure, impenitent, unthankful, and carnal-minded men, that attribute all to natural causes, and will acknowledge no supreme power, that have cauterized consciences, or live in a reprobate sense: or such desperate persons as are too distrustful of his mercies.[62]

By running into either of the two extremes, says Burton, "wee become fooles, madmen, without sence." In Burton's view the atheist is, essentially, an insane person:

> That grand sin of Atheism or Impiety, *Melanchthon* calls it, *monstrosam melancholiam,* monstrous melancholy. . . . A company of *Cyclopes* or Giants, that war with the gods, as the Poets feigned, Antipodes to Christians, that scoff at all Religion, at God himself, deny him and all his attributes, his wisdom, power, providence, his mercy and judgment. . . . *They seem to me* (saith Melanchthon) *to be as mad as Hercules was, when he raved and killed his wife and children.*[63]

---

[62] *Anat.* III. iv. 1. 1, ed. Shilleto, III, 367.
[63] Shilleto, III, 434 and 438. Note that Tamburlaine, in warring against the gods and in killing his own child, merely follows the pattern behavior here described.

Substantially the same view is found also in Nashe.[64]

The importance for literature of this heightening of the ethical element is considerable. Since atheists are by definition insane, such "atheists" as Machiavelli, the Pope, the Guises, and all "tyrants" must be shown in drama as monsters of iniquity. The callousness of certain villains of the Elizabethan stage, and the artificiality in their characterization and action, is certainly not unconnected with the morality tradition we have been discussing. Professor Hardin Craig[65] has made the point that De Flores and similar monsters of Jacobean tragedy seem to be manufactured by a formula based on the psychology of Stoicism as revived by Burton. And Professor Merritt Hughes[66] has remarked that Spenser's "mythical caricatures of exaggerated passion in figures like Corflambo and Busyrane" owe something to conceptions of Love Melancholy like Burton's. These critics are certainly correct—only we may quite as well say also, I think, that Burton's rationalistic psychology is but one piece in a vast store of humanistic philosophy rediscovered by the Renaissance and put to use by artists.

Seneca and Calvin were popular because they were thought to stand so directly over against "atheism" and Machiavellianism. The literary artist who was interested in educating his public against irreligion (and what loyal Elizabethan would have been ashamed to be a propagandist in this sense?) knew where he could turn both for illustrations of hated doctrines and for their antidote and confutation. The battle between the two camps was, first of all, over the issue of the interpretation of the Law of Nature. "Nature doth teach us all to have aspiring minds," says Tamburlaine

---

[64] *Christs Teares*, ed. McKerrow, II, 114-5.
[65] *The Enchanted Glass* (New York, 1936), pp. 116-7.
[66] "Burton on Spenser," p. 558.

voicing Machiavellian doctrine; but that was not the Stoic or the Calvinist notion of what Nature teaches. According to the Stoics, Nature teaches a cosmic providence, a rational law of reward and punishment: Nature is a principle of moral order, not of amoral energy. This Stoic view, taken over by Zwingli and by Calvin into their conceptions of Providence, furnishes the characteristic religious thinking of the Renaissance. Professor Quirinus Breen has suggested [67] that Calvin's commentary on Seneca's *De Clementia* can very well be regarded as a "Muzzle for Machiavellianism"; for Calvin, while agreeing with the Machiavellian view that the Prince is not subject to his own laws, diverges abruptly from Machiavelli's conclusion by insisting that the Prince is subject to the moral world-order, that even the Prince cannot escape responsibility to the laws of God. In short, Calvin's commentary is a sort of Mirror for Princes, in which Calvin shows himself wholly in agreement with Seneca's attempt to combat all forms of arbitrary despotism and tyranny.

Protestant Humanism was thus in polar opposition to Machiavellianism.[68] Queen Elizabeth, as head of English Protestantism, was supposed to be the antithesis of Machiavelli. Simon Patericke writes in 1577 that "the most renowned Queen"

hath hitherto preserved the State of her realme, not only safe but flourishing: not by Machiavelian artes, as Guile, Perfidie, and other Villaines practising: but by true vertues, as Clemencie, Iustice, Faith.[69]

The Elizabethan prejudice against Machiavelli is to be traced

---

[67] *Calvin*, pp. 80 ff.

[68] On this point see especially Hans Beck, *Machiavellismus in der englischen Renaissance* (Duisburg, 1935), pp. 21 ff.

[69] Gentillet, *A Discovrse Vpon The Meanes of Wel Governing*, etc., trans. Patericke (London, 1602), The Epistle Dedicatorie, dated 1577.

not, as Edward Meyer supposed, almost wholly to Gentillet, but more broadly to the Huguenot movement and to Protestantism generally. We find Elizabeth's Protestant tutor Ascham raising the cry against Machiavelli's "irreligion" already in the *Scholemaster;* and the term "Machivilian" is opprobrious in ballad literature, as Mario Praz has shown, as early as 1568. Thus Machiavelli's name had become, even before the publication of Gentillet's book, a sort of "rallying-point for whatever was most loathsome in statecraft, and indeed in human nature at large." [70] Gentillet does not inaugurate but merely illustrates Protestant sentiment when he calls the Florentine "un vray atheiste et contempteur de Dieu" and says that "son but a esté d'instruire le Prince à estre un vrai Tyran, et à luy enseigner l'art de Tyrannie."

An obvious parallel in our own day is Liberalism's bitter hatred of the Communazi Dictator. If only Gentillet could see our portraits of Hitler! Machiavelli—there he stands; and ours is an all-out war against him. But in Elizabeth's time—as today—the enemy fascinated as well as horrified. Those who cried out most loudly against him felt compelled occasionally, alas, to use his doctrines for their own self-preservation. Such instances of hypocrisy under duress served only to convince them of the insidiousness of the disease.

The religion which Humanism opposed to Machiavellianism was latitudinarian. It is interesting to discover, for example, that Swift gets his famous fable of Latitudinarianism not from his own eighteenth century but from Gentillet. The *Tale of a Tub* has its source, as D. E. Baughan has shown,[71] in a tale in Gentillet's Preface to the section of his book attacking Machiavelli's views of religion. Along with the tale, Gentillet brings forward a lengthy discourse, in which it is argued that Protestants and Catholics are basically

---

[70] Praz, pp. 52-54.
[71] "Swift and Gentillet," *Studies in Philology,* XXXVII (1940), 67-68.

of one religion. The common people among the Catholics, our author thinks, do not really believe the "subtle distinctions and sophisticall tearmes" which their Sophist-priests would make them believe. If we will but appeal to "such points of Religion, whereof the Catholikes have some knowledge by the apprehension of sence and common iudgement," we will find that we can reject the Romish doctrines of transubstantiation, supererogatory works, merits of saints, wearing of special vestments, and the pope. In "the articles which are necessary for our salvation" Protestants and Catholics agree. For surely we must believe that God has given us a religion which is "simple, cleare, and intelligible, that even plaine people might comprehend and understand it." [72]

Liberal Humanism has, as Gentillet indicates, no great respect for sophistications and subtleties. In art its genius is for caricature: for simple, bold distinctions and broad, sharp strokes. Swift's satires and Marlowe's dramas are in this tradition.

We may say of Elizabethan religion, in summary, that while it has really no new elements not in the medieval background, it has them in a somewhat new arrangement. In theory the hierarchical subordination of classical culture to Christian revelation still holds; but in practice the importance of the classical is magnified, and fundamental Christian concepts tend to be defined from the standpoint of Seneca and Plato. The tendency in philosophy is syncretistic; in Faith, latitudinarian. The Ship of Souls is less emphasized than the School of Nature. And Penance, the medieval "medicine of the soul," is largely superseded by Moral Philosophy, which Sidney calls "a medicine of cherries." [73]

---

[72] Gentillet, pp. 80 ff.
[73] *Defence of Poesie*, ed. Feuillerat, p. 21.

RALEIGH'S RELIGION

꿹 꿹

SIR WALTER RALEIGH, like Marlowe, was a brilliant man and considerably misunderstood. His life, also, was dramatic and tragic. Nowadays he is commonly named together with Marlowe in a supposed friendship, though the contemporary evidence for a close association of these two Elizabethans is rather scant.[1] The conjecture of a relationship between them is attractive largely for intangible reasons. Somehow both men seem to represent the "spirit" of the Renaissance. Both have long carried with their names the stigma of atheism. That Raleigh's views on philosophy and religion correspond roughly with Marlowe's it would be rash to claim, for we know as yet too little about Marlowe. But we can investigate Raleigh's religion as a topic worth some consideration in its own right; and our study may serve incidentally to reveal attitudes and concepts which will aid the intelligent approach to Marlowe's dramas.

It is interesting to note that our most recent critics of Raleigh have been inclined to rescue him from the scandal of atheism.[2] They find that Raleigh's views are orthodox,

---

[1] The likelihood of some sort of association between Raleigh and Marlowe can be inferred from the following pertinent facts: 1) A spy's report of the testimony of Richard Cholmley that "Marloe tolde him that hee hath read the Atheist lecture to Sir Walter Raleigh & others." 2) Baines' report of Marlowe's blasphemy that "Moyses was but a jugler & that one Heriots being Sir W. Raleighs man can do more than he." 3) Kyd's report that Marlowe "conversed with Hariot. 4) The fact that Raleigh wrote answering verses to Marlowe's *The Passionate Shepherd to His Love.*

[2] See G. T. Buckley, *Atheism in the English Renaissance* (Chicago, 1932), pp. 137-52; J. Beau, "La Religion de Sir Walter Ralegh," *Revue Anglo-Américaine,* XI (1933-34), 410-22; E. A. Strathmann, "Sir Walter Ralegh on Natural Philosophy," *Modern Language Quarterly,* I (1940), 49-62, and *"The History of the World* and Ralegh's Scepticism," *Huntington Library Quarterly,* III (1940), 265-87. Buckley concludes that Raleigh "may in his youth have

his piety notable, his ethical concern thoroughgoing, and his handling of Scripture reverential. Actually, as Professor Strathmann points out,[3] Raleigh is very far from the vulgar blasphemy that Moses was a juggler (the blasphemy attributed to Marlowe), for Raleigh considers the miracles of Moses quite opposite in character to the conjurings of Pharaoh's sorcerers. In short, Raleigh is not an atheist, not even a religious skeptic; he does, however, inherit much of the superstition of his time regarding astrology and witchcraft.[4]

This modern view—fundamentally, I think, a correct one—needs, however, further clarification. For if Raleigh was actually orthodox, how shall we explain his reputation for atheism? The rumor of his unconventional opinions was prevalent enough to inspire an investigation in 1594; and though nothing was adduced before the Queen's Commission to convict Raleigh of heresy, certain Elizabethans held doubts of his strict orthodoxy even to the time of his death. By what perspective, then, shall we reconcile the "atheist" of Elizabethan rumor with the Christian apologist of Mr. Buckley's modern interpretation?

I

Let us begin by examining the nature of the popular charge against Raleigh. It had, apparently, two grounds: 1) his bold social criticism; and 2) his associations with

---

passed through a period of doubt, but age at any rate found him orthodox and even one of the defenders of the Christian dogma." Beau speculates that Raleigh may have discarded all belief except in the moral governance of the world, until reborn by his prison experiences he found a God vaster than the God of the Christian sects—a religion of adoration, without dogma, composed of some essential truths. But, as Strathmann points out (*H. L. Q.*), there seems to be no evidence for any chronological demarcations in Raleigh's views. What he says publicly in 1614 in the *History of the World* is in harmony with what Ironside reports of his views in 1594.

[3] *M. L. Q.*, I, 54.
[4] *Ibid.*, p. 61; *H. L. Q.*, III, 287.

men who met together for secret discussions of the sciences and philosophy. Example of the first is his poem *The Lie,* a heatedly righteous denunciation of corruption and hypocrisy in both the Court and the Church, for which Raleigh received the rebuke:

> The Court hath settled sureness
> In banishing such boldness
> The Church retains her pureness
> Though Atheists show their coldness
> The Court and Church though base
> Turn lies into thy face.[5]

Illustration of the second ground of criticism appears in 1592 in the notorious charge, generally attributed to Parsons but probably by Creswell,[6] that Raleigh was conducting a "schoole of Atheism" wherein

both Moyses, & our Sauior, the olde, and the new Testaments are iested at, and the schollers taught amonge other things, to spell God backwarde.

Interestingly, the charge can be inferentially supported by the reported testimony of Richard Cholmley in 1593:

that one Marlowe is able to shewe more sounde reasons for Atheisme then any devine in Englande is able to geiue to prove divinitie and that Marloe tolde him that hee hath read the Atheist lecture to Sir Walter Raliegh & others.[7]

Since Creswell's charge appears in a propagandist tract, and Cholmley's testimony is that of a double-dealing spy

---

[5] See Edward Thompson, *Sir Walter Raleigh* (New Haven, 1936), p. 74.
[6] C. F. Tucker Brooke, "Sir Walter Ralegh as Poet and Philosopher," *E. L. H.,* V, 108.
[7] Harleian MSS 6848, fol. 190; reprinted by F. C. Danchin, "Etudes Critiques sur Christopher Marlowe, II.," *Revue Germanique,* IX (1913), 575-76.

whom Marlowe may have wished to deceive, the two pieces
of evidence must be viewed with caution. But even if Creswell and Cholmley have misinterpreted the facts, the evidence nevertheless suggests that behind the misinterpreta-
tions lies the fact that Raleigh was much interested in philosophic discussions of occult matters. And this, I think, is
significant. Occultism is one of the characteristic interests
of radical Puritanism: neither our Salem ancestors nor John
Milton were immune from the fascinations of esoteric learning. And the other note we find in Raleigh is equally
characteristic of Puritanism: an impulsive concern for morality. The genuineness and seriousness of Raleigh's ethical
interest cannot be doubted. Not only *The Lie* but also the
poem *His Pilgrimage* and especially the exceedingly moral
History of the World argue it. We may accuse him, of
course, as we so often accuse the Puritans, of hypocrisy; but
our criticism will not gainsay the fact that in his own
eyes Raleigh was an earnest champion of morality.[8]

The chief source for these two themes of Puritanism—
morality and occult philosophy—is the revived Platonism
of the Renaissance. This point deserves note and comment.
We need to remember that all forms of Neo-Platonism have
as their central concern the conversion of the moral life, and
that the Neo-Platonic metaphysics, which interprets nature
as a vast scheme of cosmic wisdom established for a moral
purpose, aggrandizes the sphere of the spiritual by introducing mystic powers throughout the framework of nature.

---

[8] The charge of Puritanism was apparently levelled against Raleigh in his
own day, for in a marginal note in the *H. W.* (V. v. 2, p. 650) he objects to
being called a Puritan. Since he elsewhere in the same work (II v. 1, pp. 296-
97) complains against the Familists, Anabaptists, Brownists, and other Sectaries,
who "in this super-fine Age" would cast away order and ceremony and bring
Church government into contempt, we must assume that Raleigh considered
himself of the Anglican party. However, his official loyalty to the Established
Church does not preclude the philosophic Puritanism which I have attributed to
him, and which is always an incipient characteristic of Anglicanism.

Whenever Neo-Platonism has been in the ascendant it has encouraged both an emphasis on virtue and a study of natural philosophy.

Raleigh's thought is dominated by this Platonic tradition. In the *History of the World* we find him using the words of the Areopagite to define his notion of God and the words of Ficinus truly to express "the will and science of Nature." [9] On the relation of God and Nature, he quotes at length a description by Proclus of the way in which the world is sustained by the Divine Being; and in his discussion of Fate and Providence he takes his stand near Plotinus and Origen, after refuting the conceptions of the Stoics.[10]　He holds with Trismegistus that the world is *Magni Dei sapiens opus*; and with Nicholas of Cusa that it is "nothing else but God expressed." [11]　And he accepts the doctrine that man is a microcosm or little world.[12]　The Platonism of his thinking is striking when he says that

True philosophy, is an ascending from the things which flow, and rise, and fall, to the things that are for euer the same.[13]

Rebellion against Aristotle was common during the Renaissance, and Raleigh shares the modern temper.　Contemptuously he speaks of "Aristotles rotten ground . . . vpon which he hath notwithstanding founded the Defences and Fortresses of all his Verball Doctrine," and he marvels that even "the iudgement of Naturall reason" has not better informed Aristotle than to cause him to deny the doctrine

---

[9] *History of the World* (1614), Preface, Sig. D4^r; E2^r.
[10] *Ibid.*, Sig. E^r; and I. i. 11.
[11] *Ibid.*, Sig. A2^r; and I. i. 1.
[12] *Ibid.*, I. ii. 5.
[13] *Ibid.*, Sig. E2^v.

of the world's Creation.[14]   Aristotle has "taught little other than *termes*."

But, for my self, I shall neuer be perswaded, that GOD shut vp all light of Learning within the lanthorne of *Aristotles* braines.[15]

Coming to the discussion of magic, Raleigh writes:

The third kinde of *Magicke* containeth the whole Philosophie of nature; not the brablings of the *Aristotelians,* but that which bringeth to light the inmost vertues, and draweth them out of natures hidden bosome to human vse.[16]

It is this interest of Raleigh in magic—that is, in Neo-Platonic natural philosophy—which is at the bottom of his vigorous rejection of Aristotle.   Raleigh is a modern in that he insists on appealing directly to the authority of nature and experience.   He is a modern also in that he has no patience with the "subtile distinctions" of the Schoolmen.[17]   To Raleigh's way of thinking, God reveals His truth in two ways: by "his word" and by "this visible world."[18]

---

[14] *Ibid.,* Sig. D2^r.

[15] *Ibid.,* Sig. D2^v.

[16] *Ibid.,* I. xi. 2, p. 202.   To support his favorable view of magic, Raleigh brings testimony from a host of Platonists—from Plato himself that "the art of *Magicke* is the art of worshipping God"; from Ficinus, that Magus is "a name gratious in the Gospell"; from Mirandula, that magic furthers us in knowing the divinity of Christ; and importantly from Senensis, that "Magic is of two sortes, the one everywhere condemned by Origen; which worketh . . . by couenants with Deuils; the other commended by Origen; which appertaineth to the practick part of naturall philosophie."

[17] *H. W.* I. ii. 1, p. 23.   Note Francis Osborne's statement in his *Miscellany* (1659): "Sir Walter Raleigh was the first that ventured to tack about and sailed aloof from the beaten track of the Schools; therefore . . . he was ever after branded with the title of an atheist, though a known asserter of God and Providence." Quoted by J. Beau, p. 421n.

[18] *H. W.* I. i. 1.

II

In illustration of the character of Raleigh's thought it will be profitable to examine his statements on three central problems: the nature of God, the nature of the world, and the nature of man. We shall discover that his Christianity rests mainly on Platonic natural religion—and risks the tendencies toward Christian heterodoxy which Platonism encourages.

On the nature of God, the earliest evidence we have of Raleigh's views is that produced at the Cerne Abbas inquiry.[19] Ralph Ironside, minister of Winterbor, testified that he had been present at an after-supper discussion among Sir Walter, his brother Carewe, and others around the table of George Trenchard at Wolverton one night in the summer of 1593. The discussion became significant when Carewe posed the question of the nature of the soul. Sir Walter answered:

> I have been (sayeth he) a scholler some tyme in Oxeforde, I have aunswered vnder a Bacheler of Arte, & had taulke with diu[ines], yet heithervnto in this pointe (to witt what the reasonable soule of man is) have I not by anye benne resolved. They tell vs it is primus motor the first mover in a man &c.[20]

Ironside then quoted Aristotle's definition of the soul: but Sir Walter thought it too obscure and intricate to satisfy anyone. He challenged Ironside to demonstrate his definition as one would demonstrate a proposition in mathematics, say, for example, the proposition that the whole is greater than any of its parts. Ironside replied that even Sir Walter's

---

[19] A full report of these proceedings is available in G. B. Harrison's edition of *Willobie His Avisa* (London, 1926), Appendix III, pp. 255-71; and in F. C. Dauchin, pp. 578 ff.

[20] Harrison, p. 266. Perhaps for "diu[ines]" we should read "diu[ers]."

proposition could be demonstrated only *that* it is (*quod est*), not *what* it is (*quid est*), and added that though there is no more certain thing than *that* God is, yet to subject Him to our imperfect senses as to *what* He is is impossible. This pleased Sir Walter:

Marrye quoth Sr. Walter these 2 be like for neither coulde I lerne heitherto what god is.

When later Aristotle's definition of God as "Ens Entium" was advanced, Sir Walter disliked the conversation and "wished that grace might be sayed; for that quoth he is better than this disputation."

The attitude here expressed looks like the *sacra ignorantia* of Nicholas of Cusa, Erasmus, and the *Devotio moderna*.[21] For while Raleigh's piety is conspicuous, he is skeptical of definitions and dissatisfied with Aristotle. He seems to wish to reduce knowledge to what is strictly demonstrable, like mathematics. He does not allow, as does Aquinas, for an indirect or analogical knowledge of God's nature.

When, at some date not exactly known, Raleigh wrote his *Treatise of the Soul* we find his view still essentially unchanged from what Ironside had reported it to be. This time Raleigh calls to his support various Church Fathers, declaring:

The substance of the soul is hardly known; Lactantius denieth that men can attain to the knowledge of the nature of the soul; and Galen confesseth, that he cannot tell what or where the substance of the soul is. And Athanasius saith, that while we live there are three things whereof we cannot attain the knowledge; the substance of God, of angels, and of our souls.[22]

---

[21] See R. H. Bainton, *Castellio Concerning Heretics* (New York, 1935), pp. 30 ff.; and Lefranc, "Marguerite de Navarre," pp. 166 ff.
[22] *The Works of Sir Walter Ralegh*, ed. Oldys and Birch (Oxford, 1829), VIII, 574.

This conclusion, typically that of negative theology, is the same as that set forth in the popular *Trewnesse of the Christian Religion* (1587), where in a chapter discussing "What it is that we can comprehend concerning God" Mornay bases his view on the testimony of Cicero, Galen, Plotinus, Moses, Trismegistus, Porphyry, and the Areopagite.[23]

The view appears again in the *History of the World,* written during the years 1607-1614. Man is ignorant of what his soul is, for no man, not even Aristotle, can define it;[24] and man can likewise not define the transcendent glory which is God.[25] However, Raleigh makes much of the doctrine that the world of creatures is a mirror which images the Undefinable Glory. In viewing the world we can "in part discerne" and "approach to the knowledge of" God—"whom the wisest men acknowledge to bee a Power vneffable and Vertue infinite, a Light by abundant claritie inuisible."

This is Neo-Platonic language: God is essentially unknowable, but Nature points us to God. God is utterly transcendent—"That infinite power of which wee can comprehend but a kind of shadow." Or again, Raleigh remarks that in respect of God's sublimity and purity what Trismegistus has said of God is true: He is not a mind, but the cause of mind; nor spirit, but the cause of spirit; nor light, but the cause of light.[26] We might say that what Raleigh

---

[23] Chap. iv. Mornay says: "Verily the most in effect that we can knowe concerning his being is that we can understand nothing at al thereof." Mornay's corollary conclusion is pietistic: we will do best to give ourselves to loving, serving, and worshipping God. Cf. Nashe's view, *Christs Teares,* ed. McKerrow, II, 118-19.

[24] Pref., Sig. D3^r.

[25] *H. W.* I. i. 1, pp. 1-2.

[26] *H. W.* I. i. 7, p. 11.

is really describing is a transrational First Cause—which he calls God.

The existence of this God, Raleigh holds, can be proved by Necessity without the aid of Faith.[27] Raleigh makes no mention of the role of Christ in revealing God, because it is Raleigh's view that the witnessing of nature, together with the testimony of the philosophers,[28] establishes beyond controversy the truth of God's existence; and to inquire further as to the essence of God and other secret matters is to "grow mad with reason." Let us be satisfied, says Raleigh, that Reason without the help of Authority "doth prove" unto us that there is a power infinite and eternal present everywhere in the world. *How* this power is present must be left to Faith, which is strengthened by our ignorance. The whole view accords clearly with what was reported of his theology in 1593: God's existence is certain; His essence, unknowable.

Raleigh's Christian apologetics is in a tradition of thought reaching back to Raymond of Sebonde. Raymond, we remember, argued that by attending to the book of Nature, which teaches by experience, every man can recognize without difficulty or toil every truth that he needs to know for salvation.[29] Even the Christian doctrine of Creation, Raymond held, can be proved, without ecclesiastical authority, from the witness of Nature alone. In contrast to Aquinas who modestly admits that Reason cannot disprove Aristotle's denial of a Creation but can only show his arguments to be insufficient, Raymond undertook to conclude against the eternity of the world without reference to Revelation.

---

[27] Pref., Sig. E2ᵛ-E3ʳ.

[28] Among philosophers Raleigh singles out the opinion of the reverent and learned Trismegistus that belief in "one true God, and euerlasting being, all for euer causing, and for euer sustaining" is an "vnresistable necessitie" (*H. W.* I. vi. 7, p. 96; Pref., Sig. D3ʳ).

[29] See the excellent chapter on Raymond in C. C. J. Webb's *Studies in the History of Natural Theology* (Oxford, 1915), pp. 292-312.

Raymond's effort is likewise Raleigh's. In the Preface to the *History* Raleigh argues that Aristotle's doctrine of the world's eternity is impossible "euen in the iudgement of Naturall reason." He declares that "euery reasonable soule" must confess that God created the world *ex nihilo* and that it is madness to hold any other view.

It is important to recognize that in Raleigh's apologetics rationalism and skepticism go side by side under the banner of a mystico-moral religion. Reason is advanced to "prove" doctrines; but skepticism is used to undermine dogma. The central interest is always morality:

Beatitude doth not consist in the knowledge of diuine things, but in a diuine life: for the Diuells know them better than men. *Beatitudo non est diuinorum cognitio, sed vita divina.*[30]

Morality is again the dominant consideration in Raleigh's view of the world. He undertakes to display in his *History* "How Kings and Kingdomes haue flourished and fallen; and for what virtue and piety GOD made prosperous; and for what vice and deformity he made wretched, both the one and the other." [31] The spectacle is religiously edifying: it illustrates the Biblical truth that "GOD will not be mockt" (*Gal.* VI. 7), that His judgments are unchangeable, that "irreligious policie" has bitter fruits in all ages. For this truth of God's moral governance of the world "the sea of examples has no bottom."

But history's great educational pageant, which Raleigh says gives "life in our vnderstanding," appears to have no life in itself, no self-action; all is a divine determinism. Raleigh utterly rejects belief in fortune or chance.[32] God's

---

[30] Pref., Sig. C2ᵛ.
[31] Pref., Sig. A2ᵛ.
[32] *H. W.* I. i. 15. and II. v. 10, p. 310. In Moses' life there is "not therefore the smallest accident which may seeme vnto men as falling out by chance."

hand holds nature "but as a pencill." [33] God has impartially written out all the parts we are to play upon the world-stage.[34] Nature is, as Plato called it, "The art, or artificiall Organ of God" and, as Nicholas of Cusa testifies, "The instrument of the diuine precept." [35] All things "work by an impulsion which they cannot resist." [36] Nature has "no other selfe-abilitie then a Clocke, after it is wound vp by a mans hand, hath." [37]

Raleigh's Platonism leads him to make a sharp distinction between God and nature: it is an "impiety monstrous" to confound the two.

It is God, that commandeth all: It is Nature that is obedient to all. It is God that doth good vnto all, knowing and louing the good hee doth: It is Nature, that secondarily doth also good, but it neither knoweth nor loueth the good it doth.[38]

Raleigh's view, we can see, has dangers: so strict a removal of reason from nature avoids Stoic pantheism only to risk mechanism. God's sovereignty is elevated, but nature's liberty is abolished. In Raleigh's philosophy secondary causes are mere agents of the First Cause.

The same danger besets Raleigh's view of man. In *The Treatise of the Soul* Raleigh places man's soul somewhere midway between the great cosmic opposites of nature and God.

The soul, and this spirit which we are endued with, is a certain mean between the body and God.[39]

---

[33] *H. W.* I. xi. 2, p. 205.
[34] Pref., Sig. D[v].
[35] *H. W.* I. i. 15, p. 19.
[36] Pref., Sig. E2[v].
[37] *H. W.* I. i. 10, p. 13.
[38] *H. W.* Pref., Sig. E2[v].
[39] Oldys and Birch, VIII, 577.

This definition, certainly, is more Neo-Platonic than Scholastic. It appears in the midst of a discussion of the orthodox Christian doctrine of Creationism, which Raleigh is attempting to defend against the Aristotelians. In his explaining how God can be the creator of each individual soul, and yet not the author of evil, Raleigh adopts a view which is fundamentally Platonic, that "body" is the immediate cause of the soul's predicament:

> And although the soul come from God, yet the sin doth not come from him; but the body doth communicate it to the soul, as the soul doth impart many things to the body; for they both make one person, and the soul in the body is straightway subject to the state of sin with the body by the just sentence of God, which took from the seed of Adam all that he bestowed on Adam. And God by his judgment forsaking it, how can it be but sinful, dwelling in a sinful body? [40]

The way in which Raleigh understands man's freedom appears in the chapter on Fate in *The History of the World*.[41] We encounter here no Lutheran notion of freedom through Christ; for the discussion moves entirely on a philosophic plane. The Stoic notion which would give Fate dominion over the mind and will of man Raleigh combats by calling upon the opinions of Trismegistus and Plotinus. Raleigh acknowledges that the stars have great influence as the instruments and organs of God's providence—but not omnipotent sway. They incline man's will by working on his constitution and complexion and by the mediation of his sensitive appetite. But St. Augustine did

---

[40] *Ibid.*, p. 579. But contrast St. Augustine (*De Civ. Dei*, xiv, 3): "It is not the corrupt flesh that makes the soul sinful, but the sinful soul that makes the flesh corrupt." It is at this point, says St. Augustine, that the views of the Platonists are censurable.

[41] I. i. 11, pp. 14 ff. The reader should compare Proclus, *On Providence and Fate*, esp. sec. 8. Proclus, like Raleigh, makes the point that the empire of Fate is entirely in corporeal natures, while intellectual natures are exempt from Fate and under Providence alone.

not avouch that stars "have rule over men's minds, which
are incorporeal"; hence we must conclude that man's mind
can be influenced directly by God.

we derogate from his [i.e., God's] eternal and absolute power and
prouidence to ascribe to them [i.e., the stars] the same dominion ouer
our immortall soules, which they haue ouer all bodily substances, and
perishable natures: for the soules of men, louing and fearing God,
receiue influence from the diuine light itselfe, whereof the Sunnes
claritie, and that of the Stars, is by Plato called but a shadow.

Raleigh seems to be saying that man, by receiving the *direct*
influence of God can conquer Fate, which is a secondary
and *mediated* influence of God. In the contest, man is
affirmed to be the chooser and responsible:

as he that contendeth against these inforcements [i.e., the stars] may
easily master or resist them: so whatsoeuer shall neglect the remedies
by vertue and pietie prepared, putteth himself altogether vnder the
power of his sensuall appetite. . . . Fate will be overcome, if thou
resist it, if thou neglect it, it conquereth.

This view, anticipating Milton, construes the world as a
theatre of moral struggle in which man's armory is religious
education. Raleigh believes "there are none in the world
so wickedly inclined, but that a religious instruction and
bringing vp may fashion anew, and reforme them."

We must recognize, however, that Raleigh's notion of religious education, so far as we are able to judge from his
writings, comprehends simply the study of history and of
nature for lessons of Puritan morality and piety. Of ecclesiastical Christianity Raleigh seems to have been rather independent. His wide reading in Platonic sources encouraged
him in the study of natural philosophy; but it is less evident
that he had any very deep appreciation for Christian dogma
or even for New Testament revelation. When arguing for

the immortality of the soul he appeals not to Scripture but to the philosophers and to nature:

> The soul of man, using will and reason, is immortal: Galen reporteth that all ancient wise men unto Plato were of that opinion. . . .

> Last of all; religion, and the fear of God, which is in man, doth shew it to be immortal; for we worship God because our souls are made to his image, and we know he is *a rewarder of them that serve him.* Now religion is grafted in men's minds by nature; for it hath always, yea before any books of it were written, and all wise men have ever minded godliness and virtue, with the study of wisdom.[42]

Religion thus understood is the religion of More's Utopia—a fundamental Natural Religion.

Neo-Platonism, which as St. Augustine discovered suffers from the lack of a doctrine of the Incarnation, has always had for Christian philosophers an Arian tendency.[43] Nominally, Raleigh is apparently trinitarian, for he holds that Christ is "of the same substance" with God.[44] But there may be some significance in Aubrey's report that

---

[42] *Treatise on the Soul,* ed. Oldys and Birch, VIII, 589 and 591.

[43] The tendency is recognizable, for example, in Lactantius, of whom Raleigh seems to have been very fond—he quotes Lactantius six times in the Preface to the *History,* twice in the *Treatise on the Soul.* Miss Kathleen Hartwell, *Lactantius and Milton* (Cambridge, 1929), pp. 97 ff., is probably correct in observing that Milton could have found a source for his Arianism in Lactantius. This "Christian Cicero" of the fourth century was particularly well read in the philosophy of Hermes Trismegistus and in the poetry of Ovid. Like Reformation apologists, Lactantius wished to establish the reasonableness of Christianity, especially against the Epicureans. His emphasis in religion was predominantly on moral philosophy. René Pichon, *Lactance* (Paris, 1901), pp. 95, 101, points out that the religious philosophy of Lactantius was eclectic, a synthesis of dogmatism and Pyrrhonism. We may regard Raleigh's effort as perhaps not altogether dissimilar—witness his treatise *The Sceptick* (a close summary, as Buckley shows, of the first three tropes of the *Pyrrhonean Hypotyposes*) and his moral dogmatism. Someone could do us a service by making a study of Lactantius and Raleigh.

[44] Oldys and Birch, VIII, 743-44.

In his speech on the scaffold I heard my cosen Whitney say (and I think 'tis printed) that he spake not one word of Christ, but of the great and incomprehensible God, with much zeale and adoration, so that he concluded he was an a-Christ, not an atheist.[45]

Also it is instructive to reflect for a moment on Raleigh's central notion that there is no Fortune at all but Providence only. The idea, certainly, makes difficult a genuine doctrine of the Fall of man. The Fall can be interpreted by this philosophy perhaps as a *mistake* to be amended, but hardly as a *mischance* from which to be ransomed. An historical Redeemer is a concept quite unrelated, even somewhat out of place among the principles of Raleigh's ethical religion.

What evidence we have, then, shows Raleigh to be a man of piety, interested in the scientific study of nature and of history, interpreting these in the light of a mystical theology which has its basis in Neo-Platonism. In this we ought not to regard Raleigh as a rebel from the thinking of his age— any more than was Milton, whose views Raleigh's in so many ways resemble.[46]

III

For our study of *Tamburlaine* the outworkings of Raleigh's thought have particular import at two points which we shall here notice: his view of tyranny, and his view of perjury. Both tyranny and perjury Raleigh regards as very great crimes, inexcusable on any grounds except those of the false Machiavellian policy which is of the devil. Against such policy Raleigh invokes the God of moral law.

Because he is confident that moral law is rooted in Na-

---

[45] Quoted by F. C. Danchin, *Revue Germanique*, X (1914), 67n.
[46] Regarding points at which Milton echoes Raleigh, see, e.g., G. W. Whiting, *Milton's Literary Milieu* (Chapel Hill, 1939), pp. 39 ff. It will be recalled that Milton edited Raleigh's *Cabinet Council*.

ture, Raleigh can present quite objectively in his *Maxims of State* and in *The Cabinet Council* a thorough description of "the false doctrine of Machiavellian policy." He outlines the Rules of tyrants at the same time that he declaims against them as being contrary to religion, inhumane, cruel, and barbarous.[47] He says:

> These rules of hypocritical tyrants are to be known, that they may be avoided, and met withal; and not drawn into imitation.[48]

We who remember Tamburlaine's attitudes of piety will note, particularly, Rule 14 in Raleigh's list of 18 "Sophisms of the sophistical or subtle tyrant": it points out that a careful pretense of religion and of serving God "hath been the manner of the wickedest tyrants." Elsewhere Raleigh speaks of tyranny as "the worst of all bastard states, because it is the perverting of the best regimen, to wit, of a monarchy." He notes that tyranny tends, as is illustrated by the history of the Turks, not to the public good but to the private benefit of the tyrant and his followers.[49] Yet Raleigh can view tyranny serenely for two reasons: because it is so obviously contrary to justice, conscience, and the law of nature; and because, since bad kings as well as good are sent by God and must be endured, the best Christian remedy is patience.[50]

The sacredness of oaths is a theme Raleigh expounds at length in his *History* when he is recounting the dealings of Joshua with the Gibeonites.[51] If ever a man had warrant to break faith and to retract his promises, says Raleigh, Joshua had it; for he had the express commandment of God to root out the Gibeonites, and they were guilty of lying and

---

[47] Oldys and Birch, VIII, 18-19.
[48] *Ibid.*, pp. 26-27.
[49] *Ibid.*, pp. 3-4.
[50] *Ibid.*, p. 85.
[51] *H. W.* II. vi. 8, pp. 327-28.

deceit, and they were known idolaters. Yet, "notwithstanding that they, to whom hee had sworne it, were wor-
shippers of the Deuill," Joshua held firm his promise, in
order that men in the future might not borrow from him
any example of truce-breaking. The "Doctrine of keeping
Faith," Raleigh declares, leaves no loophole for that "horrible deceit of this latter age, called *Equiuocation."* A promise sworn to a man, or a state, or a king in the name of the
living Lord is, if broken, a promise broken not to man but
to God. He that breaks faith has no Faith to break: for
whoever has Faith dares not break faith.

Raleigh adduces two *exempla.* The Christians in the
Holy Land were at the height of their empire beaten out,
because (according to the Reverend Bishop William of
Tyre) the Christian king Almerick broke faith with the
Caliph Elhadech:

neither would the woodden Crosse (the very *Crosse,* say they that
Christ died on) giue them victorie ouer Seladine, when they brought
it into the field as their last refuge: seeing they had forsworne themselues in his name, that was crucified thereon.

The second illustration is even more interesting, for it happens to be the very piece of history which Marlowe used as
pattern for the subplot of *Tamburlaine* II. Here is how
Raleigh tells it:

It was *Eugenius* the Pope, that perswaded, or rather commanded the
King of *Hungarie* after his great victorie ouer *Amurath* the *Turke,*
and when the said King had compelled him to peace, the most
aduantagious that euer was made for the Christians, to breake his
faith, and to prouoke the *Turke* to renew the warre. And though
the said King was farre stronger in the field than euer; yet he lost
the battaile with 30,000 *Christians,* and his owne life. But I will
stay my hand: For this first volume will not hold the repetition of
Gods iudgements vpon faith-breakers; be it against *Infidels, Turkes,*

or *Christians* of diuers Religions. Lamentable it is, that the taking of oathes now-a-daies, is rather made a matter of custome than of conscience.

This is good anti-Catholic polemic. We shall find that Marlowe, when he presents the story in drama, omits the Pope from a share in the perjury and thus sidesteps the antipapal theme; yet Marlowe presents oath-breaking, as Raleigh views it, as a sin against moral law, punished providentially by the overthrow of the sinner.

CHAPMAN'S RELIGION

G EORGE CHAPMAN has been called by Havelock Ellis "the moralist of the English Renaissance."[1] Of the various men whose names have been linked with Marlowe's, Chapman would seem to be the one in whose works we might look most profitably for a system of ideas to help us in understanding Marlowe's mind,[2] for we know that in continuing Marlowe's *Hero and Leander* Chapman claims a spiritual affinity with the deceased poet. He says that Marlowe, who stood "up to the chin" in the waters of poetic truth, "drank to me half this Musaean story" and that now he, Chapman, will return the pledge. He calls upon the powers of intellectual inspiration to bear his message to the "free soul" of the dead poet and to "Tell it how much his late desires I tender." He hopes that the "most strangely-intellectual fire" will make his own "soul's dark offspring" as immortal as Marlowe's.[3]

The intellectual fire which Chapman here invokes is a quality we readily sense when we read either his poetry or Marlowe's. Both poets load their verses with learning and with passion. The dramatic personages who speak these verses live grandly in the kingdoms of the mind. In *Bussy D'Ambois,* as in *Tamburlaine,* the drama is spectacular and violent, loaded with ethical reflections, and built about a single titanic figure.

---

[1] *George Chapman* (Bloomsbury, 1934), p. 74.

[2] Ellis regards Marlowe as "Chapman's master" (p. 74) and speaks of "the school of Marlowe out of which Chapman came" (p. 20). Ellis supports the judgment by comparing stylistically the verse of the two poets. He does not, however, attempt to discuss their ideas.

[3] See *Hero and Leander,* III, 182-98.

Also there are elsewhere, as recent critics have pointed out,[4] certain bits of biographical and literary evidence which seem to indicate that the two poets shared a common interest in certain dark and esoteric matters. It is now supposed that Marlowe—together with Raleigh, Hariot, Roydon, and possibly others—was included in the so-called "School of Night," which it is thought Shakespeare attacks in *Love's Labour's Lost,* and which is commonly identified with what a Jesuit pamphleteer called "Sir Walter Raleigh's School of Atheism."

These observations would lead us to expect in Chapman and Marlowe a similar temper of mind. How are we to explain, then, the fact that Anthony Wood describes Chapman in words which hardly seem to fit at all with what modern biographers say of Marlowe? Wood describes Chapman as "a person of most reverent aspect, religious and temperate, qualities rarely meeting in a poet."[5] Could Wood's Chapman and Baines' Marlowe have been bosom friends?

However we may answer that question, there can be no doubt but that Wood's picture of Chapman's moderation and piety is fully substantiated by the revelations which Chapman gives us of himself in his nondramatic verse. We are very fortunate in Chapman's case (in contrast to Marlowe's) not to have to rely for our knowledge of the author's opinions solely on his dramatic works—from which a poet's beliefs are so easily misread. Chapman has left us a goodly amount of occasional verse, in which the salient concerns and convictions of his mind may easily be seen. And we find there that the following pious verses *For Good Men* are typical of the poet's spirit:

---

[4] See the New Cambridge *Love's Labour's Lost,* ed. A. Quiller-Couch and J. D. Wilson, pp. xxix ff.; also M. C. Bradbrook, *The School of Night* (Cambridge, 1936.)

[5] See "Chapman," *Dict. Nat. Biog.*

And I obey, I follow, and I praise
My good Commander. All the cloudy days
Of my dark life, my envied Muse shall sing
His secret love to goodness: I will bring
Glad tidings to the obscure few he keeps;
Tell his high deeds, his wonders, which the deeps
Of poverty and humblesse, most express,
And weep out (for kind joy) his holiness.[6]

Or, equally characteristic, is the doctrine Chapman gives
Prince Henry, that a king is truly kingly when he keeps

His whole life's actions in the royal bounds
Of virtue and religion, and their grounds
Takes in to sow his honours, his delights,
And complete empire. . . .[7]

Genuine piety is also evident in the poem *The Tears
of Peace,* which is a description of the nature of Chapman's
devotion to learning, love, peace, and the religious life of
kindliness and self-control. The author heaps particular
scorn on ambitious men, whom he terms "scarecrows"
rather than men,

Those giants, throwing golden hills 'gainst heaven,
To no one spice of one humanity given.[8]

He discriminates among the foes of Peace three classes: 1)
those Active men who "consume their whole life's fire in
thirst for State-height," 2) those Passive men who give
themselves up to their appetites and lusts, and 3) those In-
tellective men who study "not to get knowledge but for
mere reward." The poet's description of the third group
is worth noting: they are "shades," he says, who serve

---

[6] *The Works of George Chapman: Poems and Minor Translations* (London,
1875), p. 154.
[7] *Ibid.,* p. 128.
[8] *Ibid.,* p. 116.

> Like errant-knights that by enchantments swerve
> From their true lady's being, and embrace
> An ugly witch with her fantastic face,
> To make them think Truth's substance in their arms;
> Which that they have not, but her shadow's charms.

Chapman, plainly, has not missed the lesson of Spenser's Red Crosse Knight and Duessa.

It is not easy to summarize the system of Chapman's beliefs, yet it is plain what their characteristic tendency was. Philosophically, Chapman's outlook is characterized by a Platonic dualism. The soul and all its faculties are highly exalted as man's means of salvation, while the body and its forces are regarded as the massy dregs that clog or obscure man's spirit. Chapman likens our souls to rays from heaven, and our bodies to dunghills.[9] Elsewhere he interprets man's flesh as a Shirt of Nessus.[10] The same Platonic logic of sharp dichotomy leads him to set Religion in opposition to Policy, and the Inner over against the Outer. There is an esoteric aloofness in his championing of Refinement against Vulgarity, and of Knowledge against Ignorance.

As regards religion, Chapman's rationalism fosters a puritan and reforming temper. In *A Hymn to Christ Upon the Cross* he proposes that religion can do without miracles and sacrifices and should rest instead on such inner realities as "simple piety" and "humble spirit."[11] Pomp and glory he thinks are enemies to true religion. He seems to put no store by ecclesiastical authority; for he declares boldly that certain professional Divines are fiends and devils. They have, he says, only the "vestments of piety" and not the "pearls within." As for Scripture, he believes that its

---

[9] "The Tears of Peace," *Poems,* p. 124.
[10] "Eugenia," *Poems,* p. 337.
[11] *Poems,* pp. 143 ff. See also *Poems,* p. 337.

meaning is very clear, and that controversy is due not to Scripture's obscurity but to man's "Ambition, lust, and damned avarice." He holds to a mystical "true Church" resting on "truth's divine simplicity."

Instead of appealing to institutional authority, Chapman appeals to the authority of the truth which God's Spirit "hath writ Graven in my soul and there eternized it." [12] Like many men of his age, he is distraught by the many varieties of faith and divisions of religion that have sprung up, and he thinks that unity can be restored only by appealing to a universal truth grounded in nature and experience and made clear to man by the inner light in him. [13]

It is significant that Chapman the humanist sees Homer as the mediator of this wisdom of inner revelation. In *The Tears of Peace* Chapman says that the blind poet, who in times past has often brought him "a flood of soul," is now sending him the vision of Lady Peace to declare the pathway to felicity. When we remember that besides Chapman the other notable translator of Homer in Renaissance times was Dirck Coornhert—like Chapman, an independent mystic and "Spiritual Reformer" [14]—we begin to realize that the Renaissance enthusiasm for Homer had other than purely literary grounds. [15] Homer was looked to for heavenly inspiration and divine revelation. The legend of his physical blindness aptly fitted him for con-

[12] "Tears of Peace," *Poems*, p. 124.
[13] *Ibid.*, p. 111.
[14] Coornhert, a translator of Boethius, Cicero, and Erasmus, published in 1561 in Dutch a translation of the first 12 books of the *Odyssey*. For a discussion of Coornhert's religion, see Rufus Jones, *Spiritual Reformers of the 16th and 17th Centuries* (London, 1928), pp. 104 ff. "Spiritual Reformers" were Reformation independents who, breaking both with the Roman Church and with Protestant scholasticism, regarded all "outer" or "external" religions as shadow-symbols of the one true inward religion of the invisible Church. Coornhert's theology, it will be remembered, was "Arminian."
[15] Note the grounds on which Nashe compliments the Countess of Pembroke in his preface to *Astrophel and Stella*: "Thou only sacrificest thy soule to contemplation, thou only entertainest emptie handed Homer, & keepest the springs of Castalia from being dryed vp."

sideration as a sort of patron Saint by contemplatives of the humanistic school of liberal Christians.

The nature of Chapman's religious thinking can be seen more particularly if we will consider it briefly under three aspects: his notions of the good life, of poetry, and of freedom.

I

Chapman is concerned for a salvation in this life through a process of religious education. The poem *The Tears of Peace* outlines the process. The goal is peace; the means to it is in man's learning how to calm his "Errors in desire." For this it is necessary, first of all,

> To count the world's Love, Fame, Joy, Honour, nothing;
> But life, with all your love to it, betrothing
> To his [i.e., God's] love, his recomfort, his reward.

Man must make the bold experiment of trusting God, making trial of God's "dear yoke." Such a commitment has practical reason to justify it: the venture will approve itself by its results. Man will find that "all earth's company" cannot be compared in taste with that sweet which arises out of the commerce between God and the soul. And the soul, when it finds God's love proving itself in the conscience, turns naturally in love towards the neighbor. As the soul's new-found wisdom irradiates and controls the body, peace is established. A man's conduct is the infallible mirror in which his soul bears witness to the true learning it has discovered.

Chapman seems to look on the world as a great school and on man's salvation as a rational process within a cosmic framework. The word "Learning" is a central term. Only "true learning" can calm man's furious appetites and subdue man's wicked thoughts. Good life is ever "the effect of learning's act." [16] And that act has three aspects: love or will leads to Learning, and Learning gives Art; and by Art we perfect Nature.

Chapman's ethical scheme is most clearly displayed in a figure which he has taken from Plotinus.[17] As a sculptor studies to cut a human image out of a block of alabaster, so man works with his own soul—the substance of God's image—cutting away the excess of humors and perturbations so that God's true image may be revealed. Nature does not of herself reject these perturbations. But man, if he be an artisan, can do so. Man becomes an artisan by having a "goodwill to knowledge."

Elsewhere Chapman sees the scheme of man's salvation in terms of a golden chain let down from heaven.[18] This chain—by which Chapman thinks Homer prefigured the Resurrection—is the soul, infused by God into the body. If the soul, holding fast to the chain of which it is a part, aims at the love of God, man can be drawn up to heaven. Chapman seems here to be translating the Christian dogma of the Resurrection in terms of the Neo-Platonic doctrine of Ascension.

But this same system has its proper complementary doctrine: man can fall as well as rise. There is also a chain shot up from hell—the chain of Ambition—which if man takes hold of will hale him headlong into misery.[19] Elsewhere Chapman speaks of man's fall in terms of a simile taken, once again, from Plotinus.[20] As Narcissus lost him-

---

[16] "The Tears of Peace," *Poems,* p. 116.

[17] *Ibid.* Cf. Plotinus, *Enn.* I. 6. 9.

[18] "Eugenia," *Poems,* p. 336. Dionysius the Areopagite (*Divine Names,* III. i.) speaks of "a luminous chain suspended from the celestial heights" by which we in attempting to pull it down pull ourselves up. This passage, either directly or indirectly, must be Chapman's source.

[19] "Epicedium," *Poems,* p. 167.

[20] "A Hymn to Christ Upon the Cross," *Poems,* p. 146. Cf. Plotinus, *Enn.* I. 6. 8. Chapman's immediate source for the Narcissus-image seems to have been, as Professor Schoell points out, the commentary of Ficinus on Plato's *Symposium.*

self by becoming rapt with his own image in the water, so the man who becomes enamoured of beauties of sense is permitting the substance of his soul to fade into shadow-land. Here again Chapman is illustrating Neo-Platonic thought. Lust (of which Ambition and Self-Love are the two chief varieties) is set in contradistinction to Love, and blamed for mans' *de*generation even as Love is honored for his *re*generation.

It is interesting to observe how Chapman's Neo-Platonism helps him to rationalize Eschatology. The poet nowhere speaks of an historical Fall of Man. Rather, he has a doctrine of the fall in a mystical sense. We fall, he declares, every hour that we sin; just as, on the other hand, we enter into (eternal) life whenever we reclaim in us God's sacred image.[21] By the same philosophy Chapman rationalizes Hell. He explains that Hell is present here and now whenever we are deprived of a good life and hence of the joys of heaven.[22] He makes plain in the poem *The Shadow of Night* that Hell is simply the this-earthly state of man's "blindness of the mind."[23] And by interpreting Hell as a sort of mental darkness, the poet reinforces his stress on Learning as the way to Heaven.

Chapman's is a philosophical theology. Because he wishes to establish it by no other authority than that of universal human experience, he appeals not to Scripture but to the universal language of mythology. As the story of Narcissus is used to depict Failure-in-Manhood, so the story of Orpheus is set up as a pattern of the achievement of true Manhood.[24] Man makes a conquest of Hell, Chapman teaches, whenever

---

[21] "A Hymn to Christ," *Poems*, p. 146.
[22] "A Great Man," *Poems*, p. 149. Compare the memorable passage in *Faustus* (312 ff.).
[23] *Poems*, pp. 4-5.
[24] *Ibid.*, p. 5. The later Cambridge Platonist, Peter Sterry, uses Orpheus and Narcissus similarly. See V. de S. Pinto, *Peter Sterry* (Cambridge, 1934), pp. 157, 161, 181.

he, like Orpheus, calms the infernal perturbations of his mind. In another poem Chapman lets us see the bold claim his philosophy involves when he says: "As we are men, we death and hell control." [25] Such a sentence marks for us plainly the central humanism of Chapman's religion.

But if Chapman's religion was humanistic, it must also be said that his humanism was religious. Chapman has great contempt for the walking-dictionary scholar and for all learning that does not aim at what he supposes is the true effort of Learning, namely to "Turn blood to soul, and make both one calm man." [26] He censures Ben Jonson for considering wit and skill merely as a key to wealth, and he admonishes him that man's true and worthiest knowledge is

> to know and be one complete man,
> And that not all the swelling ocean
> Of arts and sciences can pour in.[27]

The arts are nothing, he elsewhere says, without the Art of Peace.[28]

II

Since Chapman's religious humanism is systematic and organic, its religious coloring pervades the definition of all his terms. Words take on for him a certain bias of meaning which a nonreligious humanist would find annoying. We have already observed that Chapman takes Learning to mean moral wisdom or self-knowledge, and that what he calls Knowledge is "holy thoughts." Similarly, when he speaks of Art he intends fundamentally the comprehensive meaning of the "Art of good life." [29] And this religious

---

[25] "A Hymn to Christ," *Poems*, p. 146.
[26] "The Tears of Peace," *Poems*, p. 118.
[27] "An Invective written by Mr. George Chapman against Mr. Ben Jonson," *Poems*, p. 434.
[28] "The Tears of Peace," *Poems*, p. 121.
[29] "Eugenia," *Poems*, p. 336.

significance reaches out, too, into his notion of Poetry. In a passage in the *Eugenia*,[30] he pictures Poesy, together with Graces and Virtues, as composing a circle of Peace, in which Religion is the precious stone that ties together the ring.

Elsewhere Chapman seems to think of Poetry as the preserver of that in religion which is essential and immortal. He speaks of

> laws, religions, all
> Offer'd to change and greedy funeral;
> Yet still your Homer lasting, living, reigning,
> And proves how firm truth builds in poets' feigning.[31]

He goes on to say that Poetry moves in perfect circles about the fountain of truth. At the same time, he speaks of Poetry as "this Divinity in earth." And he indicates that Poetry has, together with Learning, an essentially sacramental office:

> For as the Sun and Moon are figures given
> Of his [i.e. God's] refulgent Deity in heaven,
> So Learning, and, her lightener, Poesy,
> In earth present his fiery Majesty.

Chapman's simile here very probably has its source in Neo-Platonic Light-metaphysics, according to which the Sun and the Moon symbolize respectively the Divine Mind (*Nous*) and the Divine Soul (*Psyche*),[32] by which the transcendent God communicates with His world. That symbolism is particularly appropriate here. For it seems to me that the Neo-Platonic Divine-Sun or *Nous* comes close to representing what Chapman means by Learning, and that the Neo-

---

[30] *Ibid.*, p. 338.
[31] "Epistle Dedicatory to Prince Henry," *Poems*, p. 129.
[32] See Plotinus, *Enn.* V. 6. 4; and also Roger M. Jones, *The Platonism of Plutarch* (Menasha, Wis., 1916), p. 49.

Platonic Divine-Moon or *Psyche* (Divine Wisdom ensouled and in contact with the sense world) is loosely equivalent with Chapman's notion of Poetry as Learning's "lightener." Another way in which Chapman indicates Poetry's function as mediator of divine wisdom is by calling Poetry a "Promethean" faculty.[33] That is, Poetry is the faculty by which heavenly light or fire is brought down to earth. "Promethean Poets," he says, have souls illumined and made genial by heavenly fire, and they are therefore able to write for their fellow men verses which can light these men on the path of moral reform.

Chapman speaks of Poetry also in terms of still another interesting figure. Man, he says, is like a tree, and the acorn of this tree is poetry. Poetry is man's kernel of immortality; it holds power to create a new man after the old man is dead.[34] The metaphor serves to emphasize a notion which elsewhere underlies Chapman's thinking—namely, that poetry is the quintessence of the whole of man's life. The great poet must be the ideal man. Chapman would have agreed with Milton that only a good man can write good poetry. In *The Shadow of Night* Chapman makes the

---

[33] See *Poems*, pp. 5, 130. This point deserves commentary. As Ernst Cassirer notes in his *Individuum und Kosmos in der Philosophie der Renaissance* (Berlin, 1927), pp. 100-01, the Prometheus-motive comes in Renaissance speculation to supersede the Adam-motive. Cassirer points out that Boccaccio has a theory of creation significantly different from that of the Church Fathers, for Boccaccio speaks of a double creation: one, the creation by which man is called into being by Nature; the other, the creation by which man's being is given spiritual Form. Boccaccio makes Prometheus the Culture-hero of this second creation. Prometheus is the bringer of knowledge and of superbly-moral order, by which man is in a real sense "reformed"—that is, given a new form and being. The Renaissance interest in this myth is a significant signpost of the transition from Medieval to Modern culture, for the Prometheus myth involves an interpretation of man's destiny different from the Biblical. It is now supposed that man is distinguished above all other creatures by a God-given power of creativity and that he therefore fulfils his destiny by being a reformer and artist. The Prometheus myth also brings to attention the price which the true man has to pay for his intellectual awakening—the price of being tortured (so the Neo-Platonists interpreted) by his own profound meditation. See Erwin Panofsky, *Studies in Iconology* (New York, 1939), pp. 50-51. This explains the fuss Chapman makes about his own heroic intellectual agonizings.

[34] "Epistle Dedicatory to Prince Henry," *Poems*, pp. 129-30.

point that Orpheus was a great poet not by accident but because he had the Wisdom and the Art of true Manhood.

We might perhaps say of Chapman that he regards poetry very much as Matthew Arnold was later to regard religion, as "morality touched with emotion." Chapman thinks of poetry as the bearer of certain heaven-born truths of the moral life, and thus as the agent of moral reform. He believes that poetry, by revealing to man the ugliness of vice and the beauty of virtue, can show him the pathway to felicity and the hope of immortality.

III

It is a fair question whether Chapman's views leave any genuine freedom of the will. In *The Tears of Peace* we find him saying that "the arbitress of all things done" is Learning.[35] It is true that he at the same time declares that Will is the first step to Learning. But the "will" of which he speaks is hard to distinguish from Platonic love (Eros); and in any case he sees man's acts as so immediately the result of man's learning that it is difficult to see any room for what we call Liberty of Indifference. The question is of some importance to our study, because Chapman's notion of freedom colors the psychology of the personages of his dramas, and hence his whole dramatic Style or Design.

Professor Hardin Craig[36] has pointed out that Chapman's ethical theory makes him the inaugurator of a pessimistic psychology that was to become characteristic of Jacobean drama. This psychology, according to Craig, is based on a sort of Determinism, for it proclaims the irresistibility of passion. After calling our attention to passages where

---

[35] *Poems*, p. 116.
[36] "Ethics in the Jacobean Drama: the case of Chapman," *Essays in Dramatic Literature*. The Parrott Presentation Volume (1935), pp. 25-46.

Bussy, Byron, and Tamyra loudly proclaim man's inability to control his blood, Craig writes:

> It is obvious that in these characters Chapman has shifted the blame from the individual to fate, not the nemesis of the ancient world, but to a sort of psychological determinism. He has, in the process, let his sympathies come over to the side of sin, and in so doing has introduced a new element into tragedy.[37]

Further, Craig speaks of "Chapman's mechanistic philosophy" and says:

> In the warfare between sense and reason, in general, Chapman firmly believes in the indomitability of a perturbation mounted in the saddle, and to concede so much is, from an ethical point of view excessive.[38]

Professor Craig's method of drawing Chapman's beliefs directly from dramatic materials, and from dramatic materials only, prevents him perhaps from seeing Chapman's views in their full perspective. Nevertheless, Craig's observations have substantial truth. In the volume of Chapman's nondramatic verse he could have found support for the argument of Chapman's determinism in lines such as these:

> When thou lett'st loose thy mind to objects vain
> 'Tis not in thee to call her back again.[39]

On the other hand, however, we must observe also Chapman's words in a gloss to *A Hymn to Christ Upon the Cross*:

> It is false humility to lay necessarily (all our Saviour's grace understood) the victory of our bodies on our souls.[40]

---

[37] *Ibid.*, p. 35.
[38] *Ibid.* p. 39.
[39] "Of Negligence," *Poems*, p. 160.
[40] *Poems*, p. 146.

Here the poet seems plainly to reject thoroughgoing necessitarianism. It can be remarked, further, that the necessitarian doctrine of the Friar in *Bussy D'Ambois,* that

> our affections storm
> Rais'd in our blood, no reason can reform (II. ii. 140-1)

still leaves room for the possibility of reform through such trans-rational means as the intuition of Divine Wisdom or the engrafting of "Virtuous Knowledge"—Chapman's philosophical equivalents for the theological terms "grace" and "new birth." Chapman does not, I think, adopt absolute pessimism. Reform is possible—is, indeed, the burden of all his preaching. But on the moot question of whether the first step in reform is due to God's initiative or to man's, Chapman does some Arminian fence-straddling:

> For virtuous knowledge hath two ways to plant—
> By power infused, and acquisition:
> The first of which those good men graft upon,
> For good life is the effect of learning's act,
> Which th' action of the mind did first compact,
> By infused love to Learning 'gainst all ill
> *Conquest's first step is, to all good, the will.*[41]

We have here the familiar Renaissance emphasis on the central importance of the human will. And the will's *freedom* seems to be interpreted in terms of the will's *power.*

It is difficult to understand Chapman's notion of freedom, I think, except as we review briefly the Platonic theology on which it is based.[42] This theology declares a universal Divine Love and Wisdom, always and everywhere available to men; so that man is pictured as self-determining

---

[41] "Tears of Peace," *Poems,* p, 116.
[42] For a study of Chapman's evident borrowings from Platonic philosophy, see F. L. Schoell, *Études sur L'Humanisme Continental en Angleterre* (Paris, 1926). For Chapman "the divine philosopher" is Plato (see *Poems,* p. 238).

his own destiny by his attention to or negligence of the offered means of salvation. In Chapman's language, God is always in contact with man through his soul, offering man Learning and hence restoration from evil. Hence, from an absolute point of view, no perturbation is indomitable, provided man will conduct himself like an earnest sculptor and exercise himself in chipping away the excess of humors and perturbations. Chapman insists that God offers the soul as powerful means of doing His love's work as the body offers for the exercise of carnal love.[43] Only, God's means must be grasped. For the proposition has also a corollary. If God's proffered means are not embraced, then sin envelops the soul, dragging it automatically to tragic misery. "In blood where both [soul and learning] fail," says Chapman, "then lies noblesse wrack'd." [44]

In the logic of this philosophy, each man's power over his own destiny is conditioned simply by the extent of the moral wisdom which he has succeeded in achieving through commerce with God. Ideally, his soul's power is absolute;[45] but when the soul, instead of attending on divine things, lapses into consenting to the "body's will," there is inaugurated a series of mischiefs progressively difficult to amend:

> But be assured that one day's soothed sin
> Will ask thee many to amend and mourn,
> And make thy mind so willing to adjourn
> That instant-due amendment, that 'twill breed
> A custom to do ill; and that will need
> A new birth to reform. "What, may I then
> (By any diligence or power in men)
> Avoid transgression," No, 'tis past thy power:
> But this thou may'st do; every day and hour,
> In that be labouring still, that lets transgression:

---

[43] See "Eugenia," *Poems*, p. 336.
[44] See "The Tears of Peace," *Poems*, p. 116.
[45] See *Poems*, p. 124, Col. 2; and cf. "Of The Will," p. 156.

And worth my counsel 'tis, that this impression
Fix'd in thy mind, and all means used in man,
He may transgress as little as he can.[46]

Chapman's view has obvious affinities with the views of
Boethius, Proclus, and Plotinus.[47] Boethius, as Professor
Patch has well pointed out, adopts the solution offered in the
Platonic tradition that the more man shares in the divine
the more he achieves freedom from Fate. The man whose
soul stands immovable in God as on the center of a circle
stands above the order of destiny; whereas whenever and
according as his soul moves from God as center he then is,
like the circumference of a circle, subject to destiny, to a
bond of causes that may not be unbound.[48]

Now what distinguishes Chapman's view is exactly the
awareness of the meshes of fate which tightly constrain
the soul which has departed from the Center. Bussy, Byron,
and Tamyra are souls of this sort. Because each is lacking
at some point in true religious wisdom, each is caught in
a chain of tragic circumstance in which each expresses a
feeling of helplessness as if under the heavy hand of fate.
The strain of necessitarianism in the psychology of these
heroes results from the fact that their acts are seen to be
directly governed by their faulty opinions. Chapman's
philosophy is "mechanistic" only in the sense that he has
left no room for fortune or chance. As in the philosophy of
Plotinus or Boethius, consequences are seen to follow closely
on causes. When Bussy follows a seeming good rather
than a real good, his nature necessarily descends from Reason

---

[46] "Of Attention," *Poems*, p. 157.

[47] See H. R. Patch, "Necessity in Boethius and the Neoplatonists," *Speculum*,
X (1935), 393-404. Professor Patch, p. 398, thinks that Plotinus preserves only
the illusion of choice. If the charge is true of Plotinus it is true also of
Chapman.

[48] See *Consolatio*, Bk. IV, pr. 6.

into the realm of the senses, and thus he falls under the control of Fate.

By this philosophy dramatic action takes on the quality of inevitability. Once started in the circuit of desire for things outward, man is carried by his passion headlong into tragedy. There is, strictly speaking, no question of further decisions, but simply the spectacle of logical development and exemplification. That, I would venture to suggest, is why *Hamlet* is so different a drama from *Byron* or *Bussy* or *Tamburlaine* or *The Jew of Malta*. Shakespeare is interested in the psychology of *decision,* whereas Chapman and Marlowe are concerned with the psychology of *frailty*. The latter view will lead to Milton's neat epitomizing of it in *Samson Agonistes* (834): "All wickedness is weakness."

THEORIES OF FORTUNE,
FATE, AND PROVIDENCE

I T is not too much to say that the doctrine of Providence was the chief apologetic interest of Reformation times. Thomas Beard undertook in his *Theatre of Gods Judgements* (1597) to show "manifest proofes that there is a God aboue that guideth the sterne of the world . . . and that is iust in punishing the vnjust and malicious." [1] To this same purpose, as we have seen, Raleigh devoted his *History of the World*. Belief in a God who rewards and punishes was central to the religion of Thomas Nashe,[2] Philemon Holland,[3] and John Calvin.[4] And John Davies of Hereford forthrightly declared: "By nought so much as by his prouidence / Is God discern'd." [5]

The characteristic features of the doctrine are nicely displayed in the verses of Sylvester's Du Bartas. Particularly is it pointed out that The Almighty is not

> an idle God
> That lusks in Heav'n and never looks abroad,
> That crowns not Vertue, and corrects not Vice;
> Blinde to our service, deaf unto our sighs:
> A Pagan Idol, voyd of power and piety,
> A sleeping Dormouse (rather) a dead Deity.[6]

On the contrary, He is the vital power that sustains our world:

---

[1] The Preface.
[2] See *Christs Teares*, ed. McKerrow, II, 115-16.
[3] See Plutarch's *Morals* (1603), p. 538. Holland's preface to chap. 37.
[4] See *The Institution of Christian Religion* (1561), pp. 56ᵛ-70ᵛ, but esp. pp. 58ʳ-60ʳ.
[5] *Mirum in Modum* (1602), ed. Grosart, I, 26.
[6] *The First Week*, Seventh Day, 114-19, ed. Grosart, I, 84.

God is the soule, the life, the strength, and sinew,
That quickens, moves, and makes this Frame continue,
God's the main spring, that maketh every way
All the small wheels of this great Engin play.[7]

And his judgments are not delayed to an other world:

God is the Judge, who keeps continuall Sessions,
In every place to punish all Transgressions.[8]

The scope given Providence in Renaissance theory is a matter for some rather careful consideration, because it has a bearing on the rationalization of history that was being attempted by Renaissance historians and dramatists. The medieval view of history, if we take Boccaccio's *De Casibus* as example, allows chief importance to the role of Fortune in bringing about historical tragedies. The significant shift in point of view that comes with Elizabethan times is, as Mr. Willard Farnham has pointed out,[9] that Fortune's share in tragedy is increasingly minimized and history becomes explained now in terms of human choices and of divine purposes.

It is difficult, however, to formulate quite precisely a single consistent theory of Providence which we may denominate as Elizabethan. Here, as in other matters of philosophic importance, the thinking of the times was eclectic and transitional. Traditional Christian views were mingled with revived Stoic and Platonic theory. Apologists for religion were interested not so much to define a metaphysical doctrine of Providence as to prove by affirmation and testimony that a God of rewards and punishments pre-

---

[7] *Ibid.*, 160-64. Note the suggestion of mechanistic philosophy in the metaphor. On the theme of God's vital, ever-present activity in the world, see also Davies of Hereford, *Mirum in Modum*, ed. Grosart, I, 18; and Nashe, *Christs Teares*, ed. McKerrow, II, 120.

[8] Lines 184-85.

[9] *The Medieval Heritage of Elizabethan Tragedy*, esp. pp. 286-290.

sides over mundane affairs. Writers were interested particularly in confuting the view

> That all things roll and run at a venture, and that there is no cause of the good and evill accidents of this life, but either fortune or els the will of man.[10]

Holland called this the view of the Epicureans; and such folk were thought by good Elizabethans to be all too numerous. Against them it was felt necessary to establish the fact of Providence—not necessarily in a particular Christian sense, but in the general sense in which such a doctrine might claim to have universal acknowledgement by all men of good sense. Davies of Hereford asserted that all men who have "a humane Soule, and common sense" must needs discern Providence.[11] Raleigh pointed out that besides the Scriptures, Hermes, Plotinus, and virtually all learned men acknowledge the Providence of God, and that even the Turks are confident of it.[12] And Mornay in his chapter on Providence in *The Trewnesse of the Christian Religion* advised his readers to turn to the opinions of Seneca and Epictetus and there note "how conformable the things whiche Christians teache, are to the wisdome of the best sort among the Heathen." [13] The very broadness of the doctrine in the hands of Renaissance writers hampers us thus from making very precise definition of it. But we can describe the emphases, the tendencies, and the climate of opinion of various Renaissance discussions of it.

I

Our first general observation is that the representative spokesmen of Elizabeth's day rule out Chance. They hold

---

[10] Philemon Holland, *loc. cit.*
[11] *Mirum in Modum*, ed. Grosart, I, 26.
[12] *History of the World*, I. i. 13. This view, as we shall see, underlies *Tamburlaine*.
[13] P. 216.

that the jurisdiction of Providence is such that Fortune is merely a fiction. Chance is "that kind of idolatry or god of fools," says Raleigh; and he quotes Melanchthon's statement that "whom the poets call Fortune we know to be God." [14] La Primaudaye, similarly, suggests that it is lawful to regard Fortune as "the ordinance of God." [15] And Mornay, whose view here as elsewhere is carefully reasoned, declares that either we must altogether deny Fortune or else we must mean by Fortune merely God under another name:

> If ye meane fortune as she is peynted by the Poets, blynd, standing on a bowle, and turning with euery wynd: it is as easie to wype her away as to paynt her. For who seeth not that there is an uniforme order, both in the whole world, and in all the parts thereof, and how then can one that is blynd be the guyder thereof? . . . Seeing then that there is so certein order in all things: it followeth that fortune beareth no sway in any thing, and therefore that there is no fortune at all. But if by the word fortune they meane as *Proclus* doth, a certain diuine power that gathereth causes farre distant one from another, all to one end: surely in that case we be more freends to fortune than they be. For we admit it, not only in things vncerteine wandering and wauering, but also euen in the things that are most certein, yea and in all things whatsoeuer; as the which is but God himself disguysed vnder another name.
>
> Nowthen to speake properly, what is Fortune? . . . it hath no ground or being but of and in our owne ignorance . . . that which is fortune to the wise man, is none vnto God. . . . Take away ignorance from men, and fortune is banished from all their dealings.[16]

---

[14] *H. W.* I. i. 15.

[15] *The French Academie,* chap. 23. The comment follows only a few sentences after the story of Tamburlaine's treatment of Bajazet. Similarly in chap. 44, entitled "Of Fortune," it is first pointed out that "prosperitie and aduersitie depend onely of the will of God"—then Tamburlaine's amazing prosperity is related.

[16] *Christian Religion,* pp. 217-18. Cf. Robert Garnier, *Marc Antoine,* 1140-41:

> Fortune que l'on craint, qu'on deteste et adore,
> N'est qu'vn euenement, dont la cause on ignore.

Now to an extent, it is true, this same view is present in the medieval outlook. Proclus, whom Mornay has cited as an authority for his view, received his theory from Plotinus and transmitted it to Boethius and thus into much of medieval thought. Both St. Augustine and St. Thomas Aquinas say that "As to the order of Divine Providence, nothing in the world happens by chance." [17]   However, Aquinas takes considerable care to correct the suggestion of absolute necessitarianism in the view of Boethius that "providence binds together human acts and fortunes by the indissoluble connexion of causes." [18]   Some things, Aquinas insists, "happen by contingency, according to the nature of their proximate causes."   This does not mean that some things happen outside God's providence, for that is never so; but it means that certain effects willed by God happen contingently, because God has prepared contingent causes for them.[19]   Aquinas thus preserves a kind of chance.[20]   He draws attention to the fact that certain things are accidental with respect to the efficient cause because not produced thereby in view of an end; and he declares that that activity in nature which lacks an end must be spoken of as fortuitous.[21]

But the writers whom Elizabethans read seem to have been concerned to eradicate the fortuitous entirely.   Calvin holds that there can be no such thing as fortuitous contingence.   Gentle rains are a testimony of God's favor, and storms are a proof of his special vengeance.   Even the falling out of lots is not left to the blindness of fortune but comes from God Himself.   When a broken bough falling from a tree kills a wayfaring man, it is not be-

---

[17] *Summa Theologica*, I. ciii. 7.
[18] *Ibid.*, I. xxii. 4.
[19] *Ibid.*, I. xix. 8.
[20] *Ibid.*, I. cxvi. 3.
[21] See Etienne Gilson, *The Spirit of Medieval Philosophy* (New York, 1936), p. 367.

cause of chance, but because God has delivered the man unto death.[22]   Calvin would have it that God is the "author" of all that happens. God "createth" both light and darkness, and He "formeth" both good and evil, so that no evil happens which He has not made.[23]   Though rejecting the naturalistic necessitarianism of the Stoics, Calvin substitutes for it a kind of divine determinism which is hardly less rigid.[24]

And La Primaudaye is apparently about as rationalistic as Calvin.   He has "no doubt but that *Fortune* . . . is nothing else but a fayned deuice of mans spirite, and an imagination without truth." [25]   The providence of God, he declares, "knoweth and ordereth casuall thinges necessarily."   Even lots "cast at aduenture" fall out according to God's judgment, and "generally all things are done by the ordinance of God."   The only sense in which we may call things "casuall and chancing" is in respect to ourselves, because the "necessitie of those thinges which are so strange" is "for the most part hidden in the counsell of God, and cannot be comprehended by the opinion and reach of man." [26]   This rigid rationalism leads La Primaudaye to attribute all events to God.   Scarcely a page after finishing his story of Tamburlaine, he remarks:

---

[22] *The Institution,* pp. 58-59. I. xvi. 4-6.

[23] *Ibid.,* p. 69ᵛ. I. xviii. 3.   More liberal Reformers argued, rather, the view of Plotinus that evil is simply privation. See Davies of Hereford, *Mirum in Modum,* ed. Grosart, I, 23; and Mornay, p. 213.   Such is the view held later by John Donne.

[24] Thus in *The Institution,* p. 60ᵛ, Calvin writes: "For we do not as the Stoickes do, imagine a necessitie by a certaine perpetual knot & entangled order of causes which is conteyned in nature; but we make God the iudge & gouernoure of al thinges, which according to his wisdom hath euen from furthest ende of eternitie decreed what he would do, & now by his power putteth in execution that which he hath decreed."

[25] *The French Academie* (1586), pp. 468-69.

[26] This is also Arthur Golding's view of chance, as set forth in the Dedicatory Epistle (lines 326-31) to his translation of Ovid's *Metamorphoses.*

it is too great blockishnesse to attribute the cause of the change
of monarchies, commonwealths, estates, of battels lost, and generally of all casuall mishaps, both generall and particular, to certaine
second causes. . . . But we must looke higher, and turne towards
him who vseth such meanes in the execution of his woonderfull
counsell, when he mindeth to chastise and to punish men for their
offences.[27]

This too was the view of Thomas Beard. He roundly
declares in his Preface to *The Theatre of Gods Judgements*
that God has

a soueraigne empire and predominance ouer all the world. And
unto him belongeth the direction and principall conduct of humane
matters, in such sort that nothing in the world cometh to passe by
chance or aduenture, but onely and alwaies by the prescription of
his will; according to the which he ordereth and disposeth by a
straight and direct motion. . . .

II

Yet, with all their emphasis on God as the efficient cause
of events, most Reformation writers desire also to preserve
the emphasis of the ancient philosophers that man is himself
the cause of what happens to him. Alongside of the passage already quoted from La Primaudaye we read:

The definition also, which the Ancients gaue of Fortune, is very
agreeable to the effect of the thing signified, and of that whereof
we haue daily experience: namely, that there is no other final end
of change and alteration in man, than that of his being. *Plato* saith,
that Fortune is an accidentall cause, and consequence in those things
which proceede from the counsell of man.[28]

In banishing Fortune, humanists did not want to banish
also human responsibility. Generally they insisted, rather,
that what is wrongly considered Fortune's realm is really

---

[27] Ed. cit., p. 477.
[28] *Ibid.*, p. 470.

governed by two seats of authority: God and man. Huarte writes in the *Examen de Ingenios:*

> we must not leaue all vpon Gods hands, neither yet may a man wholly affie on his owne wit and sufficiencie, but it will doe best to ioine both together; for there is no other Fortune, saue God, and a mans owne good indeauour.[29]

Philemon Holland, too, in his translation of Plutarch's *Morals* (1603) places by the side of his own emphasis on God's skill Plutarch's emphasis on man's.[30] Holland says that because of his own Christian heritage he has a heavenly wisdom hidden from Plutarch—namely, that Fortune is "an idole forged in their braine" by men "ignorant in the providence of the True God." But Plutarch, "poor Pagan and Ethnike though he were," has yet been able to confute the dangerous opinion that all things are carried by chance. Plutarch has proved that man, by the prudence and wisdom that rise from his mastery of the arts and sciences, can overrule "blind fortune." Holland does not make altogether clear how he would relate his own Calvinistic emphasis on God's omnipotence to Plutarch's humanistic emphasis on the power of man's will. But he is plainly anxious that both seats of authority be recognized.

The author of the *Mirror for Magistrates* (1559), who likewise locates causality both in God and in man when he has Jack Cade say that

> The skill of God ruleth all, it is so strong,
> Man may by skill guide thinges that to him long [31]

seems thus to indicate for us the manner in which the two powers are related. Man's jurisdiction is subsidiary to God's.

---

[29] *The Examination of Mens Wits,* trans. R[ichard] C[arew], (London, 1604), p. 218.

[30] P. 229. Holland's "Summarie" of chap. 17, "Of Fortune."

[31] Ed. Joseph Haslewood (London, 1815), II, 158. Cf. Plotinus, *Enn.* III. 3. 4.

And man's power is directly dependent on his God-given reason. Jack Cade goes on to say that

> through the skyl God hath in Reason wrought
> And geuen man, no lust nor wyl to course
> But may be stayed or swaged of the sourse,
> So that it shal in nothing force the mynde
> To worke our wo, or leaue the proper kynde.

That the stars and the body's humours have influence on us Cade grants. But he declares that they can accomplish no work unless aided by man's will. "Our lust and willes our euils chiefly warke."

Higgins, editor of the later *The First Parte of the Mirror for Magistrates* (1574), seems remarkably confident that man can by wisdom avoid tragedy. He indicates in his preface that the unhappy end of such heroes as Caesar and Hannibal could have been prevented if they had known the wisdom of Temperance as taught by Plotinus. And he further declares that any man who follows the four classic virtues will find it impossible "euer to fall into the infortunate snares of calamity, or misfortune." [32]

The view seems to accord with the doctrine we have already noted in the writings of Chapman and Raleigh. Chapman, we remember, holds that man, when true learning is given him through commerce with God, has the skill to curb the body's humors and to resist the tragic downfall with which his bodily passions threaten him. And Raleigh, similarly, holds that man, because he can draw upon a transcendental power above the circuit of destiny, can easily defend himself against an evil Fate. In this same line of thinking we may add the testimony of La Primaudaye:

---

[32] "To the Nobilitie and all other in office," ed. Haslewood, I, 5.

The stars influence men onely that in disposing their bodies, beeing compounded of the elements, vpon which the planets worke, they serue to aide them to abound in vertues or vices, according as their minde being moderatrix of all their actions, doth dispose her faculties to intend good or euill . . . . the minde of the faithfull and well instructed doth correct the nautines of the stars, and deliuereth himselfe from all peruerse inclination.[33]

III

The catch in the theory is that the "moderatrix" must be "well instructed." Virtue is not possible without knowledge. La Primaudaye goes on to say that "to those which want the gifts and graces of Gods spirit, all things cannot but succeed badly, and the influence of the spheres hurts them rather than otherwise." [34]   And the view compares with statements we have elsewhere noted—with Chapman's doctrine that "In blood where both [soul and learning] fail, then lies noblesse wrack'd;" and with Raleigh's declaration that "whatsoever shall neglect the remedies by virtue and piety prepared, putteth himself altogether under the power of his sensuall appetite." These authors are agreed that unless man makes use of God's wisdom he falls into the power of fate and becomes bound by its chain of tragic causality.

In discussing Renaissance notions of Fate, it is particularly profitable, I think, to compare Neo-Platonic conceptions; for Renaissance writers in denying Stoic necessitarianism generally fall back upon the view of Plotinus. Plotinus had argued[35] for the existence in man—and in the universe—of some principle not bound in the chain of causes that operates in things bodily. This principle, he had said, is Soul—bodiless, and therefore free. It follows in this philosophy

[33] *The French Academie* (ed. of 1616), p. 703, as quoted by Ruth L. Anderson, *Elizabethan Psychology and Shakespeare's Plays,* Univ. of Iowa Studies, III. 4. 59.
[34] *Ibid.*
[35] *Enn.* III. 1. 6-8.

that man finds freedom when he reclaims his soul by turning attention to the Divine, or he sinks into fate's meshes when his soul is lost in the love of things earthly.

Sir John Davies is following Neo-Platonic philosophy when in *Nosce Teipsum* he argues "That the soule is a thing subsisting by it selfe without the body," and when he says, using a well-known image from Plotinus, that the soul's relationship to the body is like that of sunlight to air.[36] John Davies of Hereford likewise exhibits Neo-Platonic doctrine when he pictures the human Soul as at the center point of two opposite series of influence: on the one side the Soul is within the Spirits, which are in turn within the Blood, which is within the Body, which is within the Elements; and on the other side the Soul is within the Mind, which is in the Understanding, which rests in God. On the one side the soul is lured to love "things bodily," while from the other side it is encouraged to pursue "divine Intelligences."[37] In Chapman, where we have observed this general theory in some detail, it is made clear that the man who yields to his lower powers suffers automatically from hot humours, strife, and disaster; while only the man who holds firm in the contemplation of transcendental values can know peace. The negative side of this proposition is the Neo-Platonic explanation of Tragedy. Greville uses it in *Mustapha:*

> soules, made to raigne, when they let down their State
> Into bodies humors, straight those humors give them fate.

---

[36] See *The Works of Sir John Davies* (1869-76), ed. A. B. Grosart, I, 60 and 99-100. Cf. Plotinus, *Enn.* IV. 3. 22. In Sir John's view, the body is a prison (p. 63)—just as in Davies of Hereford's view it is a "Clog" (*Microcosmus*, p. 27n).

[37] *Mirum in Modum,* ed. Grosart, I, 10-11. A little reflection makes one realize that this view of the soul and body relationship prepares the way for Descartes and mechanism. The soul is no longer, as with Aristotle and St. Thomas, "the form of the body," but it is the spiritual vitalizer of the shells or husks which envelop it.

Such souls, the Chorus goes on to say, are bound in Disorder's chain and feel Error's destiny.[38]

The view of Du Bartas on fate[39] seems to differ only in that he uses the language of Calvinist theology. That is, he appeals to Grace rather than to a mystical Divine Wisdom as the principle by which man's soul can be saved from the power of the stars. Against the Stoics, he insists that the stars do not bind God. Nevertheless, they have by God's disposition a "fatall influence" and a "charge precise." They represent the powers of tyranny to which we have become thrall by our Parent's fall. Study of the stars will teach us to beseech God

> To give us Curbs to bridle th'ill proclivity
> We are inclin'd to, by a hard Nativity:
> To pour some Water of his Grace, to quench
> Our boyling Fleshe's fell Concupiscence;
> To calm our many passions (spirituall tumours)
> Sprung from corruption of our vicious humors. (532-37)

Here is a rigid Calvinistic view of man's depravity, which sees man as fated to tragedy by the Fall—given by the Fall into the power of the Stars, and able to resist that power only by Divine Grace.

The significance of these views for Elizabethan drama is that they lend to tragic action a pronounced inevitability. Characters interpreted in the light of Platonic or Stoic or Calvinistic theories of freedom are attended by a sense of necessary *nemesis* comparable, if not quite identical, with that which gives Greek tragedy its awesome power to evoke pity and fear. Elizabethans make a rapprochement with the philosophy of Senecan drama at this point: they are

---

[38] *Works of Greville,* ed. Bullough, II, 122-23.
[39] See *The First Week,* Fourth Day, 442 ff., ed. Grosart, *Works of Sylvester* (Edinburgh, 1880), I, 56.

willing to grant that Fate has a jurisdiction over human affairs—not ultimate jurisdiction as Seneca held,[40] but nevertheless a subsidiary jurisdiction under the decree of Providence. When man's "tragic flaw" is judged theologically as a lack of Grace, or philosophically as a lack of the wisdom of temperance and piety that comes from commerce with God—then Seneca's heroes can be regarded as men fate-bound by this flaw. This was a chief reason why Seneca's methods were widely imitated. Calvinists and humanists could regard Seneca's dramas as mighty warnings against irreligion. Seneca's slaves-of-passion furnished *exempla* which by teaching negatively might drive the sinner in fear to God.

To illustrate this way of reasoning from Fate to Grace, one needs only to turn to the pages of Zwingli. The Zurich reformer takes the view that a knowledge of sin must precede and prepare us for a knowledge of Christ. In the treatise *On True and False Religion* we read:

> Therefore, just as grace is first rightly known when sin has been effected through the law, as Paul says, *Rom.* 7:25, that is, when sin has been weighed and known through the law, so also Christ, who is the pledge of grace, nay, is grace itself, is first rightly taught and known when from close observation of sin we have learned that by its interposition the way to heaven has been closed to us. . . . In order, therefore, rightly to know Christ, we must first rightly know ourselves; for they that think themselves righteous receive not Christ . . . and he that feels no sickness wants not the help of a physician.[41]

The study of spiritual sickness, or the anatomy of the sinful self, thus appears as the proper task of religious education. Measured by this standard, *Faustus* and *Tamburlaine* are obvious masterpieces.

---

[40] As, e.g., in *Oedipus*, 980-92 (Loeb ed.).
[41] *The Works of Zwingli*, ed. C. N. Heller and G. W. Richards (Philadelphia, 1929), p. 99.

THE THEORY OF PUNISHMENT

A SURVEY of the attitudes of Renaissance writers to the problem of punishment furnishes us an excellent barometer of the secularizing and rationalizing temper of the times. For the drama, Professor Willard Farnham has made such a survey in his very fine study of *The Medieval Heritage of Elizabethan Tragedy*. He has shown that in Boccaccio's stories and in the early morality plays there is almost no attempt to show the wages of sin in terms of the material world, but that beginning with *Mundus et Infans* (1522) and with Skelton's *Magnyficence* we find physical suffering in the mundane sphere presented as retributive justice. Somewhat later, the Protestant dramatists Bale and Wager quite abandon the merciful denouement of the early moralities and lay stress instead on the heavy vengeance of God working in physical events to display the reward of tyrants. "In *Cambises,*" writes Farnham,[1] "the English morality comes to the climax of its concern for mundane retribution. . . . Preston's play has no touch at all of mercy. It centers in a single concrete sinner and leaves him with the utmost lack of hesitancy to the wages of sin which his acts might be expected to gather in this world." Mr. Farnham finds this point of view continuing dominant in the *Mirror for Magistrates* and its progeny of tragedies, and epitomized in Munday's *Mirror of Mutabilitie* (1579).

The sources for this revival in literature of a strict tragic justice are many. The influence of Plato, Plutarch, Origen, and Plotinus can hardly be overemphasized. Each of these authors makes much of the theory of inevadable retribution;

---

[1] P. 269.

and each was widely studied by the Reformers. In Plutarch, for example, Renaissance moralists found the attractive theory that a sinful act at the very moment of its committing engenders within itself its own punishment—so that wicked persons "have no need either of God or man to punish them," for their own depraved lives and desperate passions are sufficient to torment them to the full.[2] Seneca and the Old Testament were other storehouses for the doctrine of direct worldly retribution. Seneca owed a large part of his popularity in Renaissance times to the fact that his dramas picture torments on this earth for evildoers. Judaism furnished the important principle of *talio*—that evil deeds are requited in kind—illustrated, for example, in the story of Absalom hanged by the hair of which he was so proud or in the story of the Egyptians drowned in the sea into which they wished to drive the Israelites.[3] *Talio* was widely employed by Renaissance authors—by Beard in his *Theatre of Gods Judgements,* by Preston in *Cambises,* by Marlowe in *The Jew of Malta,* and by Whitney in his emblem of the thief choked to death by the sack of loot he had tied about his neck.[4] It can be said that resurrected classical and Hebrew theories of justice dominate the intellectual milieu of the Elizabethans.

The law of punishment, as proclaimed by representative Elizabethans, was believed to be grounded in the law of nature and in the testimony of experience, but was attributed always to God. God, it was held, has two ways of punishing the wicked: internally, by perturbations and maladies of the mind and the passions; and externally, through the work of tyrants who serve God as His Scourges. Since both

---

[2] *Morals,* trans. P. Holland (1603), pp. 545-48.
[3] See G. F. Moore, *Judaism* (Cambridge, Mass., 1927), II, 251.
[4] See *Choice of Emblems* (1586), p. 41. The emblem is entitled "Poena sequens."

of these methods are operative in *Tamburlaine,* we shall give to each some detailed consideration.

I

Psychological infelicity represented a form of retribution that was regarded as certain in all cases of sin. The evil-doer, as La Primaudaye declared, finds even within himself a Judge to take vengeance "by meanes of the affections, which God placed in man to that ende." [5] The evil man, Calvinists held, loses that quiet conscience which is the best testimony of his Election. The good man is described by George Buchanan in *The Baptist*:

> O pure in heart, happy are ye!
> For never at the inward bar
> Stand ye arraigned of villainy;
> Nor scourged with fiery whips ye are
> By the Avenger that doth dwell
> Within the bosom's narrow cell.[6]

Interior punishment did not need to be proved out of the Scriptures; it could be proved out of pagan poets:

we haue the testimonie of nature imprinted with such characters in our harts, that it did euen compell the ancient poets to finde out and to faigne *Furies,* as reuengers of our sins, which are nothing else but the torments of euill consciences.[7]

---

[5] *The French Academie* (1594), Pt. II, p. 327. See also pp. 383-84, where La Primaudaye indicates that he is following Plutarch.

[6] Trans. Archibald Brown, *The Sacred Dramas of George Buchanan* (Edinburgh, 1906), p. 135. Buchanan's words are:

> O ter beatum & amplius
> Qui purus animi, ad judices
> Non fit reus domesticos!
> Clauso nec in praecordiis
> Tortore semper vapulat! (III. iv.)

Buchanan intended his drama as a vivid picture of the "miseries of TYRANTS, even when they appear to be most fortunate." A translation in 1642 bore the title *Tyrannical Government Anatomised.*

[7] *The French Academie* (1586), p. 68.

When discussing sin, Elizabethan Calvinists seem quite content to appeal to the authority of Nature rather than of Church. Discussing in *Caelica* the punishment of sin, Greville writes significantly:

> But grant that there were no eternity,
> That life were all, and pleasure life of it;
> In sinne's excesse there yet confusions be,
> Which spoyle his peace, and passionate his art;
> Making his nature lesse, his reason thrall
> To tyranny of vice vnnaturall.[8]

And in his dramas, too, Greville places authority at the bar of nature and experience. The Chorus of Good Spirits in *Alaham* challenges the Evil Spirits to "take all the world, if it one soule content."

> But if your legions here do in their glories raue,
> Tormented while they liue on Earth, and much more in the graue;
> ... Your subtile orbes, to reall beings, then must needs be thrall.[9]

Apparently guided by the same outlook, Chapman has built *The Revenge of Bussy D'Ambois* on the notion of a Justice which "in the act itself Includes th'infliction." Crime and its punishment, he says,[10] are tied together like chained shot; the one follows the other as necessarily as thunder follows the lightning. He laments that in his day Religion, which is the body of Felicity, is so split by Christendom's dissentions that ignorant men boldly overthrow all law but their own lusts. If these men, says Chapman, will not recognize the laws of Faith that are above Reason, let them at least note the laws of the world, which they cannot deny. Let them note that the world stands by proportion, and from

---

[8] Sonnet CIII, ed. Grosart, III, 132.
[9] Grosart, III, 254.
[10] See *R. of B. D.*, V. i. 1-32. The words are those of the Shade of Bussy; but I think we may assume in this instance that they represent the dramatist's own view.

thence conclude that the law of rewards and punishments is no more easily broken than the joints and sinews of nature.

Theory of similar vein can be widely adduced from other Renaissance authors. Sidney believed that the Everlasting Justice uses "ourselves to bee the punishers of our faultes" and makes "our owne actions the beginninge of our Chastisement." [11] He could have got the theory from many authors; but by none is it more eloquently stated than by his good friend Philip Mornay. Note that the doctrine inspires in Mornay a serene patience with the world's injustices:

And whereas it spyteth thee to see Tyrants reigne, and to stout it out, and to triumph, yea and that some of them come to their Crownes by doing the same things for which othersome come to the Gallowes: doth it not greatly skill (thinke you) whether a man be tormented in a coate of Veluet or in a coate of Canuas? Whether he be manacled and fettered in gyues of gold or of yron? or whether in so short a showe, he play the great Lord or the poore Begger? . . . Be thou of high or low degree, be thou rich or poore, be thou Prince or Peazant; assoone as thou hast giuen ouer thy selfe to vyce and wickednesse, by and by thou are become their prisoner and slaue.[12]

Many men, says Mornay, are not content with God's justice unless they see the offender led to the Gibbet; but these men ought to know that the Gibbet is not the beginning of punishment but rather the end of a punishment which has begun with the crime.

On the margin opposite Mornay's discussion here, the English translation by Sidney and Golding gives us the notation: "Wickednes is a punishment to itselfe. Seneca in his Thebais." The note ought to call our attention, I think, to a fact much neglected by modern critics of Senecan

---

[11] *Arcadia*, ed. Feuillerat, IV, 247.
[12] *The Trewnesse of the Christian Religion* (1587), p. 201.

plays—namely, that Seneca's closet drama, with its attention to the psychological, furnished Elizabethan humanists
evidence of divine justice exactly in that area which they
considered centrally important.

Let us follow Mornay's suggestion and look closely at
the *Thebais*.[13] We will observe that Oedipus is punished
with remorse, rage, and virtual madness—whips that are
largely psychological. His mental affliction is emphasized:
he longs to dash out his brains. Further, he is tormented by
the realization that he has sown in his sons the seeds of his
own disease: "their hearts are mad with the lust of empire."[14] As it happens, fortunately, the madness of the
two sons is allayed by Jocasta, the one person in the play
who has kept her sanity. She prevents war between
them by using an argument based on the dreadfulness of
psychological retribution. She argues that Eteocles can triumph only like Cadmus to his own ruin, because Eteocles
will have to bear as punishment the mental torment of his
own sense of guilt together with the hatred of his people.

It is central to Seneca's teaching in the *Moral Essays* that
when contentment of mind is lost all happiness is lost.
What man should most fear is insanity.[15] Seneca's dramas
but illustrate this doctrine. And since Seneca's dramas set the
style for so much of Renaissance tragedy, it will be worth our
while to note in a few more of them how the theory of
tragic justice operates.

Medea is a play exhibiting the unhappy progress of un-
bridled desire. The Chorus warns Medea that

The youth who dared drive the everlasting chariot, heedless of his

---

[13] Edward Phillips, perhaps because he recognized a spiritual affinity between
Senecan drama and *Tamburlaine*, reported Thomas Newton to be "the Author
of three Tragedies; *Thebais*, the first and second parts of *Tamerlane*."
[14] Loeb edition, 302.
[15] See "On the Happy Life," Loeb ed., Vol. III.

father's goal, himself caught the fire which in his madness he scattered o'er the sky.[16]

But Medea, to encompass her revenge, opens her breast to the Furies—wrath, violence, and rage. The misery of being driven by these passions is the only punishment Medea suffers, even up to the end of the play. Since she refuses the consciousness of guilt, she does not even suffer remorse. She rides off safely through the air on a winged car, and Jason is utterly distracted by what seems to him a failure in divine justice. He calls after her:

> Go on through the lofty spaces of high heaven and bear witness, where thou ridest, that there are no gods.

In *Hercules Furens,* again, there is no poetic justice except in the fact that Hercules' soul has become a house of mad passions. His self-imposed misery begins in his desire for conquest, reaches a climax in the blasphemous proposal to invade heaven, and results finally in his killing his own son. Then at last he discovers his own madness and is assailed by remorse and fear. In mental anguish he calls out, as Faustus in Marlowe's play, "Whither shall I flee? Where shall I hide me, or in what land bury me?"[17] But here the drama ends. There is no devil, as in *Faustus,* to provide the prospect of further retributive justice.

Atreus in Seneca's *Thyestes* is another example of successful villainy—accomplished with ridiculous ease—that goes outwardly unpunished. Thyestes calls loudly on heaven and earth to punish Atreus. Like Jason in *Medea,* Thyestes finds his faith in a moral universe sorely tried. He wonders how the earth can bear a crime so monstrous; it seems to him the gods have fled away, because heaven does not answer his prayer for thunderbolts and lightnings upon Atreus. There

---

[16] Loeb ed., 599-602.
[17] Loeb ed., 1321-22.

is no retribution whatever for Atreus, unless we reckon it
in the fact that from an early moment in the play he has
welcomed the "dira Furiarum cohors." Equally significant,
of course, is the way in which Thyestes is being punished.
Atreus has rejected both fire and sword as methods of
scourging Thyestes and has chosen instead the most devas-
tating retribution he can think of—agonies of soul for
Thyestes.[18]

When we find such criminals as Thyestes, Atreus, Hercules, and Medea all alive at the end of the plays, we are
forced to conclude either that Seneca had no concern at all
for poetic justice, or else that his sense of justice was quite
satisfied with the spectacle of psychological retribution. The
second of these two alternatives is quite plainly the correct
one. The dramatist's rigorous notion of a moral world order
is evident when Theseus says in *Hercules Furens*:

What each has done, he suffers; upon its author the crime comes
back, and the guilty soul is crushed by its own form of guilt. . . .
   Ixion whirls, racked on a flying wheel; a huge stone rests on the
neck of Sisyphus; in mid-stream an old man with parched lips
catches at the waves . . . . the impious Cadmeids roam in their
madness. . . .[19]

This mythological language, when we consider it, means
simply that each man's punishment is tied to his sin.

It is significant that occasionally Elizabethan stage-plays,
like Seneca's closet dramas, end with the monster-hero outwardly unscathed. This is the case, for example, in John
Pickering's *The History of Horestes* (1567). Falling under
the influence of the Vice, Horestes rejects Nature's arguments
against revenge and decides that blood must have blood.
When his mother is captured after a long seige of her city,
she falls repentant at Horestes' feet and begs pardon and

---
[18] See Loeb ed., 258.
[19] Loeb ed., 735 ff.

mercy; but Horestes ruthlessly commands her death. Menelaus later describes the cruelty of "this tyrant" by saying that he brought to the ground all cities that he entered and that he showed no pity even for the aged, the maids, and the widows. Yet Menelaus is persuaded to give his daughter in marriage to Horestes, and the play ends happily with Horestes in possession of the kingdom. He is even crowned by Truth and Duty; for Pickering shows him as now a reformed character who has forsaken the Vice, Revenge.

No such reformation, however, overtakes the wicked and successful hero of the anonymous *The First Part of the Tragicall Raigne of Selimus* (1594). Selimus announces himself as "The perfect picture of right tyrannie," and then boldly declares the Machiavellian doctrine that religious teachings are "Onely bug-beares to keepe the world in feare." He poisons his father, murders his brother and many others, and when he has strangled his last competitor for the crown of Arabia he "Sits downe among his friends, and with delight/Declares the trauels he hath ouerpast." There is nothing to mar his bliss. One of his victims promises that the Heavens "beare an equall eye" and that "vengeance followes thee euen at the heeles;" but we behold no catastrophe for Selimus. An epilogue promises that applause will bring a second part to the drama, with "greater murthers." No second part has survived.

More strictly Senecan is Greville's *Alaham,* where a good deal of attention is given to the psychological retribution that attends successful villainy. Alaham is a usurper who brings about the death of his father, brother, and sister. He receives a punishment both physical and psychological. He is poisoned by a Triumphant Robe given him by his wife Hala, and also he is tormented by remorse and the ghosts of conscience—"Disease, or Griefe (I know not which) or both / Languish my powers." And Hala, in turn, receives a punishment self-inflicted and wholly psychological. By mistake she murders not Alaham's child, but her own and Cain's, and thus brings upon herself great torments of remorse and woe. Here the drama leaves her—the greatest villain of the play, yet outwardly unpunished.

Greville's method in tragedy is, as he has told us, to let wickedness grow until it destroys itself by its own excess. His purpose is

> to trace out the high waies of ambitious governours, and to shew in the practice of life that the more audacity, advantage, and good successe such soveraignties have, the more they hasten to their own desolation and ruine.[20]

He says he does not wish to depict, as Ancient Tragedy has done, the punishment of innocent people: for such scenes stir up murmurs against Divine Providence, which it is his purpose to defend. As a result of Greville's theory, we discover in *Alaham* that even the noble and attractive Caelica is not without fault, but is "seduced by glory." There are no virtuous characters in Greville's plays. There are, instead, various forms of error battling each other. So Senecan a notion of tragic justice fits well with Greville's Calvinism.

II

Greville's notion of tragic justice brings us also to a consideration of the second aspect of the Renaissance theory of punishment—namely, the significance of external punishments, such as wars and tyrannies. These evils of our social life Calvinists commonly explained as chastisements of God, inflicted on wicked and degenerate men by certain great wrongdoers commissioned by God. This theory stems from Isaiah's concept of the "Scourge of God" (*Isaiah* X. 5-16), widely revived by Reformation writers. It demands our particular examination because it furnishes Tamburlaine his title and is our key to the interpretation of his tragedy.

---

[20] *Life of Sidney*, ed. Grosart, IV, 220.

Calvin, in his commentary on Isaiah,[21] makes much of the point that the Assyrian whom God uses to punish Israel is a furious, proud, and blasphemous person. He treads his enemies under foot,

> which is the vttermost of all rage, for what can men do more then with shame and contempt to stamp them *vnder feete* whom they haue vanquished?[22]

He recites his conquests, boasts of the ease of his victories, and finally vaunts himself against God. But then, says Calvin, the Assyrian's boastings are "so many bellowes (as it were) to kindle the wrath of God." God in the end burns and utterly consumes the Assyrian's glory.

Calvin did not hesitate to apply Isaiah's doctrine to the interpretation of Renaissance history:

> So at this day there are diuers diseases in the Church which the Lord will purge and heale. . . . Wherefore wee must not maruell if he lets loose the bridle to tyrants, and suffreth them still to exercise their crueltie against his Church: for the consolation is readie, to wit, *hauing vsed them as his vassals to correct his people, he will visit their pride and arrogancie.*[23]

And others besides Calvin found the concept useful in explaining the miseries suffered by Christendom at the hands of the Turks. Peter Ashton declared in his *Shorte Treatise upon the Turkes Chronicles* (1546) that "God suffereth the wicked and cursed seed of Hismael to be a scourge and whip

---

[21] *A Commentary Vpon the Prophecie of Isaiah*, trans. C. Cotton (1609), pp. 115-22. I quote, by permission, from the copy in the Huntington Library. The commentary appeared in Latin in 1551, in French in 1552, both editions dedicated to Edward VI. Later Latin editions appeared in 1559, 1570, and 1583. Cotton translated from a 1572 French translation of the 1570 Latin edition.

[22] It is therefore a particularly appropriate sign of Tamburlaine's rage when he treads Bajazet under foot, and when he orders his horsemen to charge (and thus to trample under foot) the virgins of Damascus (*Tamb.* 1458, 1898).

[23] *Commentary*, pp. 119-20.

us for our synnes." [24]   Richard Knolles in his popular *The Generall Historie of the Turkes* (1603) gave the same explanation. The "first and greatest" cause for the scandalous successes of the Turks, he said,

is the iust and secret iudgement of the Almightie, who in iustice deliuereth into the hands of these mercilesse miscreants, nation after nation, and kingdome vpon kingdome, as vnto the most terrible executioners of his dreadfull wrath, to be punished for their sinnes.[25]

Philip Mornay applies the Scourge concept to more ancient history. He explains how Cyrus, Titus, Attila, and Judas— each led on by his own evil passion—were made by God the unwitting instruments of His providence.[26] In writing of Attila, Mornay states the theory most clearly:

Ye must thinke that when this great Robber cast lots in his Countrie of Scythia, whether he should leade the third part of that land, he had another meaning than to reforme the world. Yet not withstanding, all men acknowledge him to be a necessary scourge of GOD, and to haue come in due season. Yea, and he himselfe considering that he had conquered much more of the Countrie, than euer he hoped at the first to haue seene, insomuch that he had ouercome euen those which were counted the strength of the World: as barbarous as he was, he fell to thinke of himself, that he was the Scurge whereby God chastised the World. Not that God is not able to chastise vs himselfe whensoeuer he listeth . . . but that as a Maister of a howshold holdeth skorne to whippe his Slaues himselfe . . . but causeth (peradventure) the groome of his stable to doe it, to the intent to shew them the iustenesse of his displeasure: Euen so doth God punish the wicked one by another. . . .

Elizabethan authors commonly define War as "a scourge

---

[24] Quoted by S. C. Chew, *The Crescent and the Rose* (New York, 1937), p. 106.

[25] "Preface to the Reader."

[26] *Christian Religion*, pp. 208-09. See also Du Bartas, *First Week*, Seventh Day, 204-09, ed. Grosart, *Works of Sylvester*, I, 85.

of the wrath of God."[27]   This definition is part of a paradoxical attitude in which war is regarded as both justified
(by sin) and condemned (by God).   Greville's *Treatie of
Warres* illustrates this outlook most clearly.   Greville con-
demns war as "the perfect type of Hell"; but also he justifies
war as, by Heaven's overruling power, "The sword of Justice,
and of sinne the terror."[28]   His explanation of war is that
it is a form of rebellious pride grounded in man's sin.

> Men would be tyrants, tyrants would be gods,
> Thus they become our scourges, we their rods.[29]

Two notable examples, he points out, are Nimrod and the
Turkish empire.   Mahomet's followers, boldly "climing vp
vnited staires" of diligent wickedness, have founded by war
a highly prosperous tyranny.   They have prevailed over the
Christians, because the Christians are split between a doctrine
of peace and a pope who stirs them up to war.[30]   The wicked
Turks punish the impious Christians.   War is of the devil,
but the devil is under the providence of God.[31]

Nimrod, whom Greville has cited, was a hero well known
to Renaissance readers in Du Bartas' popular story.[32]   An
attentive reader of Du Bartas' account will note at once the
general similarity of Nimrod's career to Tamburlaine's.
Nimrod, we are told, begins at an early age by tyrannizing
over shepherds.   He knows well that whoever aims

---

[27] See Nicholas Breton's characters of "War" and of "An Unworthy King"
(*Works*, ed. Grosart, II. q. 8; II. r. 5.); also Gascoigne's "Dulce Bellum Inex-
pertis," stanzas 12 ff. (*Works*, ed. Cunliffe, I, 143 ff.); Greville's "A Treatie of
Warres," esp. stanza 6 (*Works*, ed. Grosart, II, 103 ff.); and Burton's Preface to
the *Anatomy of Melancholy* (ed. Shilleto, I, 61).

[28] Stanzas 29, 50.

[29] Stanza 25.

[30] Stanzas 18, 65 ff.

[31] Stanza 31.

[32] "Babylon," *Second Week,* Second Day, 51 ff. ed. Grosart, I, 138 ff.   This
part of Du Bartas had early and separate English translation by William L'Isle,
who included also the commentary of Simon Senlisien, in an edition entitled
Babilon (1596).

At fancied bliss of Empire's awful lustre
In valiant acts must passe the Vulgar sort,
Or Mask (at least) in lovely Vertue's Port.

So he ambitiously avoids ease, hardens himself, and wins fame as a hunter. Then "snatching Fortune by the tresses," he "hunteth men to trap." Winning some men by promises, others by presents, and others by "rougher threats," he "Usurps the Child-World's Maiden Monarchy." Next he builds the high tower of Babel. At this point God says:

> ... I meant to be their Master,
> My self alone, their Law, their Prince, and Pastor;
> And they, for Lord a Tyrant fell have ta'en them;
> Who (to their cost) will roughly curb & rein-them
> Who scorns mine arm, & with these braving Towrs
> Attempts to scale this Crystall Throne of Ours.

So God confounds the people's language. Senlisien, the French commentator on Du Bartas, remarks upon the internal nature of the punishment chosen:

God ... sendeth not lightning, winde, nor tempest against the tower; but contenteth himself to strike the proud and puffed vp braines of the builders. ... Who would have thought that God had had so readie such kinde of rods to punish mankinde withall? ... God ... treading as it were with woolen feete, and stealing on softly, is able with an arme of Iron to surprise and seize upon these builders, and turne by diuers means their vaine purposes and weake endeauours to naught.[33]

Moralists were comforted by the fact that the "Scourge of God" notion commonly includes an ultimate mundane pun-

---

[33] *Babilon* (1596), pp. 21-22. The reader should compare also Du Bartas' story of the Assyrian ("The Decay," ed. Grosart, I, 251 ff.). When Rabsakeh, on behalf of Sennacherib, blasphemes:

> I am the Scourge of God: 'tis vain to stand
> Against the pow'r of my victorious hand

God presently sends a "winged champion" to slaughter the Assyrians, and Sennacherib is slain by his own sons.

ishment for the Scourge. The tyrant Caesar, so Philip Mornay said, was slain miserably

> To shewe vnto Tyrannes that the highest step of their greatnesse is tyed to a halter, and that they be but Gods scourges which he will cast into the fyre when he hath done with them. . . .[34]

And La Primaudaye affirmed that for tyrants God has His owne secret but sure stroke of revenge—"God will returne into their bosom the euill which they haue done." [35] This faith sustained the important Elizabethan doctrine that men should not for private reasons take God's revenge into their own hands.

The concept of the Scourge of God has, therefore, two complementary aspects: it serves to explain historical calamities by showing that they are chastisements of sin permitted by God; and it assures tyrants that God is not helpless before their power but that He will, when He has used them, destroy them utterly.

---

[34] *Christian Religion,* p. 196. Mornay here uses the language of Isaiah's concept, as does Marlowe in *Tamburlaine.* But we should remember also that the theme of providential death for the wicked has notable primitive exponents besides Isaiah. *Acts* 12 tells how Herod was eaten by worms "because he gave not God the glory"; and this story furnished Lactantius a model for his gory *De Mortibus Persecutorum.*

[35] *The French Academie* (1594), Pt. II, p. 326.

THE MORAL USES OF POETRY

❀ ❀

THERE is a notable passage in St. Augustine's *De Doctrina Christiana,* quoted both by William Baldwin and by Thomas Bowes, reminding Christians that

the Egipcians had not onely Idoles and great burdens which the Israelites dyd hate and flee, but also vessels, ornaments, and goodli Jewels of gold and siluer, which the Israelites departing from Egipt, vnder the coloure of borowing, stole priueli from them, not of theyr own mynd, but by the commaundement of god, to turne that to a better vse, which the Egipcians abused.[1]

Here was a made-to-order proof-text for the humanists! It could be used to justify a widespread investigation of pagan literatures and an open display of their merits. When the humanists exhibited to the public the treasure of heathen poetry—which they were most anxious to salvage, because in their view all the arts are comprehended in poetry—they were careful to argue that the ancient authors foreshadow Christian wisdom and that their verses hold instruction helpful to man's salvation. Seneca, Ovid, and Homer might be beloved as stylists, but they were recommended principally as seers.

Seneca was venerated because, as Lydgate said, he "Wrot tragedies of gret moralitie." The Elizabethans, with their concern for simple and practical religion, preferred moral pageants to abstract philosophy. For this reason Sir William Cornwallis thought Seneca a more profitable teacher

---

[1] "The Prologe to the Reader" of Baldwin's *A Treatise of Morall Phylosophye* (1547). See also Bowes, "The Epistle Dedicatorie" of *The French Academie* (1586).

114

than Aristotle[2]—just as, later, Milton was to place Spenser above Aquinas. The appeal of Seneca's dramas was not, as we sometimes suppose, a matter simply of the theatrical attractiveness of madmen and ghosts. To his English editor, Thomas Newton, Seneca was an author who "beateth down sinne." Newton's words are significant enough to be quoted at length:

And whereas it is by some squeymish Areopagites surmyzed, that the readings of these Tragedies, being enterlarded with many Phrases and sentences, literally tending (at the first sight) sometime to the prayse of Ambition, sometyme to the mayntenaunce of cruelty, now and then to the approbation of incontinencie, and here and there to the ratification of tyranny, cannot be digested without great daunger of infection: to omit all other reasons, if it might please them with no forestalled judgment, to mark and consider the circumstances, why, where, and by what manner of persons such sentences are pronounced, they cannot in any equity otherwise choose, but find good cause ynough to leade them to a more fauourable and milde resolution. For it may not at any hand be thought and deemed the direct meaning of Seneca himselfe, whose whole wrytinges (penned with a peerelesse sublimity and loftinesse of Style) are so farre from countenauncing vice, that I doubt whether there bee any amonge all the Catalogue of Heathen wryters, that with more grauity of Philosophicall sentences, more waightynes of sappy words, or greater authority of sound matter beateth down sinne, loose lyfe, dissolute dealinge, and unbrydled sensuality: or that more sensibly, pithily, and bytingly layeth doune the guedon of filthy lust, cloaked dissimulation and odious treachery: which is the dryft, whereunto he leueleth the whole yssue of ech one of his Tragedies.[3]

The Calvinist John Studley, in dedicating his English translation of the *Medea* in 1566, did not hesitate to call Seneca

---

[2] Essay 46, "Of Essayes and Bookes," *A Second part of Essayes* (1601): "Thus do I thinke of *Seneca*, and *Aristotle*, the first's moralitie is easily to bee vnderstood, and easily digested to the nourishment of vertue; the others more high, and to the reader more questionable, whether it will make him curious or honest."

[3] In the Dedication to *Seneca His Tenne Tragedies translated into English* (1581).

"that . . . Most Christian Ethnicke." And in somewhat the same spirit Thomas Lodge, when he translated *The Workes both Morrall and Natural of Lucius Annaeus Seneca* (1614), declared that Seneca's "diuine sentences" and "serious exclamations against vices" might well put Christians to shame.

Would God Christians would endeauour to practice his good precepts, to reform their owne in seeing his errours; and perceiuing so great light of learning from a Pagans pen, ayme at the true light of deuotion and pietie, which becometh Christians.[4]

Ovid was welcomed in a similar manner. Golding, in a long and careful preface to his translation of the *Metamorphoses* (1567), stresses the point that Ovid's intent was not to allure to vice but rather to promote self-knowledge and to recommend reason and temperance. It is true that Ovid has presented vices in "lyvely colours"; but the reader must remember that the function of poetry is imitative, and he must therefore be no more offended than if he saw these happenings in a crystal glass.[5]

Homer's Renaissance champion was Chapman, likewise no dispassionate antiquarian but a militant humanist, who translated Homer with large freedom. The *Iliad* and the *Odyssey* are construed by Chapman as two notable *exempla* of opposite purport: the one an exhibition of *wrath* or *predominant perturbation* or "the body's fervor"; the other, on the contrary, of *man* or *overruling wisdom* or "the mind's inward empire." [6] Chapman holds that the "soul" of poetry is allegory, and he looks to allegory to express the loveliness of Virtue and the ugliness of Vice in a fashion excelling the art which life can delineate. Poetry has, Chapman bold-

---

⁴ "To the Courteous Reader."
⁵ Epistle Dedicatory, 557 ff.
⁶ *Poems* (London, 1875), p. 237.

ly claims, "the most material and doctrinal illations of truth" regarding manners, justice, and even Christian piety.

I

Chapman's is a liberal interpretation of "doctrine" and a large claim for poetry; but it accords with the representative thought of the times, which makes moral values the first line of poetry's defense. Poetry is defined by Sidney as fable-making. The poet is no mere rhymester or versifier; he is a "right popular philosopher" who invents notable images of virtues and vices. He is an imitator of the ideal,[7] seeking to beautify history according to "that which is most reasonable," to make his fictional histories "more doctrinal" than the factual accounts of mere historians. Jesus and Plato are considered master poets because they present moral commonplaces in examples which delightfully bait our imaginations.

The common praise for poets is that their stories show virtues and vices in "Speaking Pictures." A "more familiar insight into anger" than the definitions of Stoics or Schoolmen, says Sidney, is Sophocles' Ajax. Even an ignorant man is sure to have his understanding enlightened when Medea exhibits the "sowre-sweetnes of revenge," or when the two Theban brothers display "the violence of ambition." Tragedy, because it makes kings fear to be tyrants, is "high and excellent." [8]

---

[7] The Renaissance takes its art theory not from Plato, who said that art imitates only the appearance of things and is thus thrice removed from truth, but from Plotinus (*Enn.* V. 8. 1-2), who said that art lays bare the inner truth of things, the ideal obscured in the real. The view accords well with Aristotle's (*Poet.* 1451-56) that poetry shows "what would and might be" and therefore excells history, which shows what "was."

[8] *Defence of Poesie,* ed. Feuillerat, p. 23. Cf. Chapman: the "soul, limbs, and limits of an authentical tragedy" consist of "elegant and sententious excitation to virtue, and deflection from her contrary." (Dedication to *The Revenge of Bussy D'Ambois.*)

Plato had held that poets should not "be trained to imitate the action or speech of men or women who are mad or bad; for madness, like vice, is to be known but not practised or imitated."[9] This was not the view of the Renaissance humanists. Sidney answered Plato by saying that Christianity has now taken away the hurt from the wrong opinions voiced in poetry. Other apologists simply defended wanton verses by citing the aphorism of the Bee and the Spider:

> as the industrious Bee may gather honie out of the most stinking weede, so the malicious Spider may also gather poyson out of the fayrest floure that growes.[10]

To which Golding adds piously:

> For too the pure and Godly mynd, are all things pure and cleene,
> And untoo such as are corrupt the best corrupted beene.

The humanists, academic and aristocratic in their outlook, seem to have taken the attitude that if the vulgar reader takes poison instead of honey from witnessing sin the fault and responsibility is his, not the poet's. Actually, no doubt, this liberal attitude toward the literary presentation of spectacles of vice contributed sometimes—as is the case with our modern "Crime Does Not Pay" cinemas—to the delinquency of juvenile minds. But the humanists—*vide* Milton—wished to cultivate no cloistered virtue.

Examples of this liberal line of apology readily come to mind. Spenser, in lusciously depicting the Bower of Bliss,

---

[9] *Repub.* III, 396. But ct. Plotinus, *Enn.* III. 2. 5, 11, 15.
[10] The words are Gascoigne's in a preface to *Posies* (1575); but the simile, a commonplace of Elizabethan criticism, is invoked also by Nashe (*Anatomie of Absurditie*, ed. McKerrow I, 30), by Golding ("Preface to the Reader" of the *Metamorphoses*), and by Francis Davidson as a motto on the title page of his *A Poetical Rhapsody* (1602). Francis Meres, who also cites the simile (*Palladis Tamia*, ed. G. G. Smith, *Eliz. Crit. Essays*, II, 309), indicates that it has its source in Plutarch. Sebastian Franck (*Paradoxa*, sec. 29) introduces the simile in his argument for free will: Will, the king in man, can make its world good or evil—just as out of the same flower the bee gets honey and the spider poison.

considered himself an ethical teacher exhibiting the meretricious allurements of vice. Lodge and Puttenham[11] justify the stage-wickedness of drama because it lays open to all the world the outrageous behavior of infamous men. Gascoigne[12] pleads that even in the worst sort of his verses his intent has been to "serve as a myrrour for unbrydled youth, to avoyde those perilles which I had passed." Boldly he refers to himself as one "professing armes in the defence of God's truth." If readers use for a spur what he has intended for a bridle he can only lament; his intent has been to exercise his pen in moral discourses.

Also, certainly, we must take into account the views of Nashe, who was Marlowe's collaborator on *Dido*. Nashe sees poetry as a way of placarding the deeds of the great mischief-makers of mankind. He expresses the wish that Marcus Agrippa and Nero may be given "such Epitaphes of disgrace, as they deserue, and that the Chronicles may record their reproch vnto all ages." [13] And elsewhere Nashe elaborates a theory of the function of drama, which it is natural to suppose that Marlowe knew and probably shared:

In Playes, all coosonages, all cunning drifts ouer-guylded with outward holinesse, all stratagems of warre, all the cankerwormes that breede on the rust of peace, are most lively anatomiz'd: they shew the ill successe of treason, the fall of hastie climbers, the wretched ende of vsurpers, the miserie of ciuill dissention, and how iust God is euermore in punishing of murther. And to proue euery one of these allegations, could I propound the circumstances of this play and that play, if I meant to handle this Theame otherwise than *obiter*. What should I say more? they are sower pils of repre-

---

[11] See Smith, *Eliz. Crit. Essays,* I, 80; II, 35.

[12] In prefaces "To the Reverende Divines," "To al yong Gentlemen," and "To the Readers" of *Posies,* ed. J. W. Cunliffe, *Works of Gascoigne,* I. Professor Boas has discovered that Gascoigne—like Marlowe—was accused of atheism. In "certain objections" laid before the Privy Council it is alleged that Gascoigne "is a notorious Ruffiane and especialli noted to be both a spie, an atheist, and a godlesse person." (*Christopher Marlowe,* p. 109).

[13] *Anatomie of Absurditie,* ed. McKerrow, I, 36-37.

hension, wrapt vp in sweete words . . . for no Play they haue
encourageth any man to tumults or rebellion, but layes before such
the halter and the gallowes, or praiseth or approoueth pride, lust,
whoredom, prodigalitie, or drunkennes, but beates them downe
vtterly.[14]

II

In addition to the moral argument that pageants of vice
serve as warnings and teach negatively, there is secondly
the esthetic argument that the skillful imitation of vice gives
dispassionate pleasure. "As wee are delighted in the picture
of a viper or a spider artificially enclosed within a precious
iewell: so Poets do delight vs in the learned & cunning de-
painting of vices." [15] Here Renaissance thinking owed much
to Plutarch, who gives a chapter in his *Morals* to "How a
Yoong Man ought to heare poets." Plutarch makes clear
that since poetry carries both danger and delight, the young
man must not receive poetry's statements as true but rather
he must praise them in so far as they befit the person or are
appropriate to the subject matter they describe. The young
man must understand that Poetry is the art of Imitation and
that

when we behold a Lizard or an Ape wel painted, or the face of
Thersites lively drawen, we take pleasure therein & praise the same
wonderfully; nor for any beautie in the one or in the other, but
because they are so naturally counterfeited . . . the skil of resembling
a thing wel, be the same faire or be it foule, is always commended.
. . . Some painters you shall have to delight in painting of strange,
foolish and absurd actions: as for example *Timomachus* represented
in a table the picture of *Medea,* killing her owne children: *Theon*
painted *Orestes* murthering his owne mother. . . .[16]

A point significant for our profit in reading *Tamburlaine*
is Plutarch's warning that poets have a dramatic license to

[14] *Pierce Penilesse* (1592), ed. McKerrow, I, 213-14.
[15] Meres, *Palladis Tamia,* 277ᵛ.
[16] *Morals,* trans. Philemon Holland (1603), p. 22.

utter impieties and blasphemies. Poets are privileged to invent "lying fables," including absurd things touching the Gods and virtue, and misconceptions of "felicity" and "honor."

> And much were he deceived, who should perswade himselfe that Poets take beatitude and blessednesse, which in Greeke is called εὐδαιμονία, so precisely as Philosophers doe . . . for many times Poets abuse this word, calling a man blessed and happie, who is rich in world goods; and giving the terme of felicitie and happinesse unto great power, fame and renowne.[17]

This ought to make us wary in our interpretation of Tamburlaine's poetic argument for the sweet felicity of an earthly crown, and careful likewise in our understanding of Tamburlaine's "honor that consists in shedding blood."

Perhaps we need to be warned, also, that poets do not use the term "God" in so strict a sense as does the Christian believer. Golding develops this point in presenting Ovid. Poets, he says, use the term God to represent moral allegiances of divers kinds:

> Whoose lawes wee keepe his thralles wee bee, and he our God indeede.
> So long is Christ our God as wee in christen lyfe proceede.
> But if wee yeeld too fleshlye lust, too lucre, or too wrath,
> Or if that Envy, Gluttony, or Pryde the maystry hath,
> Or any other kynd of sinne the thing the which wee serve,
> Too bee accounted for our God most justly doth deserve.[18]

With this in mind we can understand Tamburlaine's statement that his God is the God of Revenging Wrath.[19] Tamburlaine behaves as wrath's thrall, and so it is appro-

---

[17] *Ibid.,* p. 32.
[18] *Met.,* Preface to the Reader, 51-57.
[19] Though burning the Koran, and denying the Godhead of Mahomet, Tamburlaine affirms (*Tamb.* II. v. i.):

> There is a God full of reuenging wrath,
> From whom the thunder and the lightning breaks,
> Whose Scourge I am, and him will I obey.

priate for him to acknowledge a God-of-wrath as his God. It is important also to remember that morality literature is type literature. It seeks to copy ideal prototypes. Characters are drawn to embody virtue or vice writ large in cosmic terms. Spenser's knights and ladies present pattern-behavior, freed from the limitations of history and carrying the value of symbol. Greene's Selimus invites us to view in him "the perfect picture of right tyrannie." [20] And Gascoigne announces in "The argument for the Tragedie" of *Jocasta* that

> Creon is king, the type of Tyranny
> And Oedipus, myrrour of misery.

The mirror notion had an amazing popularity.[21] It symbolized the chief aim of the humanists: self-knowledge and the reformation of manners. La Primaudaye, one of the many who invoked the mirror idea as his literary theory, cited Seneca as his authority:

> Seneca the Philosopher reporteth (gentle Reader) that the looking glasse was first inuented to this end, that man might vse it as a meane to know himself the better by. . . . In which respect this Book may most fitly be resembled to a glasse . . .[22]

Greville applied the concept even to the Bible:

---

[20] *The First Part of the Tragicall Raigne of Selimus*, 284, ed. W. Bang (1908).

[21] Witness, for example, the following titles: Whetstone, *A Mirour for Magestrates of Cyties* (1584); *A Mirror of Treue Honnour and Christian Nobilitie* (1585); *The English Myrror* (1586). Gascoigne, *Glass of Government* (1575); *Steel Glass* (1576). Queen Elizabeth, *The Mirror of the Sinful Soul* (trans. in 1544). Lodge, *A Looking Glasse for London and England* (1598). Baldwin, Higgins, et al., *The Mirror for Magistrates* (1559, etc.). T. T[urswell?], *Myrrour for Martinists* (1590). *The Myrrour of the Multytude* (S. R., 15 Dec., 1586). *A Mirrour of . . . Sir Philip Sidney* (S. R., 15 June, 1587). *A Myrrour to all that love to followe the Warres* (S. R., 20 Jan., 1589). *A Christall Glasse for Christian Women* (S. R., 15 June, 1591). See also the dozen titles under "Mirror" and "Glass" in the *Short Title Catalogue*.

[22] "To the Christian Reader," The Second Part of *The French Academie* (1594). Peter Ashton attributed the Mirror idea to Plato (see L. B. Campbell's edition of the *Mirror for Magistrates*, p. 49).

This Sacred Word is the eternal glass,
Where all men's souls behold the face they bring;
Each sees as much as LIFE hath brought to pass.[23]

Philosophically the mirror idea is grounded in the Neo-Platonic belief that the world of Nature is continually mirroring deeply-hidden cosmic truth, and that the artist's task therefore is to copy this world in its symbol aspect and pattern—to present history with the clarity of fable. For in this philosophy the macrocosm is regarded as the mirror of the microcosm, and man is supposed to see and learn to know himself by studying the world. The Elizabethans believed, as Miss Lily B. Campbell well says,[24] that history when exhibited "in a poetical mirror of political truth" could teach men the way to righteousness, life, and immortality.

There is no reason for supposing that Marlowe disagreed with this prevailing mirror-theory of the function of poetry. When he writes in the prologue to *Tamburlaine*

> View but his picture in this tragic glass
> And then applaud his fortunes as you please

we have every right to assume that the dramatist intends to maintain in his treatment of history the artistic detachment that accords with the imitative office of poetry.

III

The great popularity of poetry—particularly the vogue of tragic drama—in Elizabethan times has, finally, one other explanation. We have mentioned poetry's moral and esthetic uses; we must also consider the theological. For besides the view that plays are moral warnings, and skillful

---

[23] *A Treatise of Religion*, stanza 58; ed. Grosart. *Works of Greville*, I, 258.
[24] *Tudor Conceptions of History and Tragedy in "A Mirror for Magistrates"* (Univ. of Calif. Press, 1936), p. 27.

works of imitation, there is the conviction that plays are revelations of Divine Purpose and Plan.

Elizabethans were awed and inspired by the idea that God was a dramatist. This world was His stageplay. The Calvinist imagination, exalted by the vision of sovereign Divine Providence, viewed the panorama of election and damnation with predestinarian equanimity.

God, who is the Author of all our tragedies, [writes Raleigh] hath written out for vs, and appointed vs all the parts we are to play: and hath not, in their distribution, beene partiall to the most mighty Princes of the world; That gaue vnto *Darius* the part of the greatest Emperour, and the part of the most miserable begger, a begger begging water of an Enemie, to quench the great drought of death; That appointed *Baiazet* to play the *Gran Signior* of the *Turkes* in the morning, and in the same day the *Footstoole* of *Tamerlane* . . .[25]

For their doctrine at this point Renaissance humanists go back to Plotinus. The Neo-Platonists alone among the great philosophers of antiquity develop the notion that history is a pageant, the work of a great Dramatic Artist.[26] The Stoics make their contribution to drama by their notion of immanent law and automatic punishment, which furnishes the ground in nature for Poetic Justice; but it is Plotinus who, coming after the Stoics, enlarges the horizon by his picture of a transcendent God, presiding over a marvellously variegated universe in which individual souls play out the various roles assigned to them by the supreme Author.[27] The following passage will illustrate the serenity and scope of Plotinus' outlook:

Murders, death in all its guises, the reduction and sacking of cities, all must be to us just such a spectacle as the changing scenes of a play; all is but the varied incident of a plot, costume on and off,

---

[25] *History of the World* (1614), Preface, Sig. D^v-D2^r.
[26] See Plotinus, *Enn.* III. 2. 11.
[27] See *Enn.* III. 2. 17.

acted grief and lament. For on earth, in all the succession of life, it is not the Soul within but the Shadow outside of the authentic man that grieves and complains and acts out the plot on this world stage which men have dotted with stages of their own constructing. All this is the doing of man knowing no more than to live the lower and outer life, and never perceiving that, in his weeping and in his graver doings alike, he is but at play . . .[28]

Through Ficinus[29] this view was passed on to the Renaissance. When Philip Mornay discusses Providence in his *Trewnesse of the Christian Religion* he says:

Surely *Plotin* hath made two or three bookes thereof, wherein he teacheth prouidence by all things from the greatest to the smallest, comming downe euen to the little flowers which wee see vnblowen in the morning and withered at night, as though he had ment to say the same thing that wee reade in the Gospell: namely, Consider me the Lillies of the field; and so forth.

Then, to summarize the truth regarding God's Providence, Mornay quotes the dictum of Plotinus: "the prosperitie of the wicked is but as a Stageplay." [30]

Elsewhere Mornay elaborates in interesting fashion the analogy between God and the dramatist. The tragic dramatist, he points out, presents before our eyes various evils. We bear with the sight of "the unmeasurable barbarous cruelties of Atreus, the wicked presumptions of an Ixion" because we think that "ere he leaves the stage, he will tye the wicked Ixion to a wheele, or make the feends of Hell to torment Atreus." God directs the great drama of history with similar regard for justice:

---

[28] *Enn.* III. 2. 15. Mackenna's translation.

[29] Probably as a result of his translating Plotinus, Ficinus himself makes a good deal of the analogy between God and the artist. See his *Theol. Plat.* II, 13; IV, 1; XIII, 3 (cited by P. O. Kristeller, *Church History,* VIII, 209n).

[30] P. 213. After still further exposition of Plotinus, Mornay finally, to avoid long discourse, tells the reader to look for himself in Plotinus' works. Then Mornay goes on to argue Providence out of Porphyry and Synesius. The influence of the Neo-Platonists on Mornay's thought is thus overwhelming.

And if God seeme erewhyles to hold his peace, and to suffer men to play their partes; ought wee not too haue so good opinion of his wisdome, as to think that he can tell when it is tyme to pay them their hyre? And that although he let the wicked walk at large vpon the stage, and the goodly to lie in prison: he can also prouide to end the braueries of the one sort with iust punishment, and the wofull complaintes of the other sort with ioyful triumph? When a Tragedy is playd afore thee, thou art not offended at any thing which thou hearest. Why, so? Because that in two howres space thou hast shewed vnto thee the dooings of ten or twelue yeres, as the rauishing of *Helen,* and the punishment of *Paris,* or the miserable end of *Herod* vpon his murdering of *Iohn Baptist.* Insomuch that although thou bee not acquainted with the storie, yet the arte which thou perceiuest, and the end which thou expectest, make thee both to beare with the matter, and to commend the thing which otherwise thou wouldst thinke to be both uniust, and also cruell in the gouerner of the Stage. How much more oughtest thou to refreine thy mislyking, if thou considerest that the world is a kind of Stageplay, conueied to a certaine end by a most excellent maker?[31]

It is probably correct to say that drama was the chief form of Elizabethan art largely because Providence was the central dogma of Elizabethan religion. Heywood began his *Apology for Actors* (1612) thus:

> The world's a theatre, the earth a stage,
> Which God and nature doth with actors fill.

God, Heywood added, "doth as a spectator sit."

The notion is the more striking when we compare it with the medieval view. St. Thomas Aquinas had thought of God as the General of an Army, governing men toward a final end, which is His victory. Renaissance humanists prefer the metaphor of the Dramatist, which honors God by removing Him from the scene of conflict to the throne of a Poet's glory. This shift of thought is one of the signposts by which we can mark the transition to modern history.

---

[31] P. 197.

ANATOMY OF *TAMBURLAINE*

MARLOWE'S USE OF
THE HISTORICAL SOURCES

翢 翢

M ARLOWE'S Tamburlaine is the Scourge of God.
This important concept gives unity to the portrait. It
furnishes the hero his role, makes his history intelligible, provides his life a destiny. The dramatist selects and
arranges his historical episodes to minister to this controlling
idea. And to embellish the action he adds symbolism and
story not taken from any history.

As preface to our study of Tamburlaine, it will be of interest to examine a typical sixteenth-century history of another Scourge of God—the history of Attila as provided by
Paulus Giovius.[1] We note, first, the characterizing lineaments of this hero. An epitaph to Giovius' account calls
Attila "monster," "torch of the world," "scourge of God,"
"accomplice on earth of angered Jove." A decorative en-
graving exhibits Attila's savage face. Giovius speaks of the
inhuman and lurid pallor of this face and says that the
fierce gleam of the eyes breathes forth an immense savagery.

Attila behaved himself, says Giovius, as if he were the
deadly scourge of a wicked age (funesti seculi dira clades),
the monstrous devastator of cities and lands. Indeed, he
wanted to be called by the high and terrible name of Scourge
of God in order that he might attribute to the wrathful
power of God his own hatred of the human race and
his own savage ill will. Under this excuse he engaged in
continual conquest. Always cruel and raging, he panted

---

[1] See the *Elogia Virorum bellica virtute illustrium* (Basle, 1575), pp. 14-17.
The book contains also an account of Tamburlaine (pp. 102-07), and of Bajazet
(pp. 107-11). My summary here is a direct but free translation, with the
omission of unimportant matter.

after the fame of the robber Alaric, who forty years earlier had devastated Rome.

Finally, Attila led his barbarians against Rome. He would have attained his hope, had not Martianus Caesar sought the sure aid of Almighty God and received in a dream the advice to throw Leo, the Roman Pontifex, in front of the approaching monster. Leo, a holy and venerable man, cheerfully undertook the business without fear, because it would bring him the glory of true sanctity. Dressed in a priestly garment and bearing a silver cross, and accompanied by a simple band of priests and elders, Leo cast himself at the feet of the tyrant. With his pious pleadings Leo so mitigated and changed Attila's atrocious spirit, which was at all other times wrathful and implacable, that Attila surrendered. The reason for Attila's mollification was that the divine power was secretly terrifying him. The leaders of the Huns, eager for Roman booty, were amazed that Attila, forgetful of his courage and fortune, should suddenly turn timid, the vigor of his spirit broken by the speech of the priestly little man. Attila, in answer to this, attributed the cause of so great a change to two heroes of rather august appearance, who standing on the right and the left of the supplicating Leo seemed to be threatening him with death with gleaming swords, unless he should give in to the pious pleadings. Christians believe these were the ghosts of the divine Peter and Paul.

But we come shortly to the account of Attila's death. Attila married Hilda, a superlative beauty; but the gods at once prohibited that from this savage marriage any progeny so dangerous to the human race should be produced. On the wedding night, when Attila was drunken and snoring heavily, so great a force of blood burst from his nose, that he who had inhumanly caused provinces to bleed with so many slaughters, suddenly breathing his last, inundated the marriage couch with a very large river of his own blood.

Comparing this story with that of Tamburlaine as generally given in the histories, we note that the careers of both heroes exhibit prominent moral elements. Tamburlaine, like Attila, is a barbarian of inhuman pallor and fiery eyes, thirsting after conquest; he is, like him, a robber who shamelessly claims the title "Scourge of God" as justification for his merciless cruelties. Also, as in Attila's history, Tamburlaine is visited by pleading emissaries from a besieged city. However, with Tamburlaine the miracle of conversion does not take place—presumably because the emissaries are not Christians and hence have no ghostly apostles to support their plea.[2] If we use the incident to compare Tamburlaine and Attila, it but serves to heighten Tamburlaine's character for cruelty, since he appears to outdo in rigor the famed Attila. Tamburlaine's invincibility is another point which compares him with Attila: neither scourge is ever overcome by an opposing army. And neither dies by outward violence: Attila's death is Providential; and Tamburlaine's, in the elaboration which Marlowe gives to the histories, is an occasion in which Heaven's intervention is acknowledged. The general similarity of the two accounts suggests that the Scourge of God notion has operated as a formal pattern—for historian and for dramatist—in determining a selection of details for the interpretation of history.

In almost any history Marlowe may have read he would have found recorded Tamburlaine's claim to be the Scourge of God. Fortescue, in the passage we have already noted in Introduction, is so far as I know the only historian who furnishes commentary to interpret the claim. But Tamburlaine's declaration of it occurs commonly in western histories, generally in connection with the story of a certain merchant of Genoa, who protested against Tamburlaine's

---

[2] In *Tamb*. II. v. i., where Marlowe invents a siege of Babylon, we find a citizen urging the Governor to send Christian emissaries to plead before Tamburlaine, but the proposal is rejected.

cruel treatment of the virgins of an unnamed besieged city who had come on the third day to ask mercy.[3] As Fortescue tells the story, Tamburlaine

answered in moste furious wrath and ire, his face red and firy, his eyes all flaming with burning Sparcles, as it were blasing out on euery side. Thou supposest me to be a man, but thou too much abusest me, for none other am I, but the wrathe and vengeance of God, and ruine of the world.[4]

Interestingly enough, Marlowe does not use this declaration at the point where the historians introduce it. The dramatist locates the episode of the supplicating virgins in connection with a siege of Damascus, but he provides no Genoan merchant to protest, and hence no retort from Tamburlaine.[5] Instead, Marlowe uses the "scourge" declara-

---

[3] See Ellis-Fermor's edition of *Tamburlaine,* Appendix, p. 295; also John Shute, *Two very notable Commentaries* (1562), p. 5; Lonicerus, *Chronicorum Turcicorum* (1578), I, 15; Pope Pius II, *Asiae Europaeque Elegantissima Descriptio* (1534), p. 85; George Whetstone, *The English Mirror* (1586), p. 82; André Thevet, *Les Vrais Povrtraits et Vies des Hommes Illustres* (1584), p. 633[r]; and (without the Genoan merchant) Paulus Giovius, *Elogia,* p. 106. The latter three works have not been listed by Miss Ellis-Fermor in her bibliography of histories of Tamburlaine. John Bakeless, *Christopher Marlowe* (New York, 1937), pp. 124-25, tells us that the works by Pope Pius and by Giovius were in the library of Corpus Christi, Cambridge, while Marlowe was a student there. Very much like the title page of *Tamburlaine,* so it seems to me, is the opening sentence of Giovius' excellent account: "TAMERLANES Schytharum Imperator, qui propter inauditam animi feritatem atque saeuitiam portentosasque vires, orbis TERROR, & CLADES Orientis apellatus est; ex humili militae loco per omnes honorum gradus ad eximiam bellicae virtutis opinionem, & denique ad summum imperium ascendit. . . ."

[4] *The Forest,* p. 70 (Second edition, 1576).

[5] Marlowe's closest parallel occurs in Part II of the drama when Tamburlaine slays his son Calyphas and draws from the captive kings a protest against his "barbarous damned tyranny." Tamburlaine thereupon answers:

> Villaines, these terrours and these tyrannies
> (If tyrannies wars iustice ye repute)
> I execute, enioin'd me from aboue:
> To scourge the pride of such as heauen abhors,
> Nor am I made Arch-monark of the world,
> Crown'd and inuested by the hand of *Ioue,*
> For deeds of bounty or nobility:
> But since I exercise a greater name,
> The Scourge of God and terrour of the world,
> I must apply my selfe to fit those tearmes,
> In war, in blood, in death, in crueltie,
> And plague such Pesants as resist in me
> The power of heauens eternall maiesty. (3820-32.)

tion both earlier and later in the story and with such frequency as to make it the running theme of the drama. A dozen times in the play[6] the protagonist calls our attention to his title; and he dies announcing with his last breath that "Tamburlaine, the Scourge of God must die."

Our study of other "scourges" has prepared us to look for certain type traits of character in Tamburlaine. The qualities we expect to see, prominently, are those of ambition, robbery and tyranny, cruelty, magnanimity, and invincibility. Marlowe's protagonist has these attributes; and it can be shown that each of the five finds a place in various portraits of Tamburlaine given by histories to which Marlowe could have turned. The dramatist did not need to invent for his hero the essential traits of a Scourge's behavior. But let us see how Marlowe used and developed his sources.

I

Nowadays we know that the actual Tamburlaine was the son of a chief. But the sixteenth-century European historians, departing from strict truth, make Tamburlaine a low-born shepherd or soldier.[7] The soldier tradition appears in Shute's translation of Cambinus; while the shepherd tradition is reported by Fulgotius—and by Lonicerus, Perondinus, and La Primaudaye, who apparently borrow from Fulgotius. Both traditions are recorded by Fortescue, Thevet, Whetstone, and others. "Tamberlayn was a man of base blud," writes Peter Ashton, quoting Cuspinian, "first of all a Nethred [i.e., neatherd], after a raskall souldier, and last of al, he rose to hye dignitie." [8] As we read the accounts

---

[6] *Tamb.* 234, 1142-43, 1475-76, 2629 ff., 3046-48, 3820-32, 3873-75, 4003, 4078, 4204, 4294-96, 4436-37, 4641. The term is used also by the Prologue, by the Souldan of Egypt (1579), by Orcanes (3523-24), and by Usumcasane (4429-30).

[7] Thevet is something of an exception, for he adds that he has seen some accounts which would derive Tamburlaine from the stock of Ciugis Cham.

[8] *Shorte treatise vpon the Turkes Chronicles* (1546), Sig. B. iiii.

in the various histories, it becomes apparent that Tamburlaine's low birth is being stressed in order to magnify his haughty ambition. Whetstone writes:

Tamberlaine being a poore labourer, or in the best degree a meane souldiour, descended from the Partians: notwithstanding the pouertye of his parents: euen from his infancy he had a reaching & an imaginative minde, the strength and comelinesse of his body, aunswered the haughtines of his heart. This *Tamberlaine* as Fulgosius reporteth, keeping beasts among other youthes of his condition his companions in a meriment chose him for their king: wherevpon *Tamberlaine* (hauing a ruling desire) after an othe of obedience, commanded euery man to sell his cattaile: and to contemn their meane estate, and to follow him as their captaine . . .[9]

Fortescue, who relates the same facts, says that Tamburlaine's "spirits were rauished with great and high matters." Even in extreme penury Tamburlaine was devising high enterprises "as though he sometimes should be a maister of many things."[10]   Thevet gives the summary judgment that "C'estoit l'homme, le plus ambitious, qu'il est possible de penser."[11]

Marlowe accepts for his drama the tradition of Tamburlaine's lowly shepherd origin. The fact receives attention both on the title page of the drama and internally in the dialogue. On one occasion the Souldan of Egypt contemptuously calls Tamburlaine a "Peasant";[12] on another occasion Orcanes calls him to his face "Shepherds issue, base borne Tamburlaine."[13]   He makes his first appearance in Marlowe's drama as the leader of a band of shepherds engaged in plundering the trade routes. How he became the shepherds' leader Marlowe does not relate. But Tambur-

---

[9] *English Mirror*, p. 79.
[10] *The Forest*, p. 67ʳ.
[11] *Povrtraits*, p. 633ʳ.
[12] *Tamb*. 1436.
[13] *Tamb*. 3579.

laine's tremendous martial ambition is from the beginning emphasized. In an invented scene of considerable symbolism Tamburlaine is shown casting off disdainfully his shepherd's garb, and exchanging for it the armor of a warrior, while he voices the dream that his companions—"silly country Swaines"—will be leaders of earth-shaking armies and will affect with him "thoughts coequall with the clouds." Not long afterward, he is described as "Thirsting with soueraignty," and Cosroe has learned to know him as "That fiery thirster after Soueraigntie." [14] Building upon the histories, Marlowe has given forceful emphasis to the fact of Tamburlaine's immoderate, insatiable, violent desire.

II

A number of European historians likewise give evidence of the robbery, craftiness, and tyranny by which Tamburlaine achieved his phenomenal rise. They report that Tamburlaine begins by corrupting his shepherd-followers into highway robbers—at first only five hundred of them, according to La Primaudaye and Fortescue. Then his activities arouse the Persian king to send forth a captain with a thousand horsemen to seize Tamburlaine, and Tamburlaine wins this troop additionally as his followers. Soon thereafter, by taking part in the civil war between the Persian king and his brother, Tamburlaine both plunders the Persian king and then treacherously despoils the brother. This is the picture of Tamburlaine's rise given by at least half a dozen of the European historians.[15]

Marlowe, evidently perceiving both the dramatic appeal and the moral significance of these details, follows them closely. As the play opens, the fame of Tamburlaine's

---

[14] *Tamb.* 474 and 842.
[15] See Ellis-Fermor, *Tamburlaine*, p. 28. Whetstone and Lonicerus must be added to Miss Ellis-Fermor's list.

brigandage is being bruited about the court of the Persian king, and Theridamas is dispatched to seize "that sturdie Scythian thiefe." When Tamburlaine himself enters on stage in scene 2, his soldiers are "loden with treasure." We learn that he has five hundred men and many "golden wedges." With these he confronts and wins over the thousand horsemen of Theridamas. Marlowe gives us one of the reasons for Tamburlaine's swift success in the words of Meander:

> This countrie swarmes with vile outragious men,
> That liue by rapine and by lawlesse spoile,
> Fit Souldiers for the wicked *Tamburlaine*. (545-8.)

Soon Tamburlaine joins Cosroe to overthrow the Persian king; then, in defiance of plighted faith, goes on to dispatch Cosroe. Later, the Souldan of Egypt accurately describes Tamburlaine as

> . . . . bloody *Tamburlaine*,
> A sturdy Felon and a base-bred Thiefe,
> By murder raised to the Persean Crowne. (1581-83.)

Whetstone says Tamburlaine's empire was "tirannous";[16] and Fortescue, as we noted earlier, includes Tamburlaine in the class of "bloody tirants." Marlowe does not seek to dodge this judgment. Repeatedly in the play Tamburlaine's enemies call him "Tyrant," and finally they accord him the glorious title "the Tyrant of the world."[17] The Governor of Babylon offers the opinion that Tamburlaine is "sent from hell to tyrannise on earth."[18]

---

[16] *English Mirror*, p. 63.
[17] See *Tamb.* 2186, 4033, 4245, and 4386.
[18] *Tamb.* 4223.

III

Tamburlaine's cruelty is revealed strikingly in the well-known story of the three tents. It was Tamburlaine's custom, the western historians tell us, on the first day of his siege of a city to raise a white tent, in sign that if the citizens yielded they should have their goods, lives, and liberty; the second day a red tent, signifying that by yielding then they might save the lives of all but their chief men; and on the third day a black tent, promising death to all and the burning of the city. The black tent signified that "he then had shut up his gates from all compassion & clemency." [19] The story does not appear in the oriental histories. That it should be repeated by nearly every European historian illustrates the extent to which Tamburlaine's career had become a moralized saga for western Christendom.

Most of these historians, moreover, confirm the story of the tents by adding to it the story of a certain city which unwisely waited until the third day to beg for mercy. Then were sent forth as supplicants

all their women & Children in white apparel, bearing each in their hands a braunch of Oliue, crying with haute voice, humbly requesting and demaunding pardon, in maner so pitiful and lamentable to beholde that besides him none other was but would haue accepted their solemne submission. This *Tamburlain,* notwithstanding that he beheld them afar off in this order issuing, so far then exiled from all kinde of pitie, that he commaunded forthwith a certain troupe of horsemen to ouer run, to murther and kil them, not leauing one aliue of what condition soeuer, and after sacking the Citie, raced it euen vnto the very foundations.[20]

---

[19] The quoted phrase is from Fortescue's account. See Ellis-Fermor's *Tamburlaine,* p. 294n, for a list of the authors who relate the story. Additionally, I find it recounted by Lonicerus, by Thevet, and by Whetstone; and Mr. Don Cameron Allen reports (*T. L. S.,* Sept. 24, 1931, p. 730) its appearance in Peter Crinitus, *De Honesta Disciplina,* which was issued as early as 1504, and of which the Bodleian lists a similarly titled edition of 1496.

[20] Fortescue, p. 70ʳ. Since the author says he is taking this story from Pope Pius, we may judge the amount of elaboration by comparing Pius' much briefer account (*Asiae,* p. 85): "Fama est, populosae cuiusdam ciuitatis, quae prima die

The story testifies, says Thevet,[21] that in cruelty Tamburlaine was hardly second to any.

But the conqueror's cruelty is exhibited most famously in his treatment of Bajazet.

> The ages that shall talk of *Tamburlain,*
> Euen from this day to *Platoes* wondrous yeare,
> Shall talke how I haue handled *Baiazeth.* (1539-42.)

Almost all the European histories relate that when Tamburlaine had overcome the mighty Bajazet he shut him up in a cage, sometimes used him for a horse block, and at mealtime fed him with scraps from the table as if he were a dog. The horse-block idea is much older than histories of Tamburlaine. Lactantius in Chapter V of his *On the Manner in Which the Persecutors Died* tells how the emperor Valerian was punished

in a new and extraordinary manner, that it might be a lesson to future ages that the adversaries of Heaven always receive the just recompense of their iniquities. He, having been made prisoner by the Persians, lost not only that power which he had exercised without moderation, but also the liberty of which he had deprived others; and he wasted the remainder of his days in the vilest condition of slavery: for Sapores, the King of the Persians, who made him prisoner, whenever he chose to get into his carriage or to mount on horseback, commanded the Roman to stoop and present his back . . .[22]

We may wonder whether Marlowe had read Lactantius. Certainly some one or more of the historians of Tamburlaine must have done so.

Other details of the Tamburlaine story are peculiar to cer-

---

deditionem neglexisset, pueros puellasque omnes in candida veste ramos oliuae praeferentes exiuisses, vt principis iram placarent. illum omnes ab equitatu conculcari atque conteri iussisse, & vrbem captam incendi."

[21] *Povrtraits,* p. 633ʳ.

[22] *Ante-Nicene Fathers* (New York, 1899), VII. 302.

tain of the historians. At least three authors say that shameful services were exacted of Bajazet's wife, and that the Turk committed suicide by braining himself against his iron cage.[23] Of eastern histories, Marlowe may very well have known that of Chalcondylas, available in the Latin translation by Clauserus; for Chalcondylas, unlike the western historians, tells of taunts hurled by Bajazet at Tamburlaine's wife, of her consequent rage, of Bajazet's protest against his own wife's ignominy, and of Tamburlaine's derisive attitude.[24]

Most of these details of spectacular and sophisticated savagery have been appropriated by Marlowe—though, of course, he could not present Bajazet's wife, as La Primaudaye says, in a "gowne cut downe to hir Nauell." But using the tradition of the three tents for his time scheme, the dramatist projects against this background in Acts IV and V of Part I a succession of Tamburlaine's cruelties, based on the histories but arranged to produce a cumulative effect. While the white tents are set against Damascus, Tamburlaine uses the Turk as a footstool; when the red tents are pitched, he offers Bajazet food from a sword's point and taunts him to make meal of Zabina; and on the day of the black tents, just after Tamburlaine has commanded the brutal slaughter of

---

[23] In pointing out that these details appear in Perondinus, C. H. Herford and A. Wagner ("The Sources of Marlowe's *Tamburlaine,*" *The Academy,* Oct. 20, 1883, pp. 265-6) concluded that Marlowe could hardly have failed to read Perondinus. However, Herford and Wagner overlooked La Primaudaye's account in *The French Academie* (1586), p. 475, and Lonicerus' account, p. 14. Lonicerus writes: "Quin & vxor eius Lazari despotae filia, quam vnice dilexerat, quam vna cum ipso captiuam traxerat, crepidulis tantum calciata, sagoque breuissimo induta militari, denudatis obscoenis dedecorose ante Baiazethis oculos, Scytharum proceribus vna discumbentibus pocula ministrare cogebatur. Quod indignissime ferens Baiazethes, ira percitus, moeroreque confectus, mortem sibimet dire imprecabatur, qui nulla vi voti compos factus, animum inexorabili obstinatione despondens, capite innumerosis ictibus ferreis caueae clathris perfracto, illisoque cerebro, altero a capiuitate anno vita excessit." It has been pointed out on other grounds (see Ethel Seaton, "Fresh Sources for Marlowe," *Rev. Eng. Studies,* V, 385-401) that Marlowe pretty certainly knew and used Lonicerus' *Chronicle.*

[24] See Ethel Seaton, p. 394.

the supplicating virgins, Bajazet and Zabina madly dash out their brains against the bars of the cage in which they are kept. It is indeed a black day. Zenocrate, coming in fresh from the sight of Damascus' streets "strowed with disseuered joints of men," and lamenting the "cruel death" which the "unspotted maids" have guiltlessly endured, stumbles on the bloody Turk and his empress—their deaths caused, as Zenocrate's maid says, by the "ruthlesse cruelty of Tamburlaine."

In Part II of the drama, where Marlowe is largely inventing his own episodes, the theme of war, blood, and cruelty is prolonged and intensified. In an early scene we behold Tamburlaine instructing his sons that if they would be kings and keep Emperors in iron cages, they "must armed wade vp to the chin in blood." To rival the massacre of the Damascans in Part I, Part II presents the drowning of the Babylonians. For violence, the scourging of the captive kings compares with the tormenting of Bajazet in Part I. And when Tamburlaine, in an unhistorical episode, slays his own son, he provides illustration of a cruelty that has passed all natural bounds.

To appreciate the moral significance of such spectacle, one needs to read in Fortescue's history not only the chapters which treat of Tamburlaine, but also such a chapter as the one entitled "How detestable a matter crueltie is." [25] There Fortescue declares that cruelty is the chief of vices. It is, quoting Seneca, "the execrable felony of the soule"; for it takes Man, a creature formed in the image of God, and transforms him into "a brute beast, terrible, furious, of nature accursed and enemye to God, who is the sole and souerain Clemencye."

IV

But a hero who commits such great atrocities needs to

---

[25] *The Forest, The First Parte,* chap. 14, pp. 30ᵛ ff.

have, additionally, certain admirable qualities;[26] for unless his character can be in some sense definitely attractive, we refuse him our credence. Marlowe does not debase his protagonist into the villain of melodrama. The dramatist can feel, as Fortescue had felt, an awesome rapture in the contemplation of the glories of Tamburlaine's natural gifts—gifts of the sort we have observed in the scourge Nimrod of Du Bartas' portrait. Prominent are the qualities of handsome stature, martial prowess, hard self-discipline, industry, and liberality. These, no doubt, are what Fortescue has in mind when he speaks of Tamburlaine's "rare virtues." None of the histories which Marlowe may have read failed to celebrate some of these finer qualities.

Pius II, Cambinus, Lonicerus, Fortescue, and Whetstone call our attention to Tamburlaine's excellent military discipline, his courtesy, his industry and dexterity in arms, and his liberality to his companions. Fortescue lays special stress on the orderliness, splendor, and amity of Tamburlaine's camp. Whetstone says that

in his armye was neuer found mutinie: he was wise, liberall, and rewarded euery souldiour with his desert . . . his gouernment and order was such, that his campe seemed a goodly City, wherein euery necessary office was found, marchants without feare of robbing, or spoyling repayred thither, with all maner of necessary prouision for his army: the reason was he suffered no theft vnpunished, and as louingly honored, praised, and payed the vertuous and valiaunt souldiour . . .[27]

---

[26] Note that Erasmus in commenting on Xerxes, Cyrus, Alexander, and other great conquerors—all of whom he terms "raging robbers"—adds: "There never was a tyrant so detestable that he did not. do some things which, if they were not done in the cause of virtue, at least may be fitted to the example of such a quality. . . . Alexander did many things like a madman, but he acted honorably in keeping aloof from the captured women of Darius." *The Education of a Christian Prince*, ed. Lester K. Born (New York, 1936), pp. 201-2. We remember, of course, Tamburlaine's boast (2268-69) that he has kept aloof from captured Zenocrate. See hereafter, page 232.

[27] *English Mirror*, p. 80.

Thevet says that for pride and severity some would compare Tamburlaine with Hannibal, because Tamburlaine, while himself "le plus grand brigand & detestable vilain," yet punished theft with the greatest severity.[28] On this point Thevet is very likely following Cambinus, who also likens Tamburlaine to Hannibal, and for the same reason. Cambinus speaks twice and emphatically of Tamburlaine's "seuere Justice againste thefts."

> he woulde not leaue vnpunished the least violence that was committed: not so much as the takyng away of one handful of grasse agaynst the owners good wil . . .

But the commentary of Cambinus is significant:

> And it is thought that he dyd it to that ende, that the feare of punishement shoulde cause them to refraine, to the ende that he alone mought robbe and spoile according to his owne desire the whole world . . .[29]

Marlowe uses these details of camp-life splendor and amity —but perhaps not so much as we would expect. The orderly scene pictured by the histories is, one feels, somewhat jarred by Marlowe's introduction of the episode of Tamburlaine's madness at Zenocrate's death; and the beauty of camp discipline, when illustrated by Marlowe with the episode of the blood covenants and later with the slaying of Calyphas, takes on a somewhat lurid cast. Also, Marlowe gives us no picture, as the histories do, of the visitations of merchants or of the punishing of theft. There is evidence here, it would seem, against the claims of critics who think that Marlowe refracts Tamburlaine's character in a more favorable light than the histories do.

However, the orderliness of Tamburlaine's camp is never

---

[28] *Povrtraits*, p. 630^v.
[29] Shute's trans., *Two Commentaries*, pp. 4^r, 5^v.

in doubt in Marlowe's picture. There is no civil dissention. The troops are captivated heart and mind by Tamburlaine, who in turn is generous with banquets and crowns. When crowning his lieutenants he enjoins on them noble behavior:

> Deserue these Tytles I endow you with
> By valour and by magnanimity.

Submissively these men repair to him with their crowns in Part II,[30] and magnanimously he returns the crowns. Generosity combined with discipline is further illustrated in the scene following the defeat of the four kings. The spoil of jewels and concubines is portioned out to the victorious troops—the captive Queens, justly, to the tall soldiers. And Tamburlaine warns:

> Brawle not (I warne you) for your lechery,
> For euery man that so offends shall die.

In courtesy, too, Tamburlaine can be spectacular. On Zenocrate he bestows the grace of his eloquence, because "women must be flatered." Both Cosroe and Zenocrate's father are charmed by his manners. Even when raging, Tamburlaine has a sort of savage courtesy.

V

Finally, there is the fact of Tamburlaine's invincibility. Shute says[31] that all historians that have ever written of Tamburlaine record a fact greatly to be marvelled at: that "he neuer fought with man, but he had the victorye ouer hym, so that he neuer tasted Fortune's bitterness." Fortescue testifies similarly that Tamburlaine

---

[30] *Tamb.* II. i. vi.
[31] *Two Commentaries*, p. 4ʳ.

neuer was vanquished or put to flight by any, that he neuer took matter in hand that he brought not to wished effect . . .[32]

La Primaudaye adds that

he ended his days amongst his children, as a peaceable gouernour of innumerable countries.[33]

And Whetstone reports simply that

In the ende this great personage, without disgrace of fortune, after sundry great victories, by the course of nature died, and left behind him two sons . . .[34]

The tradition of Tamburlaine's peaceful and natural death being thus firmly established,[35] we must recognize that Marlowe's opportunities to make of the history an example of God's punishing of sin were definitely limited. The histories were attributing to this Scythian scourge a long life of unobscured glory—a career which looked like a blasphemous challenge to the Puritan dogma of Providence. Yet Marlowe promises in the prologue to Part II to show how "murdrous Fates throwes al his triumphs down." How can the dramatist manage this without distorting the facts? The typical modern critic of Marlowe's drama complains that

no avenging ghosts dog the footsteps of the Scythian conqueror. He simply continues his wild career till the weapons of war fall from his nerveless hands . . .[36]

But such a critic has not read carefully the play. The avenging ghosts, by Marlowe's superb skill, have been track-

---

[32] *The Forest*, p. 71ʳ.
[33] *The French Academie*, p. 475.
[34] *English Mirror*, p. 82.
[35] Lonicerus, however, p. 15, gives an interesting variant of the tradition. He says that Tamburlaine choked to death in his sleep during a nightmare in the fiftieth year of his age.
[36] F. S. Boas, *Shakspere and His Predecessors* (London, 1896), p. 45.

ing the protagonist for a long time. When the death scene comes, the event appears not to distort what is said in the histories, yet it presents this historical moment in a double light: what is from one point of view simply a natural event takes on by another perspective the cast of a supernatural intervention. The invincible warrior is revealed to be, after all, overthrown. Of this we shall say more in our next chapter.

But here let us note with what care earlier in the drama Marlowe has built up the notion of Tamburlaine's invincibility. It appears as the conqueror's most cherished illusion:

> sooner shall the sun fall from his Sphere
> Than *Tamburlaine* be slain or ouercome. (371-2.)

Or again, he boasts that

> The chiefest God . . .
> . . . Will sooner burn the glorious frame of Heauen
> Then it should so conspire my ouerthrow. (1452-55.)

Further, Marlowe strengthens the general impression of Tamburlaine's invincibility by two methods. First, he goes even beyond the histories in painting the marvel and ease of the victories. The battle between Tamburlaine and Bajazet, says Fortescue,[37] was "the most cruell and most terrible battail that erst was euer hearde of," the fight continuing doubtful till night. But Marlowe makes the battle short, though Tamburlaine's army is contending against superior numbers.[38] In Part II there is an equally amazing victory over four kings and six hundred thousand soldiers. Even when at last Tamburlaine is sick unto death, the mere sight of him riding to battle causes Callapine's army to melt away in fear.

---

[37] *The Forest*, p. 69ʳ.
[38] See *Tamb.* 1109-10.

Secondly, Marlowe makes also Tamburlaine's enemies swell the chorus which proclaims the conqueror's invincibility. So convinced of it are his victims that they lose faith in God and become fatalists. Bajazet concludes that

> such a Star hath influence in his sword
> As rules the Skies, and countermands the Gods
> More than Cymerian Stix or Distinie. (2013-15.)

Zabina realizes that "Then is there no Mahomet, no God." And she and her husband, thus driven to atheism, commit suicide.

The first check to Tamburlaine's power comes with the death of Zenocrate, an episode entirely invented by Marlowe. Here Tamburlaine is made to admit, for the first time in his life, that he, the Scourge, is being scourged. The mental wound is more significant than a physical wound. He feels Death's darts "pierce the Center of my soule," and he retaliates in vain gestures of rage. The episode prepares us for the second check to Tamburlaine's will, which comes with his own death. Here Marlowe has so enlarged upon the histories as to change the fact of natural death into an affair involving Tamburlaine in torments of soul and in impotent raging against what he believes to be Heaven's intervening hand. There is both physical and psychological defeat in the fact that Tamburlaine must "admit necessity" and confess that "the Scourge of God must die."

VI

One further matter remains to be considered—Marlowe's treatment of Bajazet's fall. Practically all the histories make this episode an occasion for moralizing. In *The Forest* we read that

This Tragidie might suffice to withdraw men from this transitory

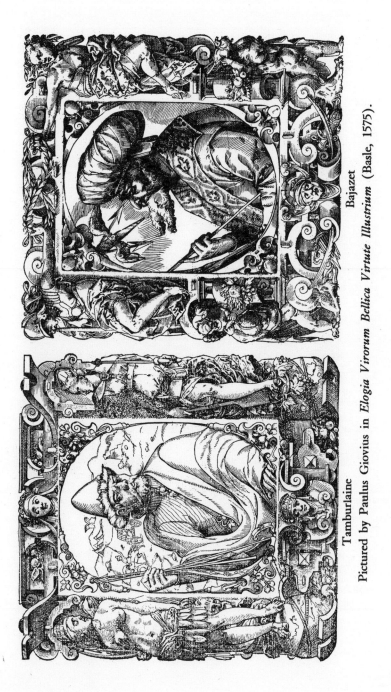

Bajazet

Tamburlaine

Pictured by Paulus Giovius in *Elogia Virorum Bellica Virtute Illustrium* (Basle, 1575).

Bajazet encaged, as pictured by Philippus Lonicerus in *Chronicorum Turcicorum* (Frankfurt, 1578).

pompe and honoure, acquainting them selues with Heauen and with heauenly things.[39]

Whetstone sees in the episode both the working of God's will and an example of the uncertainty of worldly fortunes:

But such was Gods will, . . . he [i.e., Bajazet] was taken prisoner, and presented to *Tamburlaine,* who closed this great Emperour in an iron cage, and as a dog fed him onely with the fragments that fell from his table . . . a notable example of the incertaintye of worldly fortunes: Baiazet, that in the morning was the mightiest Emperor on the earth, at night, and the residue of his life, was driuen to feede among the dogs, and which might most grieue him, he was thus abased, by one that in the beginning was but a poore sheep-heard.[40]

It is interesting that Giovius sees in the episode, besides Tamburlaine's barbarity, a singular example of severe justice. Giovius makes Tamburlaine declare that the punishment of Bajazet is deserved, because Bajazet has murdered an elder brother.[41] Elsewhere Giovius describes Bajazet as rapacious, cruel, and impious; and like other historians he calls attention to the title "Heaven's Lightning" popularly given Bajazet.[42] There are details here which Marlowe does not use. He omits the story, so derogatory to Bajazet's character, of the murder of an elder brother; and he does not

---

[39] Fortescue, p. 69^r.

[40] *English Mirror,* p. 81.

[41] Giovius writes, *Elogia,* p. 105: "Sed ab hoc inexorabili barbaroque Tamberlanis ingenio, singulare iustae saeueritatis exemplum prodiit. Quum enim homo Ligur gemmarum insignis mango, ob idque Tamerlani qui magnopere gemmis oblectabatur, familiaris, inducto sermone de Baiazetis miseria, illum humanitatis atque clementie blande admonuisset, & vt meminisse vellet Baiazetem inter Mahometanos reges victoriis & opibus fuisse clarissimum. Tamerlanes obducta fronte, contortisque in illum oculis, verbum redargutus respondit: se non regem nobilitate atque potentia superbum; sed hominem improbum, impieque nefarium digna poena plectere, qui maiorem natu fratrem inhumaniter occidisset." Cf. Perondinus, *Magni Tamerlanis Vita* (1553), p. 32; and Lonicerus, p. 14. Lonicerus, perhaps by a slip, reports Bajazet as the slayer of his *younger* brother.

[42] Giovius, p. 111. Cf. Thevet, p. 632^r, Lonicerus, p. 12; and Anthony Munday, *A Briefe Chronicle, of the Successe of Times, from the Creation of the World, to this instant* (1611), pp. 91-92.

give Tamburlaine a speech justifying the hard treatment of
Bajazet. It is enough for Marlowe that Tamburlaine is the
Scourge of God—the concept implies justice in the op-
pressor and wickedness in the victim.

Marlowe's Bajazet is, so far as I can see,[43] simply another
such warrior as Tamburlaine is—proud, valiant, sure of his
own invincibility[44]—but less fortunate. The difference between these two pagans is only in the matter of success.
Bajazet threatens to make his enemies draw his chariot;[45]
Tamburlaine actually succeeds in such a plan. The spirit is
the same in both men. Bajazet, it is true, seems to contrast
unfavorably with Tamburlaine when the latter declares that
he will free the Christian slaves whom Bajazet has been
abusing in the galleys.[46] But there is no later indication that
Tamburlaine actually does so; and certainly Tamburlaine's
treatment of his own captives of war is not more humani-
tarian than Bajazet's treatment of the Christians. Both
heroes boast, slay, and rage with comparable violence.

Bajazet's fall can be interpreted from two vantage points.
The Christian reader can see in it—as Fortescue apparently
does—example of Tamburlaine's not unjust chastening of
"kings and proud people of the earth." And the pagan
observer can at least take from it—as Fortescue plainly takes
—a warning against ambition and the instability of worldly
fortune. This second meaning is what Tamburlaine's wife
sees when she comes across the spectacle of the suicides.
Whereas formerly she had been as proud as Tamburlaine,
she now knows pity and fear, and the tragedy serves as a
mirror in which she sees warning of the gulf that threatens
the similarly proud career of Tamburlaine. Her words are

---

[43] See, however, Leslie Spence, "Tamburlaine and Marlowe," pp. 612-14,
where it is argued that Marlowe, debasing the character of Bajazet as given in
the histories, shows him a coward, a vain boaster, and an impudent snob.
[44] *Tamb.* 925.
[45] *Tamb.* 1177-78.
[46] *Tamb.* 1142 ff.

the echo of Fortescue and others regarding the slipperiness of earthly pomp.

More profound, however, than the workings of Fortune are the ways of Providence. And the spectator who surveys the scene from the truer vantage point can see in Tamburlaine's title "Scourge of God" the key for the interpretation of Bajazet's fall—and also of Mycetes' defeat and of Cosroe's overthrow. These kings suffer deserved punishment. At the same time it is recognized that Tamburlaine is morally no better than they; merely, he excels them in the arts of the devil. His progress of world conquest is to be admired as the judgment of God—a judgment which will be complete when the Scourge himself is cast into the fire.

The history in Part II, therefore, is by no means a purposeless mélange of episode, used to piece out the hour's traffic of the stage. It is true that Marlowe, now without the aid of historical material, has to invent almost all the action; but his ordering of the spectacle is guided by knowledge of the role which Tamburlaine must play. It cannot be said that Marlowe has distorted the Tamburlaine of sixteenth-century European saga; but it must be said that he has developed a grander and more complete fable. His drama is—as Sidney said poetic history should be—more doctrinal than mere factual history.

EXTRA-HISTORICAL
MORALITY ELEMENTS

❧ ❧

T HE *Tamburlaine* drama may be likened to a fabric set with jewels. The fabric, the history of a mighty conqueror, would be bald spectacle if it were not decorated with resplendent scenes of moral instruction, sewn in with care to create the tapestry. As bits of brilliant spectacle these scenes gain significance from their place in the fabric of the history; yet as jewels they have independent value in themselves and are easily detachable for separate consideration. Their presence in the drama gives it its "purple patches," makes it seem episodic and a thing of parts, despite the continuity provided by the hero and his life span. Indeed, it is plain that the *Tamburlaine* drama has no plot in the modern sense of entanglement and resolution. The play is a pageant. Its successive scenes have a continuity not dissimilar to that provided by the guild-wagons of the early Corpus Christi day dramas.

I

We have discovered in our previous chapter some of the morality episodes—semihistorical and pseudohistorical—with which the Tamburlaine saga had been decked by the European historians before it came to Marlowe's hands. Adding to these materials, the dramatist drew upon other stores of his own. Of the episodes which must be credited to Marlowe's own invention in Part I of the drama, Miss Leslie Spence has listed the following five:[1]

---

[1] "The Influence of Marlowe's Sources on *Tamburlaine I*," *Modern Philology*, XXIV (1926), 181-99.

150

1) Tamburlaine's discarding of shepherd weeds for full armor and a curtal axe. (*Tamb.* I. i. ii.)
2) The display of captured treasure to dazzle Theridamas. (*Tamb.* I. i. ii.)
3) The naked dagger offered to Agydas. (*Tamb.* I. iii. ii.)
4) The messenger Bajazet boasted he would come and get. (*Tamb.* I. iii. i.)
5) The conspicuous use of crowns.

Miss Spence believes these additions are "dazzling trappings rather than meaningful episodes." [2] Obviously, they do add spectacle to the history. But have they no further significance? I think they plainly have.

In the first we behold a shepherd renouncing the shepherd life. It is Tamburlaine's very initial act on stage, and therefore especially to be remarked. We must remember that the Elizabethans idealized the shepherd life. Spenser in the July eclogue of *The Shepheardes Calender* points to "the first shepheard" Abel as a paradigm of what a true Christian life should be—simple, humble, lowly, meek. For contrast, Spenser cites the story of the false-shepherd

> Whom Ida hyll dyd beare,
> That left hys flocke to fetch a lasse,
> Whose love he bought to deare.

This allusion to Paris, whose love of Helen caused him to leave the tending of sheep for a life of costly and tragic warfare, points a paradigm for what Marlowe's Tamburlaine does. When the "Scythian Shephearde" enters on stage he comes bringing the lass Zenocrate; and now, to win her love by making her "Empresse of the East," he abandons shepherding.

Professor W. R. Parker has suggested to me that it is chiefly in the pastoral poetry of the Renaissance that we find

---

[2] *Ibid.,* p. 192.

the warning against the kind of ambition Tamburlaine typifies. The pastoral tradition was in full swing by the time Marlowe's play appeared. What, Professor Parker asks me, did the author of *The Passionate Shepherd to his Love* think about Tamburlaine the shepherd? The answer can only be inferred. If pastoral verse was anything more than a polite convention with Marlowe, he must have conceived and judged Tamburlaine by the ideals of pastoralism. And the ideals of pastoralism are those of Renaissance humanism, represented typically in Erasmus and Burton. These authors set sharp antithesis between shepherding and the brigandage of warfare. "There is a very great difference," says Erasmus,[3] "between a shepherd and a robber;" the true king should be, as Homer says, a "shepherd of his people." [4] Erasmus thinks that war is called Belum—that is, "Fair"—because it has nothing good or fair; for "nothing doth worse become a man than war." [5] Heathen people are led to it by covetousness or cruelty or, more likely, by furies sent from hell.[6] What is yet more to be lamented, according to Burton,[7] is that these martial men persuade people that war's hellish course of life is holy: "they promise heaven to such as venture their lives *bello sacro* . . . they put a note of divinity upon the most cruel, & pernicious plague of human kind." The reader of *Tamburlaine* will recognize how aptly this observation applies to Marlowe's hero.

The other episodes in Miss Spence's list require only brief comment. The display of treasure to dazzle Theridamas is

---

[3] *The Education of a Christian Prince*, ed. L. K. Born (New York, 1936), p. 170.

[4] Since Techelles in Marlowe's scene describes Tamburlaine as a "princely Lion," we might note also Erasmus' comment, *ibid.*, p. 168, that "Lion" is Plato's term (*Rep.* IX. 558) for the cruel and rapacious prince.

[5] *Erasmus Against War* (reprint of the first English translation of 1533-34), ed. J. W. Mackail (Boston, 1907), pp. 13, 4. A chief source in Christian literature for such rationalistic condemnation of war is Lactantius—an author who was widely popular in the Renaissance.

[6] *Ibid.*, p. 33.

[7] *Anat.*, ed. Shilleto, I, 64.

such spectacle as Spenser might have employed in his description of the Cave of Mammon. The gold pieces represent in substantial form the golden arguments with which Tamburlaine is to tempt and win Theridamas. The scene has in a general way the type of moral significance provided by Milton in *Paradise Regained,* where Satan tempts his adversary with the promise of the kingdoms of the world.

The story of Agydas, thirdly, offers a stock example of the fate of virtuous philosophers under tyrants. The emperor Tamburlaine does not care to be guided by moral philosophy (nor does the would-be empress Zenocrate); so Agydas, like Seneca under Nero, is advised to dispatch himself. The episode serves to call attention to the tragic flaw that will henceforth explain the drama—the protagonist's rejection of Reason.

The fourth addition, the matter of Bajazet's messenger, is not of much importance. It illustrates the boastful vaunting of martial prowess which pricks on these pagan heroes to their combats with each other.

But the reiterated introduction of crowns is highly significant. It serves to give constant emphasis to the lust for empire, which is the ruling theme of the drama. The chief characters snatch at crowns, parade with crowns, and discourse of the felicity of crowns. The extent of the symbol-pageantry can be appreciated if we attempt to make a list of the occasions in the drama where crowns figure prominently. Part I includes the following points:

1) The concern for his crown evidenced by the silly Mycetes, who wants to hide it in a "simple hole."
2) Cosroe's desire for a crown, which results in his being crowned by his followers. Later, Tamburlaine offers him the crown he has taken from Mycetes, which Cosroe refuses. Still later, when Tamburlaine attacks Cosroe, his triumph is indicated by the stage direction: "Tamburlaine takes the Crowne and puts it on." Cosroe complains:

Barbarous and bloody *Tamburlaine*,
Thus to depriue me of my crowne and life.

3) Tamburlaine, Bajazet, their wives, and their followers show great
concern for crowns. Before going to battle Tamburlaine and
Bajazet give their crowns to Zenocrate and Zabina respectively.
The fighting over, Tamburlaine resumes his crown, while
Bajazet's crown is wrenched from Zabina's head and given to
Zenocrate. The soldiers of Tamburlaine have returned from the
battle with "each man a crown." They announce: "We haue
their crownes their bodies strowe the fielde." They are told to
deliver up the crowns to the treasurry. Later, there is a "course
of Crownes" (presumably sweetmeats shaped like crowns)
brought in to them at the banquet. Tamburlaine says: "Here are
the cates you desire to finger, are they not?"

4) Part I concludes with the coronation of Zenocrate.

And in Part II we may note the following:

1) Callapine corrupts his jailor Almeda with promises of "many
crownes of burnisht gold." Later Callapine actually crowns
Almeda, while Tamburlaine scoffs at the procedings.

2) Tamburlaine instructs his sons what they must do in order to
wear the crown of Persia.

3) Tamburlaine's lieutenant kings offer up to him their crowns and
receive them again from his hand.

4) Amyras observes covetously "the golden crowns" of the proud
Turks. His brother, the slothful Calyphas, shows no interest
even in his father's crown.

5) Part II concludes with the crowning of Amyras, while Tamburlaine instructs him.

Perhaps none of these additions in Part I can be called
major episodes. But they are such additions as add moral
significance to the quality of the action. Presumably, a
crown is to a pagan what the cross is to a Christian: Marlowe's symbolism at least lets us know that he is telling the
story not of crusaders but of world-conquerors.

Of more prominent importance is Marlowe's introduction
of Zenocrate, for which there are only the very slightest

hints in the histories. The significance of this addition we shall discuss in a later chapter.

One other point, however—a very significant one—must be added to the list of Marlowe's use of nonhistorical details in Part I. That is the dramatist's employment of ceremony in the famous banquet scene (*Tamb.* I. ɪv. iv.). While the treatment of Bajazet in this scene has basis in the histories, the historians nowhere describe Tamburlaine's behavior in supping with his followers. Marlowe therefore draws certain details, as Zabina's speech in reference to Progne would indicate, from Seneca's Thyestean banquet scene; but also, I think, from another source not so easily recognizable. Fundamentally, Tamburlaine's banquet is Paganism's unconscious travesty of The Lord's Supper. The meal has sacramental pattern. First come "Full bowles of wine vnto the God of war." Then is brought in "a second course"—pastries in the shape of crowns. Tamburlaine, the tyrant-Lord, hands this worldly-bread to his lieutenant disciples. At the same time he invests them with titles promisory of the rewards they are to have for service in his kingdom; and he exhorts them to the pagan virtues of "valour" and "magnanimity." Then, invoking "holy Fates" (Paganism's counterpart to Christian Providence), he goes forth to his triumph by the sword (counterpart of the Christian cross). This is appropriate ritual for hallowing the false Religion of War. The travesty is Marlowe's contrivance for presenting spectacularly the moral significance of an anti-Christ's career.

II

For Part II Marlowe had almost no further help available from the histories. He proceeded, therefore, to improvise such interludes and entertainments as would appropriately illustrate the life of camps and warfare, and also to construct such episode as would fulfil the tragic destiny of his protagonist.

The most important of the interludes in Part II, the story of Sigismund and Orcanes, is introduced as a subplot. Its theme concerns perjury and providence, as these moral matters are illustrated in the arena of peace and war. The events comprising the episode as Marlowe tells it are mainly historical (i.e., they appear in Bonfinius'[8] moralized history), but they are anachronistic to the history of Tamburlaine. Moreover, the episode does not further the main plot of the drama in any appreciable way. Why, then, has the dramatist introduced it? Unless we wish to believe that Marlowe uses events merely haphazardly in a desperate effort to fill space, we are obliged to conclude that he has chosen this story for its morality elements. We have already noted (ante, page 67), that the episode is one in which Raleigh saw an important moral lesson displayed.

First, let us note that the events here ascribed to Sigismund and Orcanes did not happen to the historical kings bearing these names. However, Marlowe's use of the names is not without logic. The dramatist had at least three good reasons for naming Sigismund as the Christian leader in the episode: the historical Sigismund (1368-1437) was a Hungarian King and Christendom's crusader against the Turks during the latter years of Tamburlaine's lifetime; he suffered humiliating defeat at the hands of the Infidels; and he is famous as a faith-breaker (not with the Turks, it is true, but in his dealings with John Hus). The name of Sigismund's Turkish opponent, if we follow history, should be either Bajazet (who defeated him in 1397 when he en-

---

[8] Miss Ethel Seaton, *London Times Lit. Supp.*, June 16, 1921, p. 388, pointed out that Marlowe's source here is the story of Amurath and Vladislaus, for which the dramatist may well have used Bonfinius, *Antonii Bonfinii Rerum Ungaricarum decades quattuor* (1543), together with Callimachus, *Callimachi Experientis de clade Varnensi* (1556). Summarizing and quoting from these authors, Miss Seaton shows that Marlowe's story adheres closely to historical circumstances for three noteworthy matters: 1) the manner of ratifying the peace; 2) the arguments for its rupture; and 3) the prayer of the Turkish leader to the Christian God.

deavored to raise the siege of Constantinople) or Bajazet's son Calapin (from whom Sigismund narrowly escaped by flight at a later battle in which he sought to be revenged of his defeat by Bajazet). But since Marlowe has already removed Bajazet from the scene of the drama, and since he is reserving Calapin for another set of events, he must find some other name for Sigismund's enemy. Orcanes happens to be the name both of Bajazet's grandfather (Turkish emperor, 1326-1359) and also of Bajazet's grandson.[9] Marlowe applies this name to a certain "King of Natolia," introduced as the Turkish adversary to Sigismund.

The events which Marlowe then provides for Sigismund and Orcanes are transposed from the history of the Turk Amurath II and the Christian Vladislaus, culminating in the battle of Varna in 1444. The story is that Vladislaus, king of Poland and Hungary, swore a truce with Amurath II, broke it and marched into the territory from which Amurath had withdrawn, was there met by the returning Amurath, was defeated and slain.[10] Bonfinius' account gives details many of which are closely paralleled by Marlowe. He tells us that the pact between the Turks and the Christians was confirmed by oath on both sides, the Christians swearing by the Gospel and the Turks by the Koran. Then Amurath withdrew his forces from Turkish Europe. Meanwhile the other members of the Christian League, displeased with the truce, brought pressure to bear on the Hungarians to break it. The Papal legate, Cardinal Julian, delivered a speech urging the following arguments: 1) that the league with the Turk was but a breaking of faith with the rest of the Christian League; 2) that it was the duty of the Christian to circumvent the infidel by any means in his power;

---

[9] See Whetstone, *English Mirror*, p. 72.
[10] See Ellis-Fermor, *Tamburlaine*, pp. 41-43, 206n. The story appears also in John Shute's *Two very notable Commentaries* (1562), pp. 8 ff. I am indebted to Ellis-Fermor for my summary of the arguments in Bonfinius.

3) that the Turk had never kept faith with the Christians and therefore could not expect faith from them; and 4) that it had ever been accounted a crime to observe oaths that were manifestly evil in themselves. In the Pope's name Julian absolved the Hungarians from their oath to Amurath.[11] Vladislaus then gathered an army and marched into Bulgaria, the Papal legate urging him on. Amurath, hearing the news, crossed the Hellespont and met Vladislaus at Varna. During the fight, which was long and bitter,

> Amurath, seeing the great slaughter of his men, and all brought into extreame danger, beholding the picture of the Crucifix in the displaied ensignes of the voluntarie Christians, pluckt the writing out of his bosome, wherin the late league was comprised, and holding it up in his hand with his eies cast up to heauen said:
> 'Behold, thou crucified Christ, this is the league thy Christians in thy name made with mee: which they haue without cause violated. Now if thou bee a God, as they say thou art, and as we dreame, reuenge the wrong now done unto thy name, and me, and shew thy power upon thy perjurious people, who in their deeds denie thee their God.' [12]

Marlowe has followed closely most of the details of this story, amplifying certain of them for his own purpose. He presents the swearing of the truce as an elaborate ceremony, in which the two chieftains make firm promises, binding them with the most sacred oaths which their respective religious faiths provide. Then in the first scene of Act II the lords Frederick and Baldwin, thinking the moment is opportune for a stroke of revenge, urge Sigismund to break the truce. They argue: 1) that Christians are not bound to keep faith with infidels, 2) that the oaths of infidels have never been trustworthy, 3) that it is superstitious to be strict in

---

[11] Cf. Shute, *Two Commentaries,* p. 9. The reader is directed marginally to "Note the commaundement of the pope."

[12] The English version here quoted is from the account of Knolles, *History of the Turks* (1603), p. 297, which relies largely on Bonfinius. For the Latin account of Bonfinius, see Ellis-Fermor, *Tamburlaine,* p. 209n.

keeping faith when dispensation is available, and 4) that here is an opportunity to be God's scourge in punishing the "foul blasphemous paganism" of the enemy. The divergence from Bonfinius' account is slight but significant. Marlowe has not attributed to an official representative of the Church the false reasonings with which Sigismund is besieged. Why? The Catholic Church's definition of perjury is a very subtle and delicate matter.[13] Perhaps Marlowe, like Raleigh, regards Catholic doctrine on this point as detestable equivocation. Or perhaps Marlowe simply does not wish, by introducing a Churchman's reasonings, to sophisticate a moral issue which can otherwise be kept simple. That is, Marlowe is keeping his presentation of the problem in line with the morality tradition, which simplifies history for the purposes of edification. Following a method which we have observed was characteristic of the humanist apologists for Reformed Christianity in Marlowe's day, Marlowe rests the moral issue on certain ethical norms which it is assumed must be accepted universally by both pagan and Christian. Keeping dogma, scripture, and the Church out of the picture, he appeals to moral philosophy.

Marlowe puts the responsibility for the perjury squarely on human passions, not on the Church. The argument which finally persuades Sigismund to perjure himself is not the fact of an official dispensation from the Pope, but the all-too-human revenge motive. Marlowe makes plain the point that Sigismund and his men are taking upon themselves to do God's punishing for Him—an assumption of authority which, as we have noted in an earlier chapter of

---

[13] Note Shakespeare's *King John* III. i., where it is presented dramatically. Shakespeare, instead of being moralistic in the manner of the moralities (and of Marlowe in this present instance), faces the hard moral problem in all its paradoxical complexity. Shakespeare's treatment is in line with Catholic theology; Marlowe's, with Reformation humanism. In *The Jew of Malta* (1074 ff.), where the problem of perjury is again raised, the words of Barabas seem to be directed against Catholic doctrine.

our study, is the most serious of sins. The Hungarians are proposing to be God's scourges.

Marlowe is now ready to make the point that such action is damnable by the religious faith acknowledged in common by both pagans and Christians. The irreligion of those who "in their deeds deny . . . their Christ" can be rebuked on the basis of a universal natural religion held in common by all religious men. Orcanes says:

> Can there be such deceit in Christians,
> Or treason in the fleshly heart of man,
> Whose shape is figure of the highest God?
> Then if there be a Christ, as Christians say,
> But in their deeds deny him for their Christ:
> If he be son to euerliuing *Ioue*,
> And hath the power of his outstretched arme,
> If he be iealous of his name and honor,
> As is our holy prophet *Mahomet*,
> Take here these papers as our sacrifice
> And witnesse of thy seruants periury.
> Open thou shining vaile of *Cynthia*
> And make a passage from the imperiall heauen
> That he that sits on high and neuer sleeps.
> Nor in one place is circumscriptible,
> But euery where fils euery Continent,
> With strange infusion of his sacred vigor,
> May in his endlesse power and puritie
> Behold and venge this Traitors periury.
> Thou Christ that art esteem'd omnipotent,
> If thou wilt prooue thy selfe a perfect God,
> Worthy the worship of all faithful hearts,
> Be now reueng'd vpon this Traitors soule,
> And make the power I haue left behind
> (Too litle to defend our guiltlesse liues)
> Sufficient to discomfort and confound
> The trustlesse force of those false Christians.
> To armes my Lords, on Christ still let vs crie,
> If there be Christ, we shall haue victorie. (2893 ff.)

It is evident that Orcanes, pagan and Turk though he be, has enough light of divine truth to believe in God and in Providence.[14] He invokes the authority and reputed power of Christ. He rests his trust, however, in the God of nature.[15] Orcanes has a very firm belief in an omnipotent, active God, who can demonstrate His just power in history in punishing sin. He believes—as Nashe, Raleigh, and Du Bartas had insisted—that God is infinite, that He sustains the world, and that He does not sleep.[16] Moreover, Orcanes has enough religion to apprehend a truth which the Christian apologists of Marlowe's day were constantly insisting upon: that the overthrow of wicked men should not be attributed to fortune alone, but that credit should be given to God. Gazellus says:

> Tis but the fortune of the wars my Lord,
> Whose power is often proou'd a myracle.

Orcanes answers:[17]

---

[14] Raleigh, as we have noted, argued for Providence on exactly this ground, that it is a truth known even to Turks and to other wise pagans. Perhaps Raleigh and Marlowe were familiar with what Mahometans regard as the most sublime of all sentences, the Koorsee (throne) verse in the second chapter of the Koran: "God, there is no God but He, the living, the self-subsistent. Slumber takes Him not, nor sleep. His is what is in the heavens and what is in the earth. . . . His throne extends over the heavens and the earth, and it tires Him not to guard them both, for He is high and grand." Trans. E. H. Palmer (Oxford, 1880), *The Sacred Books of the East*, VI, 40.

[15] Perhaps Orcanes' invocation of *Cynthia* in this connection is to be understood in the light of Chapman's use of Cynthia (see his "Hymnus in Cynthiam") as symbol of the divine power that rules the natural world. That is, Orcanes' call to Cynthia is appropriate language for invoking the truths of natural religion.

[16] The tragedy of Bajazet and Zabina in *Tamb.* I. iii. iii. is that they lose their faith in Providence, which means their faith in God. "O Mahomet O *sleepie* Mahomet" (italics mine), cries Bajazet in desperation. "O cursed Mahomet," adds Zabina, unable to bear the fact that God does not descend immediately to punish the wicked.

[17] This elaboration is Marlowe's own invention. Compare, however, Shute, *Two Commentaries*, p. 12: "When Amorathe had thus obtained the victorie and rested wholly maister of the fielde, he had no great desire to folow the chase of his fliyng enemies, nor yet did glorie wyth great wordes as the maner of the Turkes is, ne yet sought in any kynde of sort to amplifie the victorie: nor shewed in his countenaunce anye kinde of ioye, and being demaunded by certayne of his familiers: the cause, that after so great a victorie, he shewed him selfe so melancholicke, he answered, I desyre not often to obtayne victorie in this sorte."

> Yet in my thought shall Christ be honored,
> Not doing Mahomet an iniurie,
> Whose power had share in this our victory.

Marlowe's moral intent is doubly plain when we observe the speech he has invented for the dying Sigismund. Sigismund cries out repentantly:

> Discomfited is all the Christian hoste,
> And God hath thundered vengeance from on high,
> For my accurst and hatefull periurie.
> O iust and dreadfull punisher of sinne,
> Let the dishonor of the paines I feele,
> In this my mortall well deserued wound,
> End all my penance in my sodaine death,
> And let this death wherein to sinne I die,
> Conceiue a second life in endlesse mercie.

Sigismund's attitude contrasts significantly with the attitude of Bajazet in his overthrow, and likewise with the attitude of Tamburlaine when overtaken by death. Presumably that is because Sigismund, after all, is a Christian, able by reason of his special Faith to have hope in salvation by God's mercy and grace. He dies therefore in pious fashion with a prayer on his lips, whereas the pagans Bajazet and Tamburlaine first give way to desperation and then die with a fatalistic attitude. As commentary on this point we may refer to a passage in John Davies of Hereford's *Mirum in Modum* (1602). Davies writes regarding Pagans, Turks, and Jews:

> So in *Afflictions* stormes these dogges will die,
> And can no praier with deuotion frame,
> But *Christians* then, can best performe the same.[18]

III

The next considerable episode in Part II is the death of Zenocrate. It seems to be wholly Marlowe's invention. It is

---

[18] *Works of Davies of Hereford,* ed. Grosart, I, 14.

introduced, pretty obviously, in order that the coming of misfortune may give opportunity for revealing Tamburlaine's character. Let us note therefore that William Baldwin in his *Treatise of Morall Phylosophye,* quoting Plato, had written:

> Euyll menne by theyr bodely strength resyste theyr mysfortunes, but good men by vertue of the soule, suffer them paciently: whiche pacience commeth not by mighte of arme, by strength of hande, nor by force of bodye: but by grace of the soule, by whyche wee resyste couetyse and other worldly pleasures, hopyng to be rewarded therefore with eternall blisse.[19]

In the light of this commentary it is plain that Tamburlaine's behavior at the death of Zenocrate illustrates the pattern of the evil man. He resists his misfortune by bodily strength, threatening to

> breake the frame of heauen,
> Batter the shining pallace of the Sun,
> And shiuer all the starry firmament. (3072-74.)

Instead of patience, we behold in him, as the title page for the 1606 quarto announces, "his impassionate furie." His Titanism, evident already in Part I when he had promised that

> Our quiuering Lances shaking in the aire,
> ... Shall threat the Gods more than Cyclopian warres,
> And with our Sun-bright armour as we march,
> Weel chase the Stars from heauen, (616-21)

now rises in rebellious rage and, finding itself impotent to

---

[19] Bk. II. ch. iii. Note also the quotation from Isocrates which Baldwin gives (II. v.): "prayse no man before death, for death is the discouerer of al his workes."

[20] That this is one of the significant episodes of the drama is indicated by the Prologue, where we are told that we shall see "with how manie cities sacrifice He celebrated her sad funerall."

harm heaven, razes and devastates the beauty of the earth,[20] setting up a pillar in memory of the event.[21]

The burning of Larissa in honor of Zenocrate has a noteworthy analogue in Alexander's burning of Persepolis for Thais.[22] The way in which Elizabethans would be expected to regard Tamburlaine's act may be judged by the way in which they regarded Alexander's act. And the Elizabethan view of Alexander's act is made very clear by John Davies of Hereford:

> The *Macedonian Philipp's* peerelesse *Sonne,*
> That over-ranne the *World* with *Sword* and *Fire,*
> This flaming *fury* yet did so ore runne,
> That for his *Thais* (that kindled his *desire*)
> He burnt *Persepolis,* sans cause of *ire*:
> Yea, did not onely that fowle *fact* command,
> But with his *Hands* he lab'red (as for *hire*)
> To burne the *buildings* which as yet did stand,
> Till he had laid al level with the *Land.*
>
> A *Wonder* worthy of all wonderment,
> That he that foil'd what ere his *force* withstood,
> Should be thus *foil'd,* and made a *President*
> Of *Lust's* fell *force,* which so enflam'd his *Blood*
> That made his *Flesh* Wild-*Fire* in likelyhood:
> A *Man* by *woman,* a *King* by a *Queane*
> To be so overcome through *Lustfull moode,*
> (Being so *effeminate* and most *obscene*)
> Argues, in *Loue* and *Lust* there is no meane.[23]

---

[21] Nashe's words in *Christs Teares* will serve for commentary: "Great is theyr vaine-glory also that will rather reare themselues monuments of Marble then monuments of good deedes in mens mouthes" (ed. McKerrow, II, 109).

[22] Compare also Whitney's *Choice of Emblems* (1586), p. 45. An emblem entitled "Furor & rabies" shows King Agamemnon brandishing his sword, while in the background are a burning city and, across the way, the tents of his camp. The initial verses read:

> The crewell kinges, that are inflam'de with ire:
> With fier, and sworde, their furious mindes suffice.

[23] *Microcosmos,* ed. Grosart, I. c. 66.

This is especially significant if we remember that Fortescue had written that Tamburlaine "in no point was inferiour to that prince of the worlde, *Alexander*." [24]

Tamburlaine's likeness to Alexander is suggested by Marlowe very early in the drama, when Tamburlaine and his lieutenants speak of riding in triumph through Persepolis, repeating the phrase twice.[25] Miss Ellis-Fermor in a note on this passage writes:

None of the historians of Timur mention it among the Persian cities when describing his conquests there—Bizarus describes its ancient glory and destruction by Alexander—and Marlowe seems to have elevated it to a position which neither history nor his sources accord to it.[26]

Very likely, I think, Marlowe is associating Persepolis with Tamburlaine in order to suggest that Tamburlaine is reviving the spirit of an Alexander. In all his behavior Tamburlaine must be the pattern Conqueror.[27] When he slays his own son Calyphas—an episode invented by Marlowe—there is analogy for such behavior in Alexander's slaying of his philosopher Callisthenes. Through Lydgate,[28] Elizabethan readers were familiar with the story of how Alexander, growing proud, presumed to be the son of Jupiter and then slew Callisthenes for daring to oppose such madness. Somewhat similarly, Tamburlaine justifies his act of murder by claiming kinship with Jove.[29]

Also, the incident of Zenocrate's death provides us a clue

---

[24] See Ellis-Fermor, *Tamburlaine*, p. 287.
[25] *Tamb.* 733 ff.
[26] *Tamburlaine*, p. 106n.
[27] Tamburlaine likens himself to Alexander, Belus, and Ninus (*Tamb.* 4181-82), to Xerxes (613), and to Julius Caesar (1250). But note how Erasmus judges these heroes (*Educ. Chris. Prince*, ed. cit., p. 203).
[28] *The Fall of Princes*, IV, 1107 ff., ed. Henry Bergen (Washington, 1923), Part II, 504 ff.
[29] *Tamb.* II. 3785-90. Cf. *Tamb.* 394-6.

to Marlowe's conception of the character of Zenocrate. In
the course of his lamentation Tamburlaine is made to say:

> And had she liu'd before the siege of *Troy*,
> *Hellen*, whose beauty sommond Greece to armes,
> And drew a thousand ships to *Tenedos*,
> Had not bene nam'd in *Homers* Iliads:
> Her name had bene in euery line he wrote:
> Or had those wanton Poets, for whose byrth
> Olde *Rome* was proud, but gasde a while on her,
> Nor *Lesbia*, nor *Corrinna* had bene nam'd,
> *Zenocrate* had bene the argument
> Of euery Epigram or Eligie. (3054-63.)

In other words, Zenocrate is to be regarded as the very
pattern of pagan, earthly beauty. We happen to know that
these pagan beauties to whom Zenocrate is here likened were
considered by Elizabethans to be as morally reprehensible
as they were physically attractive. The Elizabethans did not
think of Helen as a "good woman."[30]　John Taylor the
Water Poet speaks of her as "the lustful Punke, Faire
Hellen."[31]　Shakespeare in *The Rape of Lucrece* refers to

---

[30] See note by Hyder Rollins, p. 187, in his edition (Cambridge, 1926) of
A Gorgeous Gallery of Gallant Inventions (1578). In a poem by T[homas]
P[roctor] entitled "The reward of Whoredom by the fall of Helen," Helen says:

> I am *Helena* shee, for whose vilde filthy fact,
> The stately Towers of Troy, the haughty Grecians sacte:
> High *Troy*, whose pompe, throughout the world did sound,
> In Cinders low, through mee was layd on ground.

Note also that in Richard Robinson's *The Reward of Wickednesse* (1574) Helen
is a soul in hell who relates her tragedy. Spenser (*F. Q.* III. 10. 12) seems to
concur in the view of Natalis Comes (*Mythologiae* 6. 23), which regards Helen
as "scelerata vitae" and interprets Paris' choice of her as a giving way to lust.
(See H. G. Lotspeich, *Classical Mythology in the Poetry of Spenser*, p. 67.) See
also Beatrice D. Brown, "Marlowe, Faustus, and Simon Magus," *P. M. L. A.*,
LIV (1939), 92-3, where it is pointed out that in medieval literature Helen is
pictured as the paramour of the false-Christ, Simon Magus, who proclaims her as
Heaven's wisdom. (Compare the boasts of the anti-Christ Tamburlaine regarding Zenocrate.) It is interesting to observe that in Renaissance times Cressida, like
Helen, is increasingly vilified when ethics become increasingly rationalized under
the impact of Humanism. See H. E. Rollins, "The Troilus and Cressida Story,"
P. M. L. A., XXXII (1917), 383-429.

[31] *Works*, 1630, Spenser Society reprint, p. 271; cited by Rollins.

Helen in the lines:

> Show me the strumpet that began this stir,
> That with my nails her beauty I may tear.   (1471-72.)

Elizabethans hated her as a harlot that had brought destruction on the Trojans, who were, so the story had it, the ancestors of the Britons. The name Helen had pattern significance as designating a type of beauty whose pursuit was dangerous to English life. This helps us understand why Faustus' love for Helen in Marlowe's later play was so plainly reprehensible. In still another drama of Marlowe's it makes clear why Dido, whose wiles almost persuaded Aeneas to forsake his divine commission, should be made to exclaim:

> all the world calles me a second *Helen,*
> ...Would, as faire *Troy* was, *Carthage* might be sackt,
> And I be calde a second *Helena.*   (1552-56.)

We may safely conclude that Zenocrate and Dido, these "Helens" of Marlowe's plays, are intended to represent earthly beauties, endowed with nature's gifts, but devoid of religion or conscience.

Olympia, in an unhistorical episode which soon follows in the play, seems plainly to be introduced by Marlowe as a foil to the character of Zenocrate. Faced by the same situation which Zenocrate faced earlier in the drama, Olympia chooses a contrary path and remains true to her first love even at the cost of death. We remember that Tamburlaine by the spectacle of his eloquence, power, and flattery had caused fickle Zenocrate to be false to her first love—thereby drawing the censure of Agydas. But here Theridamas, employing the same methods with Olympia, fails. It is not because his promises are less splendid than Tamburlaine's;

for he uses arguments which are definitely reminiscent of Tamburlaine's courtship of Zenocrate. He promises:

> Thou shalt be stately Queene of faire *Argier*,
> And cloth'd in costly cloath of massy gold,
> Vpon the marble turrets of my Court
> Sit like to *Venus* in her chaire of state
> Commanding all thy princely eie desires,
> And I will cast off armes and sit with thee,
> Spending my life in sweet discourse of loue. (3920-26.)

Theridamas fails because Olympia is a woman of true love and virtuous conscience, who would rather choose death than to be an empress; while Zenocrate, on the other hand, delights above all else to be an empress. Thus we are presented in Olympia's history an *exemplum* similar in type to the well-known morality tales of Constance, and of Appius and Virginia. Olympia is in the tradition of Susanna, Lucrece, and Avisa—the direct opposites of Cressida and Helen.[32]

The actual source of the Olympia episode in Marlowe seems to be the *Orlando Furioso,* Cantos XXVIII and XXIX, where Ariosto relates at length the story of Isabella.[33] Isabella, to avoid the persecution of Rodomont, adopts an expedient similar to Olympia's. Marlowe's story resembles Ariosto's, however, only in its general outlines. Marlowe, if he used Ariosto's story, has freely adapted it to his own special purpose.

---

[32] See *Willobie His Avisa,* ed. G. B. Harrison, esp. pp. 170, 178.

[33] See Ellis-Fermor, *Tamburlaine,* pp. 44-5. This source for the episode of the deceit practised by the captive Olympia was first pointed out by J. P. Collier, *History of English Dramatic Poetry* (1831), III, 119. Ariosto's episode, however, does not provide a source for the earlier part of the Olympia episode, where Olympia kills her own son at his consent to prevent his falling into the hands of Tamburlaine. Miss Ethel Seaton, *Rev. Eng. Studies,* V (1929), 395-6, points out that this may be derived from Belleforest's account (*Cosmographie Universelle,* 1575, II, 750) of an incident in the siege of Rhodes, where the mistress of the Governor of the fort killed and burned her children to keep them from falling into the hands of the infidels.

IV

The scene immediately next in the drama is also plainly introduced for a morality purpose. The stage directions read:

> Tamburlaine drawen in his chariot by Trebizon and Soria with bittes in their mouthes, reines in his left hand, in his right hand a whip, with which he scourgeth them.

As he drives the chariot, Tamburlaine invites us to "see the figure of my dignitie"; and after likening himself to the god who drives the horses of the sun and also to Hercules, he loudly proclaims himself "the Scourge of highest Ioue."

The source for this scene goes back to Plato's picture of the tyrant driving his chariot of State.[34] But the idea had been recently utilized on the stage by George Gascoigne and Francis Kinwelmershe in the Dumb Show preceding Act I of *Jocasta* (1566). The directions for the Dumb Show read:

> Firste, before the beginning of the first Acte, did sounde a dolefull & straunge noyse of violles, Cythren, Bandurion, and such like, during the whiche, there came in uppon the Stage a king with an Imperial crown upon his head, very richely apparelled: a Scepter in his righte hande, a Mounde with a Crosse in his lefte hande, sitting in a Chariote very richely furnished, drawne in by foure Kinges in their Dublettes and Hosen, with Crownes also upon their heades. Representing unto us Ambition, by the hystorie of *Sesostres* king of *Egypt,* who beeing in his time and reigne a mightie Conqueror, yet not content to have subdued many princes, and taken from them their kingdomes and dominions, did in like maner cause those Kinges whome he had so overcome, to draw in his Chariote like Beastes and Oxen, thereby to content his unbrideled ambitious desire.[35]

As for Marlowe's addition of the whip, we can get an explanation of its significance from the Dumb Show to Act I of *The Misfortunes of Arthur* (1587):

---

[34] *Republic,* 566.
[35] *The Works of Gascoigne* (Cambridge, 1907), ed. Cunliffe, I, 246.

Sounding the musicke, there rose three furies from vnder the stage. . . . The thirde with a whippe in the right hande and a *Paegasus* in the left. . . . By the third with her whip and *Paegasus* was prefigured the crueltie and ambition which . . . continued to th'affecting of this tragidie[36]

Perhaps, also, Marlowe had seen the following paragraph in George Whetstone:

S. Bernard saith, that the accursed chariot of couetousnesse, is drawen with foure disloyall wheeles of vices, *vz. Pusalanimite, Crueltie, misprising of God, and forgetfulnesse of certaine death.* The two horses are named *Theft, & Hardnesse.* The waggoner is *Earnest desire to haue,* who vseth two sharpe whippes: the one called *Disordered appetite to get,* the other, *Feare to loose.*[37]

It could be said that all the vices which St. Bernard enumerates (except for pusillanimity) are well exhibited in the character of Tamburlaine, and that Tamburlaine therefore fulfils the portrait of Covetousness.

A similar spectacle is introduced for similar purpose in Thomas Lodge's *The Wounds of Ciuill War* (c. 1588), a drama which is thought to owe its inspiration to Marlowe's *Tamburlaine.* In Lodge's drama we see the conqueror Scilla returning from the war against Mithradates "in his chare triumphant of gold drawn by foure Moores." To leave no doubt of his moral intention in the play, Lodge later brings it about that Scilla, beholding the desperate suicide of his rival Marius, is convinced of the vanity of worldly power. In other words, Marius offers Scilla the same object-lesson which Bajazet offers Tamburlaine. That Marlowe did not make Bajazet's suicide the occasion for a repentant reformation by Tamburlaine need not indicate that Marlowe was less moral than Lodge; to have made Tam-

---

[36] *Early English Classical Tragedies* (Oxford, 1912), ed. J. W. Cunliffe, p. 225.
[37] *An Addition: or Touchstone for the Time,* p. 29; bound in the same volume with *A Mirour for Magestrates of Cyties* (1584).

burlaine remorseful would have required the obvious distortion of the well-established historical accounts of Tamburlaine's career.[38]

V

But let us turn, finally, to Marlowe's treatment of Tamburlaine's blasphemy and death. Blasphemy, we have noted in an earlier chapter of our study, was from the Reformation point of view the worst of crimes. The Calvinist insisted that man exists for God's glory. Blasphemy is a most impious denying to God of the glory due Him. It is the opposite of genuine religion, which consists in reverence and in obedience to Divine Law as set forth in Scripture. When Tamburlaine burns his Book of Scripture the act dramatically epitomizes his flouting of Divine Law, and is a bold proclamation of religious antinomianism. The Koran, of course, is not Christian Scripture; yet for a Moslem to burn it in boastful contempt of *all* authority outside himself is an act epitomizing sacrilege.

We will remember that Isaiah in describing the Scourge of God made the prediction that the wicked Assyrian after having been used by God to punish other wicked nations would proudly say (*Isaiah* X, 13):

By the strength of my hand I have done it, and by my wisdom; for I am prudent; and I have removed the bounds of the people, and have robbed their treasures, and I have put down the inhabitants like a valiant man;

and that then God would Himself "punish the stout heart of the king of Assyria and the glory of his high looks." This is the point which Tamburlaine's history reaches with

---

[38] Besides, there is good moral theory to support the view that it would not be proper to let Tamburlaine suffer remorse. George Whetstone, who regards envy as Tamburlaine's special vice, remarks elsewhere that "In the conscience of the enuious, remorse hath no place, for that his thoughts are continually busied with diuelish imaginations as well as his forces bent to the ruine of his neyghbours." (*English Mirror*, p. 3.)

the overthrow of Babylon. As he rides into Babylon he likens himself to two notable Assyrian kings—Belus[39] and Ninus[40]—and to Alexander.[41] An alert Elizabethan could be expected to recognize in these names history's prototypes of ambition and impiety, and to recall, further, that when the conquering Alexander took Babylon he reached a summit and a sudden doom.

To a Christian audience, Babylon is the traditional symbol of wickedness. Tamburlaine's overthrow of the city is a fulfilling of his function as God's Scourge. His work being now accomplished, we may expect him, like the Assyrian, to boast himself against God. Tamburlaine fulfils our expectation. Even while his soldiers are still engaged in the work of destroying Babylon, he calls out:

---

[39] Belus, sometimes credited with building the tower of Babel, was variously identified by historians. Fortescue, p. 20ᵛ, says that some authorities call him the "second Ninus." Bodenham's *Belvedere* refers to him as the son of Nimrod. Raleigh, significantly, reckons that the worshipping of images began from Belus ("the first of all men that was euer honored by their subiects with the title of Deitie") and was established by his successor Ninus ("the first that commaunded the exercise of Idolatrie"). See *H. W.* (1614), I. x. 7 and 8, pp. 195-98.

[40] Nearly all writers of history, says Orosius, "definitely state that kingdoms and wars began with Ninus," who "for fifty years . . . maintained a reign of bloodshed throughout Asia." (*Against the Pagans*, ed. I. W. Raymond, New York, 1936, pp. 32, 42.) Fortescue, p. 11ᵛ, explains that though there were wars before Ninus, yet he was the first who for avarice undertook wars of conquest. Spenser refers to Ninus as the builder of the tower of Babel (*R. of T.,* 511; *F. Q.* II. 9. 21). The wickedness of both Ninus and Nimrod is commented upon in Bale's *God's Promises*, III, 13-17. The *Stationers' Register* under date of 10 May 1595 lists a play unfortunately not now extant: "The Tragedie of Ninus and Semiramis, the first Monarchs of the World." Thomas Heywood in *An Apology for Actors* (1612) says that Ninus is presented on the stage as a warning against ambition. (See *Shaks. Soc. Rep.,* 1841, p. 53.)

[41] Cf. *F. Q. I.* 5. 48, where Spenser lists Alexander, Nimrod, and Ninus as men whom Pride has caused to fall. In following stanzas, Spenser adds the names of Sylla, Marius, Caesar, Pompey, Semiramis, and others. This entire list of Pride's victims should be compared with the list of companions-in-hell given by Caesar's ghost in the anonymous *Caesar's Revenge*, II. i. The author, following Lydgate and Spenser, attributes to Alexander the fault of wishing "to fetch his pedigree from Heauen." For other comment on the madness of Alexander, see Seneca, *On Benefits*, VII. ii. 6; and Erasmus, *Educ. Chris. Prince*, ed. cit., p. 201, and *Against War*, ed. cit., p. 43. Alexander and Nimrod are the two names which Spenser sees engraved on the "riven walls" of Ate's dwelling (*F. Q.* IV. 1. 22).

Now *Casane,* wher's the Turkish *Alcaron,*
And all the heapes of supersticious bookes,
Found in the Temples of that *Mahomet.*
Whom I haue thought a God? they shal be burnt.
...In vaine I see men worship *Mahomet.*
My sword hath sent millions of Turks to hell,
Slew all his Priests, his kinsmen, and his friends,
And yet I liue vntoucht by *Mahomet.*

Then, as the books are burning,[42] Tamburlaine reveals to us
that he has reached the moral stand which Greene called
"atheist," and which is, to speak accurately and according to
Calvin's interpretation, the epitome of blasphemy. He dares
God out of heaven in a manner obviously analogous to the
daring words of certain Jews addressing Christ at Calvary.
He repudiates God's laws and openly questions the existence
of God. His words are:

Now *Mahomet,* if thou haue any power,
Come downe thy selfe and worke a myracle,
Thou art not woorthy to be worshipped,
That suffers flames of fire to burne the writ
Wherein the sum of thy religion rests.
Why send'st thou not a furious whyrlwind downe,
To blow thy Alcaron vp to thy throne.
Where men report, thou sitt'st by God himselfe,
Or vengeance on the head of *Tamburlain,*
That shakes his sword against thy maiesty,
And spurns the Abstracts of thy foolish lawes.
Wel souldiers, *Mahomet* remaines in hell,

---

[42] Tamburlaine's burning of the Koran has a significance analogous to that of
a rebel Christian burning his Bible. Compare John Bale's *Three Laws,* where
Infidelitas attempts to burn Christi Lex—and is visited with fire from Deus Pater.
But perhaps the burning of books has also further symbolism. Greville, *Treatie
of Warres,* stanzas 9 and 10, sees in wars a pride which "will no more the yoke
of heauen beare" and which shows itself in the burning of books:

Here bookes are burnt, faire monuments of minde;
Here ignorance doth on all Arts tyrannise;
Vertue no other mould but courage findes.

He cannot heare the voice of *Tamburlain,*
Seeke out another Godhead to adore,
The God that sits in heauen, if any God,
For he is God alone, and none but he.[43]

Such talk contrasts magnificently with the pious prayer of
Orcanes earlier in this same Part II of the drama. Indeed,
Orcanes and Tamburlaine can now be seen to be contrast-
ing types of the "religious" and the "irreligious" man. Tamburlaine has here rejected *that kind of* a God which Orcanes
held to and which Elizabethans regarded it incumbent upon
everyone to believe in: a God of moral law. The affront
rightly precipitates his doom. Not so much as twenty lines
later we hear Tamburlaine cry, "But stay, I feele my selfe
distempered sudainly." He has his answer. God is casting
His Scourge into the fire.

The fire is in the conqueror's own blood. A physician
called to examine Tamburlaine tells him, "Your vaines are
full of accidental heat," and predicts his death. We shall
note in another chapter that this parching of the blood is
the ultimate extreme of the choleric humour and that it is
the final fate predicted for the man who lets violent passions go unmoderated. The fever, therefore, is a physiological phenomenon which can be explained by psychological
causes. But that does not mean God has not had a hand in
it. All "secondary causes," we remember the humanists

---

[43] If the last three lines are somewhat puzzling, we should compare the
scepticism of the mockers at Calvary, whose blasphemy showed itself not in a
denial of the existence of God, but in a violent challenging of the truth of his
providence. Though Mahomet is in Christian eyes a false God, nevertheless
Tamburlaine's blaspheming of Mahomet must be regarded as indication of general impiety; for Calvin says that if idolaters lift themselves up against their own
forged gods they thereby show themselves contemners of all divine power.
(*Commentary on Isaiah,* ed. cit., p. 118.) Similarly, Raleigh says that Xerxes
was justly punished for impiety when he sought to challenge the power of his
false-god Apollo. (*Hist. Wld.,* III. 6. 4.) Bodin, too, held that irreverence to
idols on the part of one who believes them to be gods is an insult to the true
God. [See G. H. Sabine, "The Colloquium Heptaplomeres of Jean Bodin," in
Persecution and Liberty. Essays in Honor of George Lincoln Burr (New York,
1931), p. 300.]

saying, are strictly ordered by God, so that *nothing* happens by chance. It is, as La Primaudaye has said, "too great blockishness" to attribute casual mishaps, either general *or particular,* to any other cause than "Him who useth such meanes . . . when he mindeth to chastise and to punish men for their offenses." A fever, then, is no accident. God has put within each man's bosom the means for punishing that man's sin. Laws of nature are engines of justice, so timed as to correspond with the purposes of Providence. If the mills of God seem to grind slow, there is purpose in the delay— and at last, surely, they grind exceeding small.

Here, then, is an enemy Tamburlaine cannot defeat.

> Death with armies of Cymerian spirits
> Giues battile gainst the heart of *Tamburlaine.*
> ... These cowards inuisible assaile hys soule,
> And threaten conquest on our Soueraigne.

Illness gives Tamburlaine the inspiration to see that his opponent is no mere secondary cause. It is some "daring God" who "seeks to conquer mighty Tamburlaine." And Tamburlaine is ready for combat—even against God:

> *Techelles* and the rest, come take your swords,
> And threaten him whose hand afflicts my soul,
> Come let vs march against the powers of heauen,
> And set blacke streamers in the firmament,
> To signifie the slaughter of the Gods.

This, as Marlowe realized, is the epitome of Titanism: to propose to set black streamers in the firmament which God has reserved for the banners of Christ's red blood streaming.

Tamburlaine's invincibility is broken. He admits that he strives and rails in vain. Impatient words but add to his malady. So he spreads out before him a map of the world and keeps repeating: "And shall I die, and this vnconquered?" It is torment befitting a conqueror. Finally, he submits to death in the spirit of fatalistic resignation. He

even gives a sort of anti-Christ discourse on immortality.
And he comforts himself with the hope that the gods

> meane t'invest me in a higher throne
> As much too high for this disdainfull earth.[44]

Surveying Tamburlaine's history as a whole it is not difficult to find in Lydgate's *Fall of Princes* stories which are
in their general outlines similar. There is, for example,
Lydgate's story of Agathocles, which the modern editor
summarizes in these marginal words:

Although he was victorious, covetousness made him err, and, true
to his low origin, he became a revengeful tyrant. He thought he
had power to bind fast Fortune's wheel, the nature of which is to
be unstable; but pride, outrageous behavior and low birth caused
him to fall.[45]

A few pages later Lydgate tells the story of Sandrocottus,
another tyrant of low birth. In this instance we have the
marginal résumé:

No one is so proud and full of cruelty as a beggar set in high
estate. For a time a churl may feign gentility, but like a serpent
under flowers he will sting in the end.[46]

It is apparent from these stories that Elizabethan moralists
disliked climbers. They feared above all the man of low
birth who rises to high estate. Thomas Nashe, in explaining the cause of atheism, declared that

---

[44] If we think it strange that the dramatist permits Tamburlaine the comfort of
this hope, we should note the remarks of Sir William Cornwallis in his *Discourses upon Seneca the Tragedian* (1631), Sig. Kk3: "Our life is nothing but
a life of hope, which if wee cannot haue with a possibilitie, we will without. . . .
It neuer leaues vs, no not when we lye a dying: men vnassisted by Christianity,
at this time, even by nature are taught, to hope of another life, from which,
neither ignorance nor impiousnesse can driue them." Barnabe Barnes in *The
Divils Charter* (1607), V. vi., pictures the dying "anti-Christ" pope Alexander VI
as daring to hope that "My soule is more diuine and cannot perish."

[45] Bergen, II, 551.

[46] *Ibid.*, pp. 559-60.

None are so great enemies to God as those that (of smal likelihoods) haue waxt greatest vnder him, and haue most tasted the gracious springs of his prouidence.[47]

Elizabethan moralists equally disliked hypocrites. What their judgment must have been of Tamburlaine's claim of divine sanction for his acts of cruelty can be inferred from Nashe's description of the "inwarde Atheist":

hee makes conscience and the Spyrite of God a long side-cloake for all his oppressions and pollicies. A holie looke he will put on when he meaneth to do mischiefe, and haue Scripture in his mouth euen whiles hee is in cutting his neighbours throate.[48]

It is against the intellectual background which these quotations illustrate that we must judge the meaning and interpretation of Tamburlaine. Elizabethans, whose ethical sense was doubly keen because of the breakdown of dogmatic religion, had a moral horror of tyrants. But on the stage they loved tyrants, as they loved the stalking Herods of the Biblical plays, for their grand spectacle of Nature's pride, for their horrible warning of sin and God's judgment. Marlowe differs from his Protestant contemporaries, I believe, not in his moral outlook, but only in his ability as an artist. He was able to write such speeches for tyrants as made them come alive. As George Peele commented, Marlowe knew how "to write passions for the souls below."

---

[47] *Christs Teares,* ed. McKerrow, II, 120. Cf. I, 173.
[48] *Christs Teares,* ed. McKerrow, II, 117.

THE INFLUENCE OF SPENSER

🎕 🎕

THERE is much in the character of Marlowe's style to suggest the influence of Spenser. Particularly is this true in *Tamburlaine,* which is the most heavily brocaded of Marlowe's dramas. It has been computed that *Tamburlaine* alone contains 400 metaphors and similes, in comparison with some 250 in four other Marlowe plays taken together; and that it has more than 90 instances of classical allusion, as compared with 20 in Edward II and very few in the other plays.[1] Added to this highly figurative style is a heavy use of alliteration. Such a line as "*T*yrant, *I* *t*urne the *t*raitor in thy *t*hroat" (Tamb. 4168) exhibits the extreme of its use. Hyperbole, too, is frequent, and poetic sentiment soars at an exalted level. We feel that many of the speeches are epic or lyric rather than dramatic. Taking the form of verse paragraphs, they often exceed the sweep of Spenser's nine-line stanza but at the same time suggest it most immediately as their model.

Specific points of Spenser's influence on *Tamburlaine* have been noticed by various scholars. Georg Schoeneich, adding to the few comparisons which Dyce, Bullen, and Crawford before him had pointed out, published in 1907 a monograph entitled *Der Litterarische Einfluss Spensers auf Marlowe,* in which almost ninety pages are given to the listing and discussing of parallels between *Tamburlaine* and *The Faerie Queene.* I shall be indebted in this chapter almost constantly to his serviceable study.[2] Additionally, there is Pro-

---

[1] See F. I. Carpenter, *Metaphor and Simile in the Minor Elizabethan Drama* (Chicago, 1895), pp. 38-39.

[2] However, there is neither room here nor need to repeat the mass of Herr Schoeneich's parallel citations, many of which present very remote resemblances. I am concerned, rather, to analyze the tendencies of the evidence and to fairly appraise the significance of certain of its details.

fessor Tucker Brooke's article on "Marlowe's Versification
and Style,"[3] which in passing notes Spenser's influence in
Marlowe's use of Alexandrine lines. Professor Brooke has
counted in *Tamburlaine* some thirty pretty definite examples of Alexandrines introduced sporadically in the blank
verse.

The plainest example in *Tamburlaine* of Marlowe's borrowing from Spenser is a passage that ends with an Alexandrine. The parallel lines, first noted long ago by George
Stevens,[4] are as follows:

F. Q. I. 7. 32:
    Like to an almond tree ymounted hye
    On top of greene Selinis all alone,
    With blossoms brave bedecked daintily;
    Whose tender locks do tremble every one
    At everie little breath, that under heaven is blowne.
Tamb. 4098 ff.:
    Like to an almond tree ymounted high,
    Vpon the lofty and celestiall mount,
    Of euer greene *Selinus* queintly dect
    With bloomes more white than *Hericinas* browes,
    Whose tender blossoms tremble euery one,
    At euery little breath that thorow heauen is blowen.[5]

Since none of *The Faerie Queene* appeared in print before
1590—the year in which *Tamburlaine* too was given to the
press—we have to suppose that Marlowe had access to a
manuscript copy of at least some of Spenser's work. But
by what conjecture are we to explain this fact? Todd in his
edition of Spenser (1805) points out that already in 1588
Abraham Fraunce's *Arcadian Rhetorike* accurately cites some
lines of the Second Book of *The Faerie Queene*. Might we

---

[3] *Studies in Philology*, XIX (1922), 186-205.
[4] *Shakespeare* (1793), IX, 90.
[5] All citations of *Tamburlaine* in this chapter are, as usual, to Brooke's text;
and all citations of *The Faerie Queene* are to the Cambridge edition of *Spenser's
Complete Poems*, ed. Dodge (New York, 1908).

suppose, then, that perhaps Marlowe, like Fraunce, was a member of the Countess of Pembroke's circle; that perhaps both men became acquainted with Spenser's poem in a manuscript sent by the author to the Countess' brother, Philip Sidney? Such a supposition can find support in the fact that Marlowe wrote a dedication to the Countess of Pembroke for his friend Thomas Watson's *Amintae Gaudia* (1592).[6]

A parallel almost as notable was pointed out in 1885 by Bullen in his edition of Marlowe. When Tamburlaine boasts to the captive kings,

> Ile make ye roare, that earth may eccho foorth
> The far resounding torments ye sustaine,
> As when an heard of lusty Cymbrian Buls,
> Run mourning round about the Femals misse,
> And stung with furie of their following,
> Fill all the aire with troublous bellowing (3860-65)

the lines seem to be modelled on Orgoglio's bellowing as described by Spenser in *F. Q.* I. 8. 11.

> He lowdly brayd with beastly yelling sownd,
> That all the fieldes rebellowed againe:
> As great a noyse, as when in Cymbrian plaine
> An heard of bulles, whom kindly rage doth sting,
> Doe for the milky mothers want complaine.

A third Spenserian passage, Una's lament in *F. Q.* I. 7. 22-23, is reflected closely in various phrases here and there throughout Bajazet's speeches of lament at his overthrow. The parallel lines are:

---

[6] The Dedication is signed "C. M." The reasons for thinking it Marlowe's are given by Mark Eccles, *Marlowe in London* (1934), pp. 162 ff. The *D. N. B.* says that Watson was Fraunce's "closest literary associate." Probably Marlowe, as Watson's companion, was also acquainted with Fraunce, may even have read with him the manuscript *Faerie Queene*.

Tamb. 2040-43:

> O dreary Engines of my loathed sight,
> ...Why feed ye still on daies accursed beams.

F. Q. I. 7. 22:

> Ye dreary instruments of doleful sight,
> ...Why doe ye longer feed on loathed light.

And again:

Tamb. 2071-74:

> O highest Lamp of everliuing *Ioue,*
> Accursed day infected with my griefs,
> Hide now thy stained face in endles night,
> And shut the windowes of the lightsome heauens.

2083-84:

> Then let the stony dart of sencelesse colde
> Pierce through the center of my withered heart.

F. Q. I. 7. 23:

> O lightsome day, the lampe of highest Jove,
> ...Henceforth thy hated face for ever hyde,
> And shut up heavens windowes shyning wyde.

I. 7. 22:

> Now let the stony dart of sencelesse cold
> Perce to my hart, and pas through everie side
> And let eternall night so sad sight fro me hyde.

Briefer and less remarkable parallels are abundant. In the matter of alliteration, for example, Marlowe uses the phrase "*w*atery *w*ildernes" (*Tamb.* 3911), which is found in *F. Q.* I. 3. 32; and the phrase "*sw*olne with *w*rath" (*Tamb.* 525) which appears in *F. Q.* I. 11. 8. The phrase "*s*turdie *S*cythian thiefe" (*Tamb.* 44) applied to Tamburlaine may be a recollection of Spenser's "*s*tout and *s*turdie thief," Kirk-rapine. Spenser's line, "And Gehons golden *w*aues doe *w*ash continually" seems to echo at two points in *Tamburlaine:*

> For all the *w*ealth of Gehons golden *w*aues. (1904.)
> Which *w*asheth *Cyprus w*ith his brinish *w*aues. (3514.)

Likewise another line containing an allusion—"When *B*oreas doth *b*low full *b*itter *b*leake" (*F. Q.* I. 2. 33)—has echo at two points:

> Fearing the force of *B*oreas *b*oistrous *b*lasts. (*Tamb.* 668.)
> Beates on the regions with his *b*oysterous *b*lowes. (2395.)

Or we may compare:

> *F. Q.* II. 7. 36:
> And with *f*orst wind the *f*ewell did in*f*lame.
> *Tamb.* 2972:
> Now wants the *f*ewell that en*f*lamde his beames.

> *F. Q.* II. 3. 22:
> But *h*evenly pourtraict of bright angels *h*ew.
> *Tamb.* 232:
> But Lady, this faire face and *h*eauenly *h*ew.

The word "hew" here is one of a number of archaic words which appear in *Tamburlaine* and seem to suggest Spenser's influence.   Herr Schoeneich calls attention to the words "blubbered," "brent," "embost," "enchaced" (which occurs no less than six times in *Tamburlaine*), "parbreak," "pourtraid," and "ysprong."

The influence of imagery is more difficult to trace, since imagery generally suffers some transmutation in the process of unconscious borrowing, and also we cannot be sure that similarities of imagery are not due to poets' independent efforts.   For example, when Tamburlaine to describe his army uses the simile of an earthquake born of "windy exhalations" tilting within the earth (244-7), we may recall that Spenser has a like notion of earthquakes in a simile which he applies to the description of Paridell (*F. Q.* III. 9. 15); but the phraseology of the two poets is not particularly close.   A better parallel is offered when Tamburlaine boasts that he will

make the starres to melt
As if they were the teares of *Mahomet.* (3871.)

This may involve Marlowe's recollection from Spenser

That molten starres doe drop like weeping eyes. (*F. Q.* I. 6. 6.)

Or, again, when Tamburlaine boasts that

Where ere I come the fatall sisters sweat,
And griesly death by running to and fro,
To doo their ceassles homag to my sword (2236-38)

the image may well be a development of Spenser's

And thousand furies wait on wrathful sword. (*F. Q.* II. 2. 30.)

We can be more certain of direct influence when the phraseology is as close as in the following instances, where both poets are describing Jove's thunderbolts:

Enrold in flames, and smouldring dreriment. (*F. Q.* I. 8. 9.)
Enrolde in flames and fiery smouldering mistes. (*Tamb.* 618.)

What Marlowe gained by transforming the imagery of epic poetry into the stuff of dramatic spectacle can be illustrated by the scene of Tamburlaine's speech to the virgins of Damascus. The speech is probably founded on the lines in *F. Q.* I. 3. 9:

he gan feare
. . . For death sate on the point of that enchaunted speare.

The dramatic method makes it possible to vivify and repeat this simple image. Marlowe employs it as an opening and closing thrust in a dramatic speech in which the last drop of significance is squeezed from it, and it is made to illumine the intensity, the savagery, the fanaticism of Tamburlaine's mind:

Tamb.
Behold my sword, what see you at the point?
Virg.
Nothing but feare and fatall steele my Lord.
Tamb.
Your fearfull minds are thicke and mistie then,
For there sits Death, there sits imperious Death,
Keeping his circuit by the slicing edge.
But I am pleasde you shall not see him there,
He now is seated on my horsmens speares:
And on their points his fleshlesse bodie feedes.
Techelles, straight goe charge a few of them
To chardge these Dames, and shew my seruant death,
Sitting in scarlet on their armed speares. (1889-99.)

Pursuing further our study of Spenserian influence in *Tamburlaine,* we must next raise a larger question: is Spenser's poetry remembered by Marlowe simply for its verbal beauties? Or are there instances when Marlowe's indebtedness to Spenser includes also a sympathy with Spenser's moral philosophy? Literary influence can be a matter of ethical outlook as well as of lyric phraseology. If the imagery and diction of *Tamburlaine* indicate Spenser's influence, may not the characterization and action likewise owe something to Spenser?

If we observe closely the parallel passages from *Tamburlaine* and *The Faerier Queene* which Herr Schoeneich has assembled, we discover a fact which Schoeneich, except in one case, does not point out, namely that certain sections of *The Faerie Queene* have been much more drawn upon than others. *Tamburlaine* seems to echo particularly four sections of Spenser's poem: the episode of Orgoglio (*F. Q.* I. 7), of Mammon (II. 7), of the House of Pride (I. 4), and of Duessa's history (I. 7). Let us examine in turn each of these cantos.

From Canto 7 of Book I of *The Faerie Queene* we have already noted two major pieces of borrowing—the passage in which Tamburlaine likens his plume to "an almond tree ymounted high," and the passage in which Bajazet expresses his despair. Other echoes from this canto are less extended. But their significance is that taken together they contribute to the detailing of Tamburlaine's portrait. For example, the phrase, "Gehons golden waves," which names the birthplace of Una in *F. Q.* I. 7. 43, is used by Tamburlaine just after he has ordered death for the virgins of Damascus:

> I will not spare these proud Egyptians,
> Nor change my Martiall obseruations,
> For all the wealth of Gehons golden waues. (1902-04.)

The hero who thereby expresses appropriately his scorn of the wealth of Paradise, borrows further details of his character from Spenser's picture of Orgoglio (Spiritual Pride) in this same canto.

The following parallels should be noted. Orgoglio makes his appearance bellowing in such manner "That all the earth for terror seemed to shake" (stanza 7). Tamburlaine is "that proud Scythian" who

> with the thunder of his martial tooles
> Makes Earthquakes in the hearts of men and heauen. (2864-66.)

Orgoglio is

> An hideous geaunt, horrible and hye,
> That with his tallnesse seemd to threat the skye (Stanza 8)

while Tamburlaine is "of stature tall" (461) and

> so imbellished
> With Natures pride, and richest furniture
> His looks do menace heauen and dare the gods. (350-2.)

Further, Orgoglio is

> this monstrous masse of earthly slyme. (Stanza 9.)

And Tamburlaine is

> grosse and like the massie earth. (882.)

Orgoglio overcomes the Red Crosse Knight, but spares his life at the request of Duessa:

> Duessa loud to him gan crye,
> 'O great Orgoglio, greatest under skye,
> O hold thy mortall hand for ladies sake!
> Hold for my sake, and doe him not to dye,
> But vanquisht thine eternall bondslave make,
> And me, thy worthy meed, unto thy leman take.'
>
> He hearkned, and did stay from further harmes,
> To gayne so goodly guerdon as she spake. (Stanzas 14-15.)

Similarly, Tamburlaine spares the Souldan's life at the request of Zenocrate, remarking:

> Thy princely daughter here hath set thee free,
> She that hath calmde the furie of my sword,
> Which had ere this bin bathde in streames of blood. (2217-20.)

Turning from his fallen foe, Orgoglio honors Duessa with every earthly pomp:

> From that day forth Duessa was his deare,
> And highly honourd in his haughtie eye;
> He gave her gold and purple pall to weare,
> And triple crowne set on her head full hye. (Stanza 16.)

Similarly, Tamburlaine turns to a coronation ceremony in which Zenocrate is proclaimed Queen of Persia.

Secondly, if we consider next *F. Q.* II. 7, we find that Marlowe's portrait of Tamburlaine contains also certain details which echo features of Spenser's Mammon. Of course, since we are dealing here with the materials of a very broad morality tradition, we cannot say boldly that

Tamburlaine "copies" Mammon; we can simply show in how close agreement the authors have conceived these two characters. Mammon says:

> God of the world and worldlings I me call,
> Great Mammon, greatest god below the skye. (Stanza 8.)

This compares with Tamburlaine's notion that he is

> The Emperour of the world, and earthly God. (3524.)

Mammon, like Tamburlaine, makes great promises of wealth and power to those who will serve him. Mammon boasts specifically that

> Riches, renowne, and principality,
> Honour, estate, and all this worldes good,
> ...Fro me do flow ... (Stanza 8.)

Such lines may be said to be dramatized in *Tamb.* II. i. v-vi, when Tamburlaine receives from his followers their crowns and gives them back again as if he were the dispenser of all the world's goods. Mammon's accomplishments are enumerated by Guyon:

> realmes and rulers thou doest both confound,
> And loyal truth to treason doest incline:
> Witnesse the guiltlesse blood pourd oft on ground,
> The crowned often slaine, the slayer cround,
> The sacred diademe in peeces rent,
> And purple robe gored with many a wound;
> Castles surprizd, great cities sackt and brent:
> So mak'st thou kings, and gaynest wrongfull government.
> (Stanza 13.)

Activities of this very nature appear abundantly in the behavior of Tamburlaine. He persuades Cosroe to treachery, sheds the guiltless blood of the Damascus virgins, slays kings and crowns slayers, and is responsible, according to Callapine, for "Kingdomes made waste, braue cities sackt & burnt" (4359). When Spenser also tells us of Mammon that no "mortal steel" can "emperce his miscreated mould" (stanza 42), this detail particularly fits Mammon to be Tamburlaine's prototype, for Tamburlaine never receives wound at the hands of mortal men.

Also, there is in this same canto a most interesting parallel which no one seems to have noticed. Tamburlaine's attitude toward Zenocrate is exactly like that of Mammon's toward Philotime. Mammon thinks

> fayre Philotime
> The fairest wight that wonneth under skye
> ... Worthie of heven and hye felicitie
> From whence the gods have her for envy thrust. (Stanza 49.)

Similarly, Tamburlaine thinks that "divine Zenocrate" is so fair that all the angels of heaven ought to be waiting to welcome her to high felicity (2983 ff.). At the same time, like Mammon, he expresses the theory that her beauty is so great that it has made the gods envious:

> Now by the malice of the angry skies,
> Whose jealousy admits no second mate, [Zenocrate]
> Draws in the comfort of her latest breath.[7]

Turning next to Canto 4 of Book I of *The Faerie Queene,* we can find various bits of imagery in Spenser's pageant of the Seven Deadly Sins to parallel certain features of the dramatic action in Marlowe's play. Meander's words,

> We haue our Cammels laden all with gold (585)

---

[7] Zenocrate, to describe her dying breath, echoes a phrase from this same canto. Compare

F. Q. II. 7. 66: Gan sucke this vitall ayre into his brest.
Tamb. 3012: Hath suckt the measure of that vitall aire.

seem to be a recollection of Spenser's portrait of "greedy Avarice"

> Uppon a camell loaden all with gold. (Stanza 27.)

The prophecy by Orcanes that devils await Tamburlaine

> All brandishing their brands of quenchless fire (3529)

has verbal echoes of Spenser's portrait of Wrath:

> in his hand a burning brond he hath,
> The which he brandished about his hed. (Stanza 33.)

Tamburlaine's dream of a ride into Samarcand in a fiery coach drawn by "princely Eagles" is paralleled by Lucifera's stately ride in a golden coach drawn by peacocks. And Tamburlaine's notion that

> there my Pallace royal shall be plac'd:
> Whose shyning Turrets shal dismay the heauens (4090-91)

can be duplicated in Spenser's picture of the House of Pride:

> A stately pallace
> ...That purest skye with brightnesse they dismaid:
> High lifted up were many loftie towres. (Stanza 4.)

Finally, we can note that when Theridamas proposes to Olympia that

> Thou shalt be stately Queene of faire *Argier*,
> And cloth'd in costly cloath of massy gold,
> Vpon the marble turrets of my Court
> Sit like to *Venus* in her chaire of state,
> Commanding all thy princely eie desires (3920-24)

Schoeneich thinks the lines bear similarity to Spenser's picture of Lucifera:

High above all a cloth of state was spred,
And a rich throne, as bright as sunny day,
On which there sate, most brave embellished
With royall robes and gorgeous array,
A mayden queene, that shone as Titans ray,
In glistring gold and perelesse pretious stone. (Stanza 8.)

Spenser's description of Duessa's history in *F. Q.* I. 2.—
the fourth episode we have chosen for attention—is an important source for Marlowe's story of Zenocrate. This fact
was pointed out by Schoeneich, who has well summarized
the evidence.[8] Both Duessa and Zenocrate are beautiful
but inconstant ladies. Duessa is chosen by Spenser as the
appropriate companion of Sansfoy (i.e. "Atheist"), who
decks her out with many jewels and crowns and bells;
Zenocrate is offered similar pomp by "atheist" Tamburlaine.
When Duessa is captured from Sansfoy by the Red Crosse
Knight, she relates a story of her past life which seems to
have given Marlowe the story with which he endows
Zenocrate. The parallel details in the histories of Duessa
and of Zenocrate are summarized by Schoeneich:

1. Both are daughters of a mighty king, and each is betrothed to
a prospective king.
2. The weddings do not take place, in both instances for the
reason that the beloved princes are killed in battle against enemies.
3. The brides lament the death of the princes.
4. A journey undertaken for the purpose of seeking out the
beloved one (in the *F. Q.* it is only the body of the beloved one
that is sought for) results in both instances in the lady being taken
prisoner.
5. The captors are besought in vain to show pity.
6. Both ladies are forced to follow new protectors; they are
unhappy over their loss and call themselves wretched.

Then, as the histories of these two captive ladies further

---

[8] *Einfluss*, pp. 60-69.

unroll, there are other points of similarity. Duessa's captor "in his falsed fancy" considers her

> To be the fairest wight that lived yit;
> Which to expresse, he bends his gentle wit.   (Stanza 30.)

Tamburlaine likewise bestirs his wits to celebrate his captive's beauty. The result in both cases is that the ladies are won and grant their love to their captor. Spenser emphasizes Duessa's inconstancy by having her soon grant her love to a new captor, Orgoglio. Marlowe points out Zenocrate's inconstancy in the speeches of Agydas and in the words of Zenocrate herself. Even while her lover the prince of Arabia still lives, Zenocrate says:

> the change I vse condemns my faith,
> And makes my deeds infamous through the world.   (2172-73.)

Our study of Marlowe's indebtedness to Spenser indicates pretty clearly that Marlowe's recollections of *The Faerie Queene* were not always haphazard or of merely lyrical import. There are times, plainly, when Marlowe's modelling of his characters in *Tamburlaine* is helped by certain portraits in Spenser's moral allegory. Thus we have discovered in the drama's protagonist certain features of Spenser's Orgoglio and Mammon—even suggestions of Lucifera. For Zenocrate we have found an extended parallel in Duessa, and a minor parallel in Philotime. Such parallels, if we accept their evidence, obviously presume an interpretation of Marlowe's characters in accord with morality tradition. That is, we must assume that the dramatist intended Tamburlaine as an exhibit of Pride and Worldliness, and Zenocrate as an example of False Beauty and Love of Honor. We can think of Marlowe as using Spenser's type-characters as touchstones, to guide him in embellishing with universal significance the portraits of the personages in his drama.

It has often been remarked that Marlowe's characters of drama, like Spenser's characters of epic, are types rather than personalities. Mr. J. A. Symonds[9] complains that there is a carelessness of fine distinctions and of delicate gradations in Marlowe's sculptured colossi. "His characters are not so much human beings, with the complexity of human attributes combined in living personality, as types of humanity." The reason for this, I think we may say, is that Marlowe is following in Spenser's tradition of moral allegory, but using the drama rather than the epic as the carrier of moral philosophy.

[9] *Shakespeare's Predecessors in the English Drama* (Second ed., 1924), p. 484.

THE INFLUENCE OF SENECA

🏵 🏵

SENSATIONALISM is the most obvious feature of Seneca's dramas. It is what Kyd saw in Seneca; and, as Nashe remarked,[1] it provided Kyd "handfulls of tragical speeches." But Nashe's words make it clear that he and the university men resented this use of Seneca. We may be permitted to suppose that among Elizabethans there were roughly two schools of Senecans: the uneducated popular playwrights, including notably Kyd; and the university dramatists, including besides Nashe such men as Daniel, Greville, and Stirling. In which of these two camps would Marlowe belong? His affinity with the first group could be argued from the great popular success of *Tamburlaine,* and from the testimony of Kyd in 1593 that he and Marlowe had been writing together in the same room two years previously. But other facts would indicate ties with the second group: Marlowe's university training, his collaboration with Nashe, and his address in *Amintae Gaudia* to the Countess of Pembroke, patroness of the academic Senecans. Perhaps we should conclude that Marlowe belongs partly to both groups—learning from one group the importance of Senecan spectacle, sharing with the other group an interest in Senecan morality.

When we read *Tamburlaine* we observe, probably first of all, those characteristics which Cunliffe noted[2] as the distinguishing marks of Senecan drama—introspectiveness,

---

[1] See Nashe's "To the gentlemen students of both universities," prefixed to Greene's *Menaphon* (1589). Nashe does not name Kyd; but the reasons for judging that Kyd is the person against whom the attack is here directed are summarized by J. W. Cunliffe, *Early English Classical Tragedies* (Oxford, 1912), pp. xcv-xcvii.

[2] John W. Cunliffe, *The Influence of Seneca in Elizabethan Tragedy* (London, 1893), pp. 16-17.

sensationalism, rhetoric, extended descriptions, mythological allusions and other various evidences of erudition. Also we are aware that Marlowe, like Seneca, has charged the dramatic action with strong moral overtones. Marlowe has put heavy accent on such Senecan themes as fate, fearlessness, scorn of fortune, revenge, madness, misery, crime. What we might call the "morbid" in Seneca colors even the passages of comedy in *Tamburlaine*. There is no humor in Seneca, and equally there is no real mirth in *Tamburlaine*.[3] What comedy the play has is of a stark sort, taking the form of mockery; and the jesting is never playful without being also hideous.

Cunliffe's basic study of *The Influence of Seneca in Elizabethan Tragedy* concludes[4] that what Marlowe took over from Seneca was the Latin tragedian's bombast and violence, his exaggeration of expression and his horror of incident, but very few of the sage reflections with which Seneca adorned his plays. Are we to assume, then, that Marlowe was a popular playwright with little or no concern for Seneca's thought?

It is true, of course, that long passages of Choral wisdom such as appear in Seneca's plays have no exact duplicate in the modern dramatic method which Marlowe uses. Yet, at the same time, we observe in *Tamburlaine* what is very much like choral comment. One example is the sage reflection of Zenocrate beginning:

> Those that are proud of fickle Empery,
> And place their chiefest good in earthly pompe:
> Behold the Turke and his great Emperesse. (2134-36.)

It is remarkable, in fact, that the speeches of Marlowe's chief characters so frequently turn about moral reflections and predictions. Typical is the speech of Orcanes:

---

[3] This is true, at least, of our printed versions. Richard Jones, publisher of the 1590 text, tells us he has omitted "some fond and friuolous Iestures."
[4] Pp. 58-59.

Now, he that cals himself the scourge of *Ioue,*
The Emperour of the world, and earthly God,
Shal end the warlike progresse he intends,
And traueile hedlong to the lake of hell:
Where legions of deuils (knowing he must die
Here in *Natolia,* by your highnesse hands)
All brandishing their brands of quenchlesse fire,
Stretching their monstrous pawes, grin with their teeth,
And guard the gates to entertaine his soule. (3523-31.)

Or again, the following reflection by the King of Jerusalem is such commentary as a Chorus might have made:

Thy victories are growne so violent,
That shortly heauen, fild with the meteors
Of blood and fire thy tyrannies haue made,
Will poure down blood and fire on thy head:
Whose scalding drops wil pierce thy seething braines,
And with our bloods, reuenge our bloods on thee. (3814-19.)

Utterances such as these just quoted can hardly be explained solely as introspection. On consideration they appear, rather, as a series of moral bulletins, spoken in character, but having the larger purpose of choral comment on
the progress of the play's action. In Part I, when Tamburlaine mounts to his throne using Bajazet as a stepping-block,
he announces:

But ere I martch to wealthy *Persea,*
As was the fame of Clymenes brain-sicke sonne,
That almost brent the Axeltree of heauen,
So shall our swords, our lances and our shot
Fill all the aire with fiery meteors. (1491-96.)

The lines are an advertisement to the reader that the ethical
significance of Tamburlaine's action is to be comprehended
in the figure of Phaeton. The moral which is thereby im-
plied is the moral that is stated by the Chorus in Seneca's
Medea:

The youth who dared drive the everlasting chariot, heedless of his father's goal, himself caught the fire which in his madness he scattered o'er the sky.[5]

Tamburlaine speaking in character cannot, as a Chorus, draw the moral; but for the alert listener it is quite enough that the actor suggest it by announcing his Phaeton-like ambition.

The way in which Senecan imagery and situation can be used to heighten the moral significance of dramatic action will become clearer as we study in detail the evidence of Marlowe's borrowings. Our most important discovery is that Marlowe has constructed a great deal of Tamburlaine's character and action from the pattern of Seneca's Hercules. To begin with, let us note how allusions are used to make Tamburlaine appear as a second Hercules:

1) Theridamas compares Tamburlaine to Hercules the capturer of Cerberus:

> His fierie eies are fixt vpon the earth,
> As if he now deuis'd some Stratageme:
> Or meant to pierce *Auernas* darksome vaults. (353-5.)

2) Tamburlaine's breadth of shoulders is said to be such "as might mainely beare Olde Atlas Burthen" (464-5)—an allusion to one of the labors of Hercules.

3) In the curtain speech to Part I, Tamburlaine refers his action to the example of Hercules:

> Hang vp your weapons on *Alcides* poste,
> For *Tamburlaine* takes truce with al the world.

---

[5] Seneca here reads:

> ausus aeternos agitare currus
> immemor metae iuvenis paternae
> quos polo sparsit furiosus ignes
> ipse recepit. (599-602.)

In the text of this chapter I have thought best to quote from the modern English translation of the Loeb edition. We may be sure that Marlowe knew Seneca in the Latin and probably also in Newton's edition of *Seneca His Tenne Tragedies* (1581).

4) As Tamburlaine drives the captive kings in his chariot he makes a grand comparison of himself with Hercules:

> The headstrong Iades of *Thrace, Alcides* tam'd
> That King *Egeus* fed with humaine flesh,
> And made so wanton that they knew their strengths,
> Were not subdew'd with valor more diuine,
> Than you by this vnconquered arme of mine. (3991-95.)

5) Bajazet takes delight in the Herculean lineaments of his sons. He announces that Zabina is

>   . mother of three brauer boies,
> Than *Hercules,* that in his infancie
> Did pash the iawes of Serpents venomous:
> Whose hands are made to gripe a warlike Lance. (1201-04.)

Though Tamburlaine does not employ this allusion, it is plain that a similarly martial pattern is what he too desires in his sons. He is troubled that Zenocrate's sons seem to have "fingers made to quauer on a lute" (2598).

Besides making these direct allusions to Hercules, Marlowe has allowed Tamburlaine's career to conform at a great many points with that of Seneca's pictures of Hercules. A full list of the parallel features will serve to indicate their significance:[6]

1) Tamburlaine calls himself Scourge of God. Similarly Hercules, addressing Jove, calls himself: "I thy son, who on earth have been in place of thy bolt and lightning flash." [7]

2) Tamburlaine regards his own life as more important than the frame of heaven. He says:

---

[6] Some of the parallels have been noted by A. Brandl in the *Göttingische gelehrte Anzeigen,* XVIII (1891), 721-2; and more recently by Mario Praz in his lecture on "Machiavelli and the Elizabethans," *Proceedings of the British Academy,* XIV (1928), 71. Praz, who seems to be observing independently and unaware of Brandl's earlier discussion, presents a list of parallels practically the same as Brandl's. I am indebted to the suggestions of Brandl and Praz for about half of the parallels which I here present.

[7]   ille qui pro fulmine
tuisque facibus natus in terris oram. (*Herc. Oet.* 1143-44.)

> The chiefest God first moouer of that Sphere,
> Enchac'd with thousands euer shining lamps,
> Will sooner burne the glorious frame of Heauen,
> Then it should so conspire my ouerthrow. (1452-55.)

Somewhat similarly Hercules, finding himself striken with death, thinks the whole frame of heaven should be sacrificed:

> Now, father, were it fitting to restore blind chaos; now this side and that should heaven's frame be burst and both poles rent asunder. Why dost thou spare the stars? Thou art losing Hercules, O father.[8]

It is an attitude which is also expressed during Tamburlaine's sickness by Theridamas:

> Fal starres that gouerne his natiuity,
> And sommon al the shining lamps of heauen
> To cast their bootlesse fires to the earth. (4394-96.)

3) Both heroes are overcome not in battle, but by an enemy within their flesh which they are powerless to combat. This makes death doubly bitter for them. Both challenge death. Tamburlaine cries:

> See where my slaue, the vglie monster death
> ... Stands aiming at me with his murthering dart,
> Who flees away at euery glance I giue,
> And when I look away, comes stealing on:
> Villaine away . . . (4459-64).

Hercules calls out:

> O pest, whate'er thou art that lurkest in my vitals, come forth—
> Why dost attack me with a hidden smart? [9]

---

[8]   nunc, pater, caecum chaos
reddi decebat, hinc et hinc compagibus
ruptis uterque debuit frangi polus.
quid parcis astris? Herculem amittis, pater. (*H. O.* 1134-37.)

[9]   Quaecumque pestis viscere in nostro lates,
procede—quid me vulnere occulto petis? (*H. O.* 1249-50.)

4) The sickness of Tamburlaine and of Hercules is of a similar sort: a hotness and a dryness which sucks up the blood. Tamburlaine's physician tells him:

> Your vaines are full of accidentall heat,
> Whereby the moisture of your blood is dried. (4476-77.)

And Hercules describes his sickness:

> My heart, once filled with pulsing streams of blood, hotly distends the parched fibres of my lungs; my liver glows, its bile dried quite away, and a slow fire has exhausted all my blood.[10]

5) Neither Hercules nor Tamburlaine can quite believe that he, who has accomplished so many mighty deeds, should be overthrown. Tamburlaine asks:

> Shall sickness prooue me now to be a man,
> That haue bene tearm'd the terror of the world? (4436-37.)

And Hercules comments in amazement:

> Lo I, who have escaped from death, who scorned the styx, who through the midst of Lethe's pool have returned with spoil, at sight whereof Titan was almost flung from his falling car, I, whose presence three realms of gods have felt, am perishing.[11]

Both heroes subsequently make long speeches recounting the number of their conquests.

6) Tamburlaine's friends in calling on heaven for help use arguments similar to those of Hercules. Hercules emphasizes the shame of his overthrow (*H. O.* 1179), and

---

10   sanguinis quondam capax
tumidi igne cor pulmonis arentes fibras
distendit, ardet felle siccato iecur
totumque lentus sanguinem avexit vapor.   (*H. O.* 1220-23.)

11   Ego qui relicta morte, contempta styge
per media Lethes stagna cum spolio redi
quo paene lapsis excidit Titan equis,
ego quem deorum regna senserunt tria,
morior. (*H. O.* 1161-65.)

prophesies that his death will put heaven in danger of invasion by the forces of hell (*H. O.* 1145 ff.). Tamburlaine's friends plead his usefulness as Heaven's instrument against devils (4420 ff.) and emphasize the shame involved in his overthrow. They conclude:

> For if he die, thy glorie is disgrac'd,
> Earth droopes and saies that hel in heauen is plac'd.

So far we have observed no impiety. The pleas of Hercules are not impious;[12] nor are the pleas of Tamburlaine's friends. Tamburlaine's own pleas, however, are a different matter. His callings upon Heaven are a command rather than a plea:

> *Theridamas,* haste to the court of *Ioue,*
> Will him to send *Apollo* hether straight,
> To cure me, or Ile fetch him downe my selfe. (4453-55.)

For this impious element in Tamburlaine's character we must turn to the Hercules of *Hercules Furens,* not the Hercules of *Hercules Oetaeus.*

7) Tamburlaine's impiety is modelled on the mad Titanism of *Hercules Furens* (955 ff.). Here Hercules decides that having subdued the threefold world of the earth, the seas, and the infernal realms, the one task remaining worthy of him is to scale the heavens. He believes that he is the darling of the gods, that "the whole company of the gods of their own will summons me, and opens wide the door of heaven." But he lets us know that he is not dependent on their favor. If they refuse to unbar the sky and take him in he will "carry off the doors of stubborn heaven." He will lead the Titans to war; and in his rage he'll use rocks,

---

[12] In fact, he emphasizes his piety in the lines:

> non minus caelum mihi
> asserere potui; dum patrem verum puto,
> caelo peperci. (*H. O.* 1302-04.)

There is no such restraint in Tamburlaine.

woods, and ridges to "construct a highway to the realms above." Amphitryon advises him: "Have done with these horrible imaginings! Repress the mad fury of thy proud heart, no longer sane." Such counsel, we realize, could with equal appropriateness be addressed to Tamburlaine. Like Hercules, Tamburlaine delights to think of himself as "Emperour of the three fold world" (*Tamb.* 4097), yet cannot rest satisfied. And since Tamburlaine's outbursts of Titanism both on the occasion of Zenocrate's death and of his own are unhistorical episodes, we may be practically certain that Marlowe in construcing them had in mind this passage in *Hercules Furens*.[13]

8) When his madness is upon him, Hercules kills his own children. This may have helped suggest to Marlowe the incident in which Tamburlaine kills his son Calyphas. On that occasion Tamburlaine's virtual madness is pointed out to us by the King of Jerusalem who speaks of Tamburlaine's "seething braines."

9) Both Hercules and Tamburlaine are proud men whom the gods punish by letting them war against themselves. Juno calls Hercules "proud one" (*superbe*) and says:

Dost then seek Alcides' match? None is there save himself; now with himself let him war.[14]

To fulfill this plan Juno calls up Crime, Impiety, Error, and Madness. These attackers are, in Marlowe's play too, the only enemies that can in any sense defeat Tamburlaine. The Scourge of kingdoms is shown as scourging himself first on the occasion of Zenocrate's death:

> Behold me here diuine *Zenocrate,*
> Rauing, impatient, desperate and mad,
> Breaking my steeled lance, with which I burst

---

[13] Possibly he also remembered a similar passage in *Medea* (424 ff.).

[14]   quaeris Alcidae parem?
nemo est nisi ipse; bella iam secum gerat. (*H. F.* 84-85.)

The rusty beames of *Ianus* Temple doores,
Letting out death and tyrannising war:
To martch with me vnder this bloody flag.   (3079-84.)

In still other ways we are permitted to see that Tamburlaine's violence wars against himself. When he kills his son
Calyphas, the King of Soria prophesies that such anger
will dry up and consume Tamburlaine's blood—a prediction
which is not long in being fulfilled. When at his death
Tamburlaine wars against the gods he succeeds only in
increasing the malady which the physician calls "the fury
of your fit."

10) Further similarities of some importance are: 1) both
heroes in the course of their histories are a rod for punishing
wicked men—Hercules destroys the tyrant Lycus, and Tamburlaine overthrows the tyrant Bajazet; 2) both heroes claim
a command over hell—Hercules by virtue of his capture of
Cerberus, Tamburlaine because he believes the inhabitants
of hell "doo their ceassles homag to my sword" (2238).

This wealth of parallel material indicates beyond doubt
that Marlowe has employed Seneca's Hercules as a type for
Tamburlaine. Beyond its literary importance the fact has
moral significance, for it is a way of telling us that Tamburlaine is to be held in the same light as Hercules. Hercules, we know, was considered by Seneca as a type, like
Alexander, of the insatiable conqueror who falls victim to
his own covetousness.[15] Renaissance authors condemned
Hercules to Hell along with Alexander and Ninus and other
antique champions. It is significant that when Burton wants
to describe "that grand sin of atheism and impiety" he
compares it (quoting Melanchton) to the ravings of Hercules.[16]

Among other instances in *Tamburlaine* where Seneca can

---

[15] *On Benefits*, VII. ii. 6 - iii. 1.
[16] *Anatomy of Melancholy*, III. iv. 2. 1.

be cited as a probable source of influence, the most remarkable is the banquet scene of *Tamb*. I. IV. iv. For sheer fiendishness this banquet compares well with that in Seneca's *Thyestes*. Tamburlaine, like Atreus, triumphs over his enemy with ridiculous ease. As Atreus caused Thyestes to eat his own sons and drink their blood, so here Tamburlaine invites Bajazet to make a meal either of his own flesh or of that of his wife Zabina:

> Sirra, why fall you not too, are you so daintily brought vp, you cannot eat your owne flesh?

Usumcasane suggests:

> Nay, twere better he kild his wife, & then she shall be sure not to be staru'd, & he be prouided for a moneths victuall before hand.

To which Tamburlaine replies:

> Here is my dagger, dispatch her while she is fat, for if she liue but a while longer, shee will fall into a consumption with freatting, and then she will not bee worth the eating.

Atreus' crime, too incredible for stage presentation, is thus adopted by Marlowe in a less bloody but no less dramatically effective form. Without cluttering the stage with human mincemeat, Marlowe is able to present imaginatively the Atreus-like quality of Tamburlaine's mind. Like Atreus, Tamburlaine is not interested in killing his enemy, but only in torturing him. Like Thyestes, Bajazet cannot understand how his hellish torturer can go unpunished, and the situation drives him to despair. Seneca has Atreus compare his crime to the banquet which Procne served the king of Thrace. Marlowe has Zabina say:

> And may this banquet prooue as omenous,
> As *Prognes* to th'adulterous Thracian King,
> That fed vpon the substance of his child. (1661-63.)

Another instance of probable Senecan influence is the attention which Marlowe gives to the theme of hereditary sin, so prominent in Seneca's dramas. We behold Tamburlaine indoctrinating his sons with his own martial spirit and binding them by a covenant of blood (the devil's covenant) to be Scourges of God, even as he. Then, at the very end of the drama, Tamburlaine's legacy to his sons is again emphasized. The Scourge says:

> But sons, this subiect not of force enough,
> To hold the fiery spirit it containes,
> Must part, imparting his impressions,
> By eqyall portions into both your breasts:
> My flesh deuided in your precious shapes,
> Shal still retaine my spirit, though I die,
> And liue in all your seedes immortally.   (4561-67.)

These passages which deal with Tamburlaine's gift to his sons of his own fiery, destructive spirit may very well owe something to a passage in Seneca's *Phoenissae,* where Oedipus talks ironically of the legacy he has given his sons:

'Tis from my crimes they seek their pattern, 'tis my example they follow now. I praise them and gladly acknowledge them as sons; I urge them on to do something worthy of such a father. Go on, dear offspring, prove your noble breeding by your deeds; surpass my fame and praises and do some deed whereat your father may rejoice that he has lived till now. You will do it, I know: of such mind were you born; no trivial, no common crime can such high birth perform. Forward your arms! With torches have at your household gods . . . confound all things, hurry all to destruction; on all sides throw down the walls, raze them to the ground; bury the gods beneath their own temples; the defiled deities of your hearths melt in the fire, and let our whole house from its foundation fall . . . (331 ff.).

Seneca's influence in *Tamburlaine* can be said, in summary, to be a matter both of rhetoric and of moral philosophy. We can hardly doubt but that the language of *Tamburlaine* is richer because of the classical allusion and the grandeur of hyperbole which Marlowe found in Seneca. Neither can we fail to see that Marlowe drew upon Seneca for certain type-situations which enlarge the plot of *Tamburlaine* and amplify its moral import.

Allan H. Gilbert has well observed [17] that in one respect the Elizabethans did not follow Seneca. Seneca's subjects, except in the *Octavia,* are from mythology; the dramatists of the Renaissance preferred history. Lord Stirling, for example, thought it "more agreeable with the Gravity of a Tragedy, that it be grounded upon a true History, where the Greatness of a known Person urging Regard doth work the more powerfully upon the Affections."

Marlowe, like Stirling, grounds his drama in history. But he embellishes history by the aid of Seneca. He does not copy Senecan method slavishly as Stirling does; yet neither does he debase both Seneca and history as Kyd does. I should say that he uses Seneca so to highlight historical tragedy that it becomes morality drama. The spectacle astounds—but in order to interpret. Marlowe is aware that history if it is to take on meaning must be penetrated by the supernatural. Moreover—and in this he belongs with the Reformation humanists—his supernatural is more Senecan than specifically Christian. *Tamburlaine* is an important mid-link between the academic drama of the Senecans and the popular drama of Shakespeare.

---

[17] "Seneca and the Criticism of Elizabethan Tragedy," *Philological Quarterly,* XIII (1934), 373.

THE INFLUENCE OF MACHIAVELLI

❦ ❦

THE dying Robert Greene in a reference commonly thought to be to Marlowe asked accusingly: "Is it pestilent Machiuilian pollicie thou hast studied?"[1] Modern students of Marlowe answer this query in the affirmative. Edward Meyer, for example, in his well-known study of *Machiavelli and the Elizabethan Drama* gives us the judgment that Marlowe

had studied Machiavelli with a vengeance: and it may be stated as an absolute certainty, that had the "Principe" never been written, his three great heroes would not have been drawn with such gigantic strokes.[2]

Marlowe plainly declares his great interest in Machiavelli in *The Jew of Malta*. But critics have been mistaken, I think, in supposing that Marlowe in his own person is a champion of the Machiavellianism he there so dramatically presents. On the contrary, Marlowe belongs almost certainly in the camp with Gentillet. *The Jew* sets forth the Florentine's doctrines with typical Huguenot irony. Machiavelli himself is brought on stage in the Prologue to declare that his spirit lives on in the Duke of Guise—who in Mar-

---

[1] *Groatsworth of Wit*, ed. Grosart, XII, 142. The typical Elizabethan view of Machiavelli is represented in Greene's comment: "What are his rules but meere confused mockeries, able to extirpate in small time, the generation of mankinde."

[2] Pp. 33-34 (Weimar, 1897). See also W. J. Courthope, *A History of English Poetry* (London, 1920), II, 405 and 421; and my discussion, above, pp. 4-6, of the views of T. M. Pearce and John Bakeless. The only show of dissenting opinion is by Miss Leslie Spence in "Tamburlaine and Marlowe," *P. M. L. A.*, XLII (1927), 616. Miss Spence thinks that the historical sources, together with Seneca's influence, are enough to account for Tamburlaine's extraordinary energy, and that the vigor of Marlowe's hero has no necessary connection with Machiavelli's *Prince*. The main point in Miss Spence's brief argument will be considered hereafter (see my footnote 9).

lowe's *Massacre at Paris* appears as the murderer of the Huguenots, a hypocritical papist, a treacherous plotter against his king, and a ruthless climber who thinks of himself as a second Caesar. Can we suppose Marlowe rebel enough to have thought such action virtuous? Critics who believe that Marlowe is a disciple of Machiavelli are driven to suppose that the dramatist is hiding a secret admiration for the wicked doctrines at the same time that he is caricaturing them for the entertainment of his audience. The more natural conclusion, however, is that Marlowe—like other moralists of his day—takes imaginative pleasure in advertising the odious character of this Italian-born "atheism." He certainly makes brilliant point of the Guise's wickedness when he has the French king say:

> Did he not draw a sorte of English priestes
> From Doway to the Seminary at Remes? (*Massacre,* 1042-43.)

These lines strike at the familiar *bête-noire* of English Protestants—Machiavellian papistry.

It has been noted that Gabriel Harvey, writing two years before Marlowe's arrival at Cambridge, makes much ado of the interest taken in Machiavelli's writing by the students at the university.[3] And we know that Harvey himself published in 1578 a Latin poem intended to exhibit the evil of the Florentine's teachings. In particular, the line "Aut nihil, aut Caesar: noster Alumnus erat" is thought by Meyer[4] to have suggested Marlowe's "What right had *Caesar* to the Empire?" in the Prologue to *The Jew.* But there are other aspects, too, of Harvey's poem which seem to anticipate Marlowe's drama. Machiavelli is brought forward to boast that he is king of kings and that no one reigns who does not follow his dogma. He then proclaims the following doc-

---

[3] See E. J. F. Scott, *Letter-book of Gabriel Harvey* (Westminster, 1884), pp. 79-80.
[4] *Machiavelli,* p. 23.

trine: 1) a delight in wars, camps, scepters, and kingdoms; 2) an aspiration which is satisfied with nothing "mediocre"; 3) the acceptance of cruelty and violence as his God. But these, we realize, are exactly the themes which Marlowe displays in Tamburlaine too. Particularly do we think of Tamburlaine when Harvey's monster calls attention to the fury that dwells in his eyes (Ecce oculos: Furor ijs habitat).

There is every reason why Marlowe should have found Machiavelli useful to him in writing *Tamburlaine.* The dramatist faced the task of making credible the amazing rise and invincible rule of an upstart prince. Machiavelli's *Prince* offered the perfect guidebook. There Marlowe could find a consistent pattern of political philosophy, strategy, and behavior with which to endow his pagan hero. Indeed, we might expect the dramatist to use *The Prince* rather closely and directly for *Tamburlaine,* whereas for drawing the businessman-villain Barabas he need have had no guide other than the popular notions regarding Machiavelli.

Our expectations are confirmed by the many parallels that can be adduced between *The Prince* and *Tamburlaine.* Professor Brandl many years ago noted the following:[5]

1) Mycetes, the weak Persian king, serves as illustration of the hereditary prince, who, according to Machiavelli (*Prince,* chap. 2), can lose the crown only if an unusual outside power advances and the prince has made himself hated because of his extravagant vices. Mycetes is threatened from without by the Turks and Tartars; within, he has aroused mistrust by his tyrannical and silly show of power. (*Tamb.* I. i.)

2) According to Machiavelli, seizure of the throne, however much infamy may attend it, is nothing unnatural. But it is shameful to be overthrown; and overthrow comes to the man whose own strength does not suffice or who calls in

---

[5] *Göttingische gelehrte Anzeigen,* XVIII (1891), 718-19.

a very powerful friend and depends on fortune. In this class Cosroe belongs. He is able to usurp the crown, because he proceeds, in accord with Machiavellian precept (*Prince* 3, 6), to use fine words to win needed support. But then, without sufficient strength of his own, he entrusts himself to the "approved Fortunes" of Tamburlaine, whom he supposes he can employ as an ally; but the Giant, once he has used Cosroe, shakes him off and brings about his death.

3) According to Machiavelli, Fortune offers merely the opportunity for success; success itself comes to the man who has the personality and greatness of spirit to command his supporters at all times. Tamburlaine fits this ideal. He has self-confidence. He is "his fortune's master." His acts for establishing his power accord with various of Machiavelli's recommendations to the tyrant: the suppression of the envious, the use of might mixed with magnanimity and craft, constant readiness for battle, continual conquest. Dying in bed, Tamburlaine leaves his sons a secure kingdom— the highest triumph of the Machiavellian upstart—and also the secret of his success in the warning that they, like himself, must keep full of fiery thoughts if they wish to avoid overthrow at the hand of "proud rebelling Jades."

But Professor Brandl's parallels can, I find, be widely supplemented and extended. I would add the following:

1) It is Machiavelli's famous dictum (*Prince* 18, 19) that a successful prince must act the part of the Lion and of the Fox. Early in Marlowe's drama Tamburlaine is likened to a lion (*Tamb.* 248) and to a fox (*Tamb.* 39).

2) Tamburlaine's policies accord with Machiavelli's advice (*Prince* 19) regarding the way a prince should behave to gain a reputation. The prince, says Machiavelli, must exhibit himself in rare trials of heroic action, and he must continually contrive great matters, so as never to give his followers leisure to rest and thus to plot against him. The acts of Tamburlaine observe these rules. He devotes himself to

the display of heroic deeds [6] and proud boasts, and he keeps his men on the move by projecting before them ever-new campaigns of action. Also, according to Machiavelli, the prince must show himself a lover of virtue and of the Arts. Tamburlaine shows himself so; he captivates us all by his frequent speeches proclaiming a love of virtue, beauty, poetry, and music.[7] Additionally, we read in Machiavelli that in order to spread abroad a fame of his magnificence and worthiness a prince ought to entertain the people with feasts and spectacles (*con le feste e spettaculi*). Tamburlaine's acts obey this injunction too: in Part I he banquets his men during the siege of Damascus; and in Part II when his lieutenants return from successful campaigns he announces a luxurious feast. To entertain his men further, Tamburlaine carries on spectacular jests with various of his humbled adversaries—the crown-loving Mycetes, the encaged Turk, and the chariot-drawing kings. That Tamburlaine is interested in the fame which he will get by such actions seems to be indicated when he says:

> The ages that shall talk of *Tamburlain*,
> Euen from this day to *Platoes* wondrous yeare,
> Shall talke how I handled *Baiazeth*. (1539-41.)

Elsewhere he announces that he means to "be renown'd as neuer Emperours were" (*Tamb.* 1779), and he looks forward to the day when

> my name and honor shall be spread,
> As far as *Boreas* claps his brazen wings,
> Or faire *Bootes* sends his cheereful light. (400-3.)

---

[6] Note particularly the exhibition of heroism early in the drama when Tamburlaine speaks to his followers before going to encounter Theridamas:

> Keep all your standings, and stir not a foote,
> My selfe will bide the danger of the brunt. (346-7.)

The episode does not occur in the histories.

[7] See *Tamb.* 1769, 1941 ff., 2620, 2994 ff.

Machiavelli's ideal prince could hardly have had a more zealous concern for his fame.

3) Machiavelli stresses the point that a successful prince must develop certain attractive qualities of character. The qualities in Tamburlaine's character which charm the modern reader—the hero's frequent magnanimity in speech and action, his liberality, his show of pity and of religion—are qualities which Machiavelli prescribes for the prince. We remember, for example, that after the battle with Bajazet, and again after the defeat of the four kings in Part II of the drama, Tamburlaine liberally shares the spoil with his men. This action may be compared with Machiavelli's advice concerning Liberality:

> And that Prince that goes abroad with his army, and feeds upon prey, and spoyle, and tributes, and hath the disposing of that which belongs to others, necessarily should use this liberality; otherwise would his soldiers never follow him; and of that which is neither thine, nor thy subjects, thou mayest well be a free giver, as were Cyrus, Caesar and Alexander; for the spending of that which is another's takes not away thy reputation, but rather adds to it . . .[8]

Elsewhere (*Prince* 18) Machiavelli insists that the prince must carefully cultivate the appearance of pity, faith, integrity, humanity, and religion; that he must "never let fall any words, but what are seasoned with the five above written qualities." When the prince is campaigning and has a multitude of soldiers under him he should then pay no attention at all to a reputation for cruelty (*Prince* 17); but at all other times he must take care not to be too cruel and ferocious, lest he incur the hate or contempt of his subjects, which is the ruin of Emperors. Heliogabalus, Macrinus, and Julian,

---

[8] *Prince* 16. I quote the earliest published English translation, by Edward Dacres in 1640 (reprinted in Tudor Translations, London, 1905). Dacres comments significantly: "liberality is to last no longer than while he [the prince] is in the way to some designe: which . . . is not really a reward of vertue how ere it seems; but a bait and lure to bring birds to the net."

being entirely despicable, came to speedy ends (*Prince* 19). But Ferdinand of Aragon became the foremost monarch of Christendom by adopting a course of pious cruelty, undertaking great enterprises always under the pretext of religion (*Prince* 21). These doctrines of Machiavelli can be used to account for a number of Tamburlaine's acts. We note that whereas Tamburlaine is mercilessly cruel to enemies, he treats his followers with consideration and is notably humane toward Zenocrate. His great enterprises have, too, a religious pretext: for he is, he proclaims, a divinely appointed "Scourge of God." Also he knows how to make a charmingly magnanimous speech of pity to the virgins of Damascus, whom he means to slaughter.

Machiavelli in his emphasis on the milder qualities of a prince's character goes so far as to say (*Prince* 8) that a prince who, like Agathocles, is utterly without faith, pity, and religion, cannot be said to have *virtue;* and that although such a prince may gain dominion, he cannot gain *glory.* In other words, only virtue gives glory; and virtue must be defined to include, in addition to might and craft, a measure of humane culture. Machiavelli's attitude at this point should be compared with Tamburlaine's well-known pronouncement that "Vertue solely is the sum of glorie." [9]

---

[9] At this point the reader needs to make a distinction between the Machiavellian doctrine elaborated in *The Prince* and Machiavellian doctrine as it was exaggerated in Gentillet's *Contre-Machiavel* (1576) and in Elizabethan ballad literature. In *The Prince,* as we see, the ruler is told plainly to acquire attractive qualities of character; whereas in popular Anti-Machiavellian literature he is seen always as following axioms more obviously villainous. Meyer holds, p. 39, that *Tamburlaine* has no trace of popular Machiavellianism, whereas Barabas is "drawn from popular prejudice based on Gentillet and not from Marlowe's own study." Meyer's antithesis is, I think, too sharp; yet it seems correct to say that Marlowe makes a more direct use of *The Prince* in *Tamburlaine* than in *The Jew.* Failure to take into account this difference is responsible, I think, for Miss Spence's misjudgment (see Footnote 2) that Tamburlaine cannot be Machiavellian because he has attractive qualities. The hero's show of fairness in challenging Cosroe, which Miss Spence cites as evidence of un-Machiavellian behavior, actually argues the truest sort of Machiavellianism—a cultured, rather than a crude, craftiness.

4) The qualities of character which Machiavelli denounces in a prince are those which Tamburlaine denounces in training his sons. Machiavelli tells the prince (*Prince* 19)[10] to shun weakness, faint-heartedness, effeminacy, and delicacy. He advises the prince to take care that his actions show magnanimity, courage, gravity, and valor. Tamburlaine, instructing his sons (*Tamb.* II. i. iv.) how they may "shine in compleat vertue," insists that they bear "A mind couragious and inuincible." He dislikes their dainty looks, which argue he thinks a "want of courage and of wit." The slothful and delicate Calyphas is slain by his wrathful father, who cannot tolerate such "follie, sloth, and damned idlenesse" (*Tamb.* II. iv. i.). Earlier in the play, when Tamburlaine makes his famous speech in praise of poetry, he feels it necessary to justify himself against the anticipated censure that he is harboring "thoughts effeminate and faint."

5) The discipline of Tamburlaine's camp accords with Machiavelli's precepts for the prince. Machiavelli advises the prince to maintain diligently the practice of the art of war (chap. 14), to abstain from taking the goods or the wives of his followers (chap. 17), and to make his word stand irrevocable, so that no man may think to turn or wind him about (chap. 19). In Marlowe's drama the first of these precepts is illustrated by Tamburlaine's care for the training of his sons; the second, by the fact that Tamburlaine never robs his followers; the third, in his proclamation to the virgins of Damascus that his commands are

> as peremptory
> As wrathful Planets, death, or destinie.

Machiavelli adds, however, (chap. 18) that princes commonly effect great matters by keeping small reckoning of

---

[10] See also Eduard W. Mayer, *Machiavellis Geschichtsauffassung und sein Begriff Virtù* (Munich, 1912), p. 21.

their word: the prince must know how to wind others about. This finds illustration when Tamburlaine effects his own rise by treachery to Cosroe. As an astute prince Tamburlaine knows when to break his word, as well as when to proclaim his word's irrevocability.

6) Machiavelli's view of the relative importance of Fortune and of Virtue seems to be reflected in *Tamburlaine*. Marlowe's hero is successful both because of his Fortune and because of his Virtue. But he speaks contemptuously of Fortune, boasting that with his hand he turns Fortune's wheel about (*Tamb.* 370); while he says admiringly that

> Vertue solely is the sum of glorie
> And fashions men with true nobility. (1970-71.)

This agrees with Machiavelli's view that Virtue and Fortune co-operate in a man's success, but that they are fundamentally opposed to each other.[11] The great men of history, Machiavelli points out, had no help from Fortune other than the occasion, which presented them with the matter wherein they might introduce what form they pleased. It is true that without the occasion the virtue of their mind had been extinguished; but without virtue the occasion had been offered in vain. In Marlowe's drama illustration of this point is given when Fortune gives Cosroe the occasion to rise to power. Menaphon says to him:

> Fortune giues you opportunity
> To gaine the tytle of a Conquerour
> By curing of this maimed Emperie. (*Tamb.* 132-4.)

Cosroe seizes his Fortune; but then his rise soon comes to

---

[11] See Mayer, *Machiavellis Geschichtsauffassung*, p. 17. Mayer finds the opposition of Virtue and Fortune expressed 12 times in *The Prince*, 16 times in the *Discourses*.

ruin because he lacks the might and courage of Machiavellian Virtue. Tamburlaine, aided by Fortune, has also *virtù*.[12] These parallels are evidence that Marlowe's reliance on *The Prince* was conscious and direct.[13] But this is not to say that Machiavelli's book was Marlowe's only or chief extra-historical source for the episode and action with which he transformed a rather bare history into richly tapestried drama. Perhaps the most interesting problem of all is that of the relationship of the various layers of influence, which we have come to see are superimposed one on another in the composite work of Marlowe's art. Machiavelli's principal importance is as a supplement to Seneca. Mr. C. V. Boyer has aptly written:

Marlowe and his fellow-dramatists probably felt themselves strongly supported by the authority of Seneca once they decided to develop the villain-hero type. But a far more definite influence than even that of Seneca was affecting Marlowe; an influence that accounts specifically, not for the villain as hero, but for the type of villain chosen as hero. As if to assist the dramatist in baring the motives that underlay the conduct of powerful and faithless princes, there aptly appeared certain works of and about Machiavelli, in which the principles of villainy were so carefully outlined that wickedness in high places was thereafter as explicable as goodness itself.[14]

---

[12] Tamburlaine "is evidently meant to be the incarnation of *virtù*" (Court-hope, II, 405). For a discussion of Machiavellian *virtù*, see Mayer. *Virtù* is wholly a natural quality, consisting of physical and mental might. Mayer, p. 16, points out that in Dante *virtù* is attributed to Satan, as well as to the divine power that rules the world.

[13] We must recognize, of course, that some of Machiavelli's counsels more or less repeat precepts given by various earlier authors in a long tradition of books of Advice to Princes. In Aristotle's *Politics*, for example, where the tyrant is advised how to gain a reputation, we find the injunction to respect the property and wives of subjects and to keep subjects ever stirred up in wars that they may have no leisure to think evil of their ruler. In fact, L. A. Burd in his edition of *The Prince* (Oxford, 1891), p. 289, holds that Machiavelli's originality consists simply in modifying the traditional idea of the Greek tyrant so as to make it the ideal of a new prince. See also A. H. Gilbert, *Machiavelli's "Prince" and its Forerunners* (Duke Univ. Press, 1938).

[14] *The Villain as Hero in Elizabethan Tragedy* (1914), pp. 29-30. See also Brandl, p. 719; and Praz's discussion, pp. 63-69, of the Machiavellianism of Cinthio's dramas.

The central contribution of Machiavelli was his doctrine of *virtù*. This furnished an intoxicating philosophy whereby the wooden tyrant inherited from Senecan drama could be enlivened, and his acts endowed with vital motives impelling tragic behavior. The new Machiavellian type of tyrant, represented in Tamburlaine, is a hero inspirited with a pagan religion; he is an anti-Christ. His most extravagant actions have a preternatural vitality. He is dynamic in a manner impossible for Spenser's Vices or Seneca's puppet orators.

TAMBURLAINE'S HUMOUR

❧ ❧

T WO articles some years ago by Carroll Camden[1] pointed out, what we ought to have suspected, that Marlowe was well acquainted with Renaissance philosophy regarding humours. When Tamburlaine remarks about

> Nature that fram'd vs of foure Elements,
> Warring within our breasts for regiment, (869-70)

it is pretty certain that Marlowe has in mind the elements of fire, earth, air, and water, which were thought by Renaissance physiologists to compose the four humours of the body: choler, melancholy, blood, and phlegm. According to accepted theory, these four humours were thought to be warring continually with each other for supremacy. Health depended on keeping the humours in harmony. Illness resulted when one humour gained an ascendency.

The humour that gains the ascendency in Tamburlaine, and eventually brings his death, is choler. The choleric humour, as we may read in John Davies of Hereford, for example, is

> in its temper . . . hot and drie
> Which is the cause it is so angery.[2]

Tamburlaine's dry, hot, and angry temperament is frequently brought to our attention in Marlowe's drama. We hear Tamburlaine likening himself to a fiery meteor and to Phaeton that almost burnt heaven.[3] Somewhat later,

---

[1] "Tamburlaine: The Choleric Man," *Modern Language Notes*, XLIV (1929), 430-35; "Marlowe and Elizabethan Psychology," *Philological Quarterly*, VIII (1929), 69-78. My discussion in this chapter is indebted to Mr. Camden at several points.
[2] *Microcosmos* (1603), ed. Grosart, *Works of Davies of Hereford*, I. c. 31.
[3] *Tamb.* 1493-96.

the Governor of Damascus expresses a hope that the sight of
the lovely virgins may be a means "to quallifie these hot
extremes" [4] he observes in Tamburlaine. The hope proves
conspicuously vain. In Part II Tamburlaine in his anger
kills even his own son Calyphas, and at this point Marlowe
has one of the spectators make a physiological judgment
and prediction:

> May neuer spirit, vaine or Artier feed
> The cursed substance of that cruel heart,
> But (wanting moisture and remorsefull blood)
> Drie vp with anger, and consume with heat. (3852-55.)

Not long after, dryness and hotness is what Tamburlaine's
physician discovers is the cause of the hero's illness:[5]

> I view'd your vrine, and the hypostasis
> Thick and obscure doth make your danger great,
> Your vaines are full of accidentall heat,
> Whereby the moisture of your blood is dried,
> The *Humidum* and *Calor* . . .
> . . . Is almost cleane extinguished and spent,
> Which being the cause of life, imports your death.
> . . . Your Artiers which alongst the vaines conuey
> The liuely spirits which the heart ingenders
> Are partcht and void of spirit . . . (4474-87.)

Tamburlaine's color also serves to mark him as a choleric
type. According to John Davies of Hereford, one of the

---

[4] *Tamb.* 1827.

[5] The hotness and dryness of Tamburlaine's humours shows itself in frenzy.
He behaves as if he were possessed by a Fury, and his heated imagination calls
forth the chimera of "the vglie monster Death." His behaviour corresponds thus
with the description Du Bartas gives of the manner in which sickness attacks
a man:

> this fell *Fury*, for fore-runners, sends
> *Manie* and *Phrenzie* to suborne her friends:
> Whereof, th'one drying, th'other over-warming
> The feeble brain (the edge of judgement harming)
> Within the Soule fantastickly they fain
> A confus'd hoast of strange *Chimera's* vain

Second Week, "The Furies," 350-6, ed. Grosart, *Works of Sylvester*, I, 117.

symptoms of a choleric temperament is a yellow complexion.[6] This symptom is called to our attention also in *The Touchstone of Complexions* (1576):

> First of Yelowe Choler is engendered Pale, or of the colour of a Pomecytron, meane betwene greene and yelowyshe.[7]

Likewise, Burton tells us that in hot choleric bodies the passion of anger is accompanied by either paleness or redness of visage.[8] And we remember Giovius' description of Attila as "inhumano luridoque pallore." Paleness was regarded by Elizabethans as a conventional symptom of madness.[9]

Tamburlaine's pale complexion is twice called to our attention. Menaphon describes him as

> Pale of complexion: wrought in him with passion,
> Thirsting with souerainty with loue of armes. (473-4.)

And Agydas, who rightly reads Tamburlaine's humour as that of Choler, tells us:

> I stand agast: but most astonied
> To see his choller shut in secrete thoughtes,
> And wrapt in silence of his angry soule
> Vpon his browes was pourtraid vgly death,
> And in his eies the furie of his hart,
> That shine as Comets, menacing reuenge,
> And casts a pale complexion on his cheeks. (1054-60.)

Tamburlaine's fiery eyes, pointed out at least four times in the play,[10] are a conventional detail in Renaissance descriptions of the passion of anger. Thus in *The Touchstone of Complexions* we read that:

---

[6] *Microcosmos,* p. 31.
[7] P. 132. The translation is by Thomas Newton from the Latin of Lemnius.
[8] *Anat.* I. ii. 3. 9, quoting Lactantius.
[9] See E. A. Peers, *Elizabethan Drama and its Mad Folk* (Cambridge, 1914), p. 20.
[10] *Tamb.* 353, 1058, 1384-85, 3849-50.

Angre (which is a passion so lyke to fury and madnesse, as nothing in the world more) what force it hath . . . appeareth chiefly by countenaunce, colour, grymme visage, cruel and fiery eyes, puffing & wrynkled nostrilles, byting lyppes, enraged mouth . . .[11]

John Davies of Hereford points out that anger is a fury which rises when the blood has been set on fire,

> From which *fire* flie out *Sparkles* through his eies,
> Who stare, as if they would their *holdes* inlarge.[12]

And Thomas Elyot explains that from anger

commeth sometyme fevers, sometyme . . . madness, fransies, deformytie of vysage: and that wars is, outragious swearynge, blasphemye desyre of vengeance . . . [13]

Marlowe presents these details in Tamburlaine. Some of them are emphasized when he shows us Tamburlaine advising his sons how they may be like their father:

> For he shall weare the crowne of *Persea,*
> Whose head hath deepest scarres, whose breast most woundes,
> Which being wroth, sends lightning from his eies,
> And in the furrowes of his frowning browes,
> Harbors reuenge, war, death and cruelty. (2643-47.)

Anger is associated by Renaissance writers with the most dangerous form of choler—namely, choler adust. According to the accepted theory, all four of the humours are liable to adustion, which is caused when a humour becomes burnt through excessive heat.[14] But the adustion of choler, according to Sir Thomas Elyot,[15] is the worst of all. Timothy Bright remarks that if this unnatural condition

---

[11] P. 59.

[12] *Microcosmos*, p. 73.

[13] *Castel of Helth* (1547 ed.), p. 64^v; cited by Lily B. Campbell, *Shakespeare's Tragic Heroes* (Cambridge, 1930), p. 82.

[14] See Timothy Bright, *A Treatise of Melancholie* (1586), chap. xviii, "Of the vnnatural melancholie rising by adustion, how it affecteth vs with diuers passions."

[15] *Castel*, p. 66; see Campbell, p. 75.

rise of choler, then rage playeth her part, and furies ioyned with madnesse, putteth all out of frame. . . . If choller haue yeelded matter to this sharpe kind of melancholie, then rage, reuenge, and furie possesse both hart and head, and the whole bodie is carried with that storme, contrarie to persuasion of reason: which hath no farther power ouer these affections, then by way of counsell to giue other direction. . . .[16]

And Burton tells us that men who have choler adust

are bold and impudent, and of a more harebrain disposition, apt to quarrel, and think of such things, battles, combats, and their manhood, furious; impatient in discourse, stiff, irrefragable and prodigious in their tenets . . . Cardan . . . holds these men of all others fit to be assassins, bold, hardy, fierce, and adventurous, to undertake any thing by reason of their choler adust. "This humour," says he, "prepares them to endure death itself, and all manner of torments with invincible courage . . ." . . . he ascribes this generosity, fury, or rather stupidity, to this adustion of choler and melancholy: for commonly this humour so adust and hot degenerates into madness.[17]

Illustration of these qualities of character can readily be pointed out in Marlowe's portrait of Tamburlaine. Bright's statement that "rage, reuenge, and furie possesse both hart and head" is fulfilled almost everywhere in the drama, but most conspicuously perhaps at the death scenes of Zenocrate and of Tamburlaine. Burton's note that men of choler adust think generally of battles finds most vivid illustration when Tamburlaine says:[18]

> Then when the Sky shal waxe as red as blood,
> It shall be said, I made it red myselfe,
> To make me think of nought but blood and war. (1497-99.)

And Burton's observation that such men are "stiff, irrefragable and prodigious in their tenets," compares with Tamburlaine's

---

[16] *Treatise*, pp. 111-2.
[17] *Anat.* I. iii. 1. 3.
[18] See also *Tamb.* 1026-28; 2232-35; etc.

> And know my customes are as peremptory
> As wrathfull Planets, death, or destinie. (1908-09.)

The "invincible courage" which Cardan attributes to men
of choler adust appears, of course, always in Tamburlaine.
"Weele fight fiue hundred men at armes to one," he boasts
at an early point in the drama.[19] And when death is upon
him he shows courage not only in his proposals to combat
Death and invade Heaven, but also in a sally against Callapine so bold and invincible that Callapine is put to flight
in incredibly brief time.

Huarte, a popular Spanish authority in the matter of
humours, says that choler adust "is drie and of a delicat
substance."[20] And Davies of Hereford notes[21] that Choler
is associated with the element of Fire, while Melancholy is
associated with Earth. Here again, the words apply with
particular appropriateness to Tamburlaine, who cherishes
a temper of delicate and fiery stuff. He cannot endure
Calyphas,

> a soule,
> Created of the massy dregges of earth,
> The scum and tartar of the Elements,
> Wherein was neither corrage, strength or wit. (3796-99.)

He insists that his boys must discipline their bodies to

> thriue . . . full of thoughtes
> As pure and fiery as *Phyteus* beames. (4629-30.)

On this point we might perhaps compare Nashe's description of "spirits of the fire," set forth in his prose tract *The
Terrors of Night* (1594). Nashe says that

A man that will entertaine them [i.e. the "spirits of the fire"]
must not pollute his bodie with any grosse carnall copulation or
inordinate beastly desires, but loue pure beauty, pure vertue, and

---

[19] *Tamb.* 339.
[20] See Campbell, p. 76.
[21] *Microcosmos*, p. 31.

not haue affections linsey-wolsey, intermingled with lust and things worthy of liking. Those spirits of the fire, howeuer I terme them comparatiuely good in respect of a number of bad, yet are they not simply well inclinde, for they bee by nature ambitious, haughty, and proud, nor do they loue vertue for it selfe any whit, but because they would ouerquell and outstrip others with the vaineglorious ostentation of it. A humor of monarchizing and nothing els it is, which makes them affect rare quallified studies. Many Atheists are with these spirits inhabited.[22]

Other Renaissance authorities provide us still further details of the choleric man, for which we can find illustration in Tamburlaine. The choleric man's favorite color, we are told, is red; his special metal, gold.[23] Of his behavior John Davies of Hereford says:

> The *Chollericke* is hasty, and inclinde
> To *Envie, pride,* and *prodigalitie*;
> As Herc'les-hardy, though with anger blinde.[24]

And in *The Touchstone of Complexions* we read that

> hoate and drye natured men (which are the Cholerique) be right well furnished and skilful in perfecte utterance, vehemence of speach and readynesse of toungue . . . the Cholerique are bitter taunters, dry bobbers, nyppinge gybers and skornefull mockers of others . . . [25]

Tamburlaine fits these prescriptions. His addiction to scarlet, blood, and gold is thematic in the play; his likeness to Hercules we have discussed in an earlier chapter; and his blind anger we have sufficiently noted. Haste and envy find illustration in his very rapid conquests—particularly in his sudden decision to overthrow Cosroe. Of pride we

---

[22] McKerrow, I, 351.
[23] See J. W. Draper, "Shakespeare's 'Star-Crossed Lovers'," *R. E. S.*, XV (1939), 22.
[24] *Microcosmos*, p. 31.
[25] P. 99 (1576 ed.).

can hardly image fitter monument than the inscribed pillar which Tamburlaine erects over burned Larissa:

> *This towne being burnt by Tamburlaine the great,*
> *Forbids the world to build it vp againe.* (3207-08.)

And prodigality is reflected in such lines as:

> Cookes shall haue pensions to prouide vs cates,
> And glut vs with the dainties of the world. (2788-89.)

As for skill in speech, Tamburlaine's gift in it is the chief marvel of the drama. By his soaring words he wins Theridamas, spell-binds Zenocrate, inspirits his whole army—and completely fascinates the reader of the drama. Fitting the portrait given in *The Touchstone,* Tamburlaine is skilled also in bitter tauntings. His jestings with Bajazet in Part I and with the harnessed kings in Part II are notable examples.

The eloquence, and at times the pathos, of Tamburlaine's speeches give his dramatic character an attractiveness which prevents him from becoming repulsive in our eyes. It is worth noting, however, that these winning qualities in his manner are quite compatible with the role of a madman. Mr. E. A. Peers has pointed out[26] that in the Elizabethan presentation of insanity outbursts of anger, "thundering," and "roaring" are often preceded by sudden touches of pathos. Moreover, the wildness of the madman's anger

is not inconsistent with considerable force and pregnancy of speech, which might lead some to doubt the actual presence of insanity; and which is "a happiness that often madness hits on, which reason and sanity could not so prosperously be delivered of." (*Hamlet,* II. ii. 212.)

Applying to *Tamburlaine* these observations of Mr. Peers, we may conclude that Tamburlaine, with all his pathos and

---

[26] *Elizabethan Drama,* pp. 21-22.

his anger, his paleness of complexion and his pregnancy of speech, is one of the grandest madmen of Elizabethan drama.

Tamburlaine's "psychology," which in our preceding chapters we have discussed for its ethical significance, we have in this chapter considered in its physiological characteristics. The two approaches are complementary aspects of Elizabethan moral philosophy. Renaissance authors regarded man as a composite of soul and body: it was thought that the body reflects the state of the soul, and that the soul by the nature of its passions fashions the body to its own demands. Since this most intimate interconnection exists between soul and body, the health of the one is reflected in the health of the other, and the disease of the one in the disease of the other. Renaissance moralists regarded themselves as physicians of both soul and body.[27] They agreed that Sin was the cause of all disorder; and they regarded both disease of the body and perturbations of the soul as marks of sin.[28] It is not surprising, therefore, that Marlowe's dramatization of the sin of ambition should include appropriate physiological illustration.

---

[27] See, e.g., *The French Academie* (1594), Pt. II, p. 235.
[28] *Ibid.*, p. 236.

TAMBURLAINE'S PASSIONS

※ ※

WHEN we read attentively what the Elizabethans had to say in criticism of the human passions, it becomes very clear why Fortescue could think Tamburlaine an "incarnate devil." The tragic flaw in Tamburlaine's nature goes deep. As judged by sixteenth-century standards, his passions have fallen victim to three ills: immoderation, misdirection, and delusion. Or, to put the matter another way, his tragedy is explainable in terms of the degenerate source of his inspiration, the mistaken goal of his aspiration, and the intemperate course of his desire. Let us examine in turn each of these considerations.

I

In studying Elizabethan theory of the passions we need to observe, first of all, that literary opinion was on the side of Aristotle and the Platonists, as opposed to the Stoics. That is to say, it was held by most authors that man's passions are beneficial, provided they are kept temperate. Philemon Holland refers to

the absurdities of the said Stoicke Philosophers, who instead of well governing and ruling the soule of man, have as much as lieth in them, extinguished and abolished the same! [1]

As champion against the Stoics, Holland recommends Plutarch; for Plutarch proclaims that virtue arises not from the abolition of the unreasonable part of the soul, but from its ordering and moderation.[2] On this same question Nashe

---

[1] Holland's "Summarie" of chap. iv. of his translation of Plutarch's *Morals* (1603), p. 64.
[2] *Morals*, p. 68.

tells us that he holds to the Peripatetic view of the passions as against the Stoic.[3] And Chapman, also, is not the Stoic many critics have thought him to be: instead of *apatheia* we get from his *Tears of Peace* the declaration that "Homer hath told me that there are / Passions in which corruption hath no share. . . . To stand at gaze / In one position, is a stupid maze, / Fit for a statue." [4]

A typical Elizabethan historian such as Higgins rests his judgments of tragedy on the view of the passions taught by Plotinus. In introducing *The First Parte of the Mirrour for Magistrates* (1574) Higgins declares that the desire of glory is admirable, provided it is kept within bounds:

> *Plotinus* that wonderfull and excellent Philosopher hath these wordes: The property of Temperaunce is to couet nothing which may be repented: not to excede the bands of measure, & to kepe Desire vnder the yoke of Reason. . . . For to couet without consideration: to passe the measure of his degree, and to lette will run at random, is the only destruction of all estates. . . . Will you that I rehearse *Alexander* the Great, *Caesar, Pompey, Cyrus, Hannibal,* &c. All which (by desier of glorye) felte the rewarde of theire immoderate and insatiable lustes. . . . I surely deme those Princes above specified (considering their factes, estates, fortunes, fame and exploytes) had neuer come to suche ende, but for wante of temperance.[5]

The view may be compared with that of John Davies of Hereford, who in the midst of a long discussion of the passions declares that Choler, if kept at a mean, "yeeldes most sweet effects," making the Wit and Courage great.

> And if with *fury* it be not disgrac'd,
> It should by al *meanes,* by *all* be embrac'd.[6]

Temperance, moderation, "mediocritie," the mean—these constitute the recurring theme of Renaissance writers. Gre-

---

[3] *Anatomie of Absurditie,* ed. McKerrow, I, 27.
[4] Chapman's *Poems* (London, 1875), p. 113, col. 2.
[5] "To the Nobilitie and all other in office," ed. Haslewood, I, 3-4.
[6] *Microcosmos,* ed. Grosart, I. c. 74.

ville speaks of "mediocrity, that reciprocall paradise of mutuall humane duties." [7] He complains that "in man's muddy
soule the meane doth not content. . . . This makes some
soare and burne." [8] Amiot, the great translator of Plutarch's
Lives declares that "the commendation of all doinges" consists in "the meane poynt, betweene the two faultie ex-
tremities of too much and too little." [9] La Primaudaye
says he takes his stand with Socrates: Temperance is "the
ground-worke and foundation of all vertues," for "no man
can find out any thing that is so excellent and woonderfull
as temperance, the guide and gouernor of the soule." [10] Most
succinctly, perhaps, the reasons for giving moderation the
primary place in ethical theory are stated by Sir William
Cornwallis:

> without moderation, the wit of man will serue a wrong master;
> without moderation, the body will rebel against the soule, without
> moderation, the soule yeelds to the body; in a word, vnmoderated,
> both soule and body perisheth. This is shee that makes the dis-
> tinction betwixt vertue and vice; this is she that makes courage
> valor, that without moderation would be anger, and then fury; this
> is she that separateth iustice and cruelty, prouidence from feare,
> power from tyranny, maiesty from pride.[11]

When we put Marlowe's Tamburlaine against the background of this commentary, it is plain that the conqueror's
dramatic career is a notable example of lack of temperance.
He belongs in the class of world-conquerors lamented by
Higgins—with Alexander, Caesar, and Hannibal—men who
"lette will runne at random" to the destruction of the world
and to their own self-misery. Lacking the moderation
which Cornwallis says is necessary to prevent a man from
serving a wrong master, Tamburlaine serves earthly glory.

[7] *Life of Sidney*, ed. Grosart, IV, 179.
[8] The Chorus of Good Spirits in *Alaham*, Act 1, ed. Grosart, III, 194.
[9] "Amiot to the Readers," Plutarch's *Lives* (1579), trans. North.
[10] *The French Academie*, pp. 180, 181.
[11] *Discourses upon Seneca the Tragedian* (1631), Sig. Ll, 4ᵛ.

Lacking the moderation which distinguishes virtue from vice, his courage becomes, as Cornwallis predicts, not valor but anger and fury. Failure in moderation causes him, Greville would say, to "soare and burne."

II

But secondly, and more basically, we must be concerned with a further question: What was the reason for Tamburlaine's failure in moderation? Here, too, the Elizabethans have well-established theory. Immoderation, and all its attendant perturbations of the soul, are due, says La Primaudaye, to *misdirected* desire. Desire is natural to every soul; but those souls who through ignorance set their desire on worldly goods can never find contentment:

The Philosophers teach vs by their writings, and experience doth better shew it vnto vs, that to couet and desire is proper to the soule, and that from thence all the affections and desires of men proceede, which draw them hither and thither diuersly, that they may attaine to that thing, which they thinke is able to lead them to the enioying of some good, whereby they may liue a contented and happie life. Which felicitie, the most part of men, through false opinion, or ignorance rather of that which is good, and by following the inclination of their corrupted nature, do seeke and labor to finde in humane and earthlie things, as in riches, glorie, honor, and pleasure. But forasmuch as the enioying of these things doth not bring with it sufficient cause of contentation, they perceiue themselues alwaies depriued of the end of their desires, and are constrained to wander all their life time beyond all bounds and measure, according to the rashnes and inconstancie of their lusts. . . . Briefly, all men whose harts are set vpon worldly goods, when they are come to this estate of life, they would attaine to that: and being come thereunto, some other newe desire carrieth them farther, so that this mischiefe of continuall, vncertaine, and vnsatiable lustes and desires doth more and more kindle in them vntill in the ende death cut off the thred of their inconstant, and neuer contented life. . . . But they, who through the studie of wisdome are furnished with skill and vnderstanding, and know that all humane and earthlie things are vncertaine, deceitfull, slipperie, and so many allurements vnto men to drawe them into a downe-fall and destruction, they I say, doe laie a farre better and more certaine foundation of their chiefe GOOD, contentation, and felicitie. . . . And deliuering their soules by the grace of God, from all those perturbations, which besiege them in the prison of their bodies, they lift vp their wishes and desires, yea they refer al the ends of their intents and actions to this only marke, to be vnited and ioined to the last end of their soueraigne GOOD, which is the full and whole fruition of the essence of God. . . .[12]

Instead of "the full and whole fruition of the essence of God" which La Primaudaye recommends, Tamburlaine knows only "The sweet fruition of an earthly crowne." This blindness-of-mind we may regard as the cause of Tamburlaine's never-contented life. His argument for thinking an earthly crown the sole felicity is that Nature teaches us to have aspiring minds. But La Primaudaye holds that "No man *by nature* [italics mine] can finde out the right way that leadeth to happines. . . . The word of God sheweth vs the right way to happines."[13] Tamburlaine's aspiration, obviously, is not rooted in the word of God. Fundamentally pagan, he knows what Nature's "foure Elements" teach him—no more. Therefore his desire looks toward a wholly earthly good and runs, naturally, headlong into Ambition.

But AMBITION, as Renaissance moralists never tired of pointing out, was the ruin of Phaeton and of Adam.

> Beware ambition, 'tis a sugred pill,
> That fortune layes, presuming minds to kill.[14]

Much of the detail with which Ambition's features were conventionally drawn has pattern-significance for the portrait of Tamburlaine. We should observe, for example, in La Primaudaye that

---

[12] The opening words of "The Author to the Reader" of *The French Academie* (1586).

[13] *Ibid.*, p. 31 marginally.

[14] Bodenham's *Belvedere* (1600), p. 109.

Ambition neuer suffreth those that haue once receiued hir as a guest, to enioy their present estate quietly. . . . And the more they growe and increase in power and authoritie, the rather are they induced and caried headlong by their affections to commit all kind of iniustice, and flatter themselues in furious and frantike actions, that they may come to the end of their infinite platformes, and of that proud and tyrannicall glory, which, contrarie to all dutie they seeke after.[15]

Or if we look into Du Bartas, at the point where he is describing the diseases of the soul in his poem *The Furies,* we find a picture of "secret-burning" Ambition

> Pent in no limits, pleas'd with no Condition;
> Whom *Epicurus* many Worlds suffice not,
> Whose furious thirst of proud aspiring dyes not
> Whose hands (transported with fantastick passion)
> Bear painted Scepters in imagination.[16]

Pierre Charron[17] furnishes us a particularly detailed portrait of Ambition. Ambition, he says, is the strongest and most powerful passion that is, surmounting all other passions. Alexander, who courageously refused to touch the most beautiful damsel that was in his power, burned nevertheless with ambition, and indeed made his victory over love serve his ambition. Ambition, furthermore, takes away a man's concern for his life; it causes him to contemn religion; and it offers violence even to the laws of nature, for it causes the murder of parents, children, and brothers. Finally,

Ambition hath no limits, it is a gulfe that hath neither brinke nor bottome; it is that vacuity which the Philosophers could neuer find in Nature; a fire which increaseth by that nourishment that is giuen vnto it. Wherein it truly payeth his master: for ambition is onely iust in this, that it sufficeth for his own punishment, and is

---

[15] *The French Academie,* p. 224.
[16] Lines 702-07, ed. Grosart, *Works of Sylvester,* I, 120.
[17] *Of Wisdome,* tr. Samson Lennard (1630), Bk. I, chap. xx. Charron's *Traité de la Sagesse* was first published in 1595.

executioner to it selfe. The Wheele of Ixion is the motion of his desires, which turne and returne vp and downe, neuer giuing rest vnto his minde.

They that will flatter ambition, say it is a seruant or helpe vnto vertue, and a spurre to beautiful actions; for it quitteth a man of all other sinnes, and in the end, of himselfe too; and all for vertue: but it is so farre from this, that it hideth sometimes our vices; but it takes them not away, but it couereth or rather hatcheth them for a time vnder the deceitfull cinders of a malitious hypocrisie, with hope to set them on fire altogether, when they haue gotten authority sufficient to raigne publiquely and with impiety. . . . An ambitious man putteth himselfe forth to great and honourable actions, the profit whereof returneth to the publique good, but yet he is neuer the better man that performes them, because they are not the actions of vertue but of passion. . . .[18]

These characteristic features of Ambition appear in Marlowe's portrait of Tamburlaine. Tamburlaine can enjoy no rest. He is insatiably greedy for glory. He loves to flatter himself in furious and frantic actions. His hands may be said to "Bear painted Scepters in imagination" at the moment when, fingering the banquet cates of crowns, he indulges in dreams of empire and bestows upon his lieutenants the as-yet-unconquered kingdoms of Egypt, Arabia, and Damascus.[19] Charron's point that Alexander for ambition's sake kept himself chaste toward the beautiful damsel finds parallel in Tamburlaine's boast that he has not violated Zenocrate:

Her state and person wants no pomp you see,
And for all blot of foule inchastity,
I record heauen, her heauenly selfe is cleare. (*Tamb.* 2267-69.)

Charron's observation that those who flatter Ambition can say it is a spur to beautiful actions also finds point, for Tamburlaine's ambition makes him valorous, magnanimous,

[18] *Ibid.*, p. 82.
[19] *Tamb.* 1747 ff.

and eloquent. To his last moment he behaves magnificently. However, his death scene also reveals plainly, fulfilling Charron's portrait, the impiety and torment of unsatisfied desire. Ambition has burned to a fever of madness in Tamburlaine so that it punishes itself.

Still there is, some of us feel, another aspect to Tamburlaine's soul. Besides his lust for power, there is his worship of beauty. We would like to think that this latter quality is a point at which we may safely approve his behavior. However, if we would be strictly fair to our Elizabethan commentary, we must regard Tamburlaine's attitude toward beauty, too, as instance of misdirected or corrupt desire. The beauties he worships are earthly rather than heavenly. Pools of blood and tongues of fire, crowns, "humaine" poetry, and Zenocrate—these his imagination exalts. He takes them, mistakenly, for heavenly beauties: he supposes that wars illustrate the life of gods, that the pursuit of crowns makes him and his men godlike, that poetry is the human mind's distillation of some "heauenly Quintessence," and that Zenocrate's beauty ranks her with the angels and the "holy Seraphins." Each of these judgments is sturdily pagan—hence (from a Christian point of view) false.

No Protestant humanist would say that Tamburlaine's pursuit of earthly crowns or his love of earthly Zenocrate makes him genuinely godlike. On the contrary, these loves make him impious. It is a mad worship which causes him to threaten heaven and to burn Larissa. His Zenocrate is a beauty like Homer's Helen, not like Dante's Beatrice or Spenser's Una. Like Helen or Cressida, Zenocrate is beautiful, sentimental, inconstant, and vain, for her character is raised wholly on a naturalistic morality. But she has, superbly, the grace of pagan loveliness. And Tamburlaine's attachment is characteristically pagan: "This fair face and heavenly hue / Must grace his bed that conquers Asia. . . ."

Also in his devotion to poetry, proclaimed in an elegant and justly famous speech, Tamburlaine cannot get above a pagan understanding. Poetry is for him "the highest reaches of a humaine wit." [20] The view contrasts strikingly with that of John Davies of Hereford, for whom "Poetry [is] no skil humaine," but a divine skill; "For holy Raptures must the Head entrance." [21] According to the doctrine generally held by Elizabethan apologists, true Poetry is a matter not primarily of art, but of inspiration; not a labor, but a gift; not, as Tamburlaine says, a beauty digested by "restless heads," but, as Spenser says, a beauty infused into mortal breasts out of the Almighty's bosom. [22] And further, since this view of Tamburlaine's on poetry comes in the drama immediately after he has commanded the slaughter of the virgins, we may note that it does not fit with Spenser's view that true skill in poetry must arise out of "Love devoyd of villanie or ill."

Tamburlaine's worship of beauty, however, is dramatically very appropriate. Sidney had pointed out in his *Defence of Poesie* that poetry is "the companion of Camps," highly honored even by Turks and Tartars. [23] Tamburlaine himself explains that he is turning to beauty's just applause for the reason that

> euery warriour that is rapt with loue,
> Of fame, of valour, and of victory
> Must needs haue beauty beat on his conceites. (*Tamb.* 1961-63.)

His behavior accords with the Platonic theory that "Mars

---

[20] *Tamb.* 1949.

[21] *Microcosmos,* ed. Grosart, I. c. 81.

[22] *Teares of the Muses.* See the discussion of Spenser's theory of poetry by M. Bhattacherje, *Studies in Spenser* (Calcutta, 1929), pp. 48-9. The Elizabethan doctrine goes back to Plato's *Ion:* "All good poets compose their beautiful poems not as works of art, but because they are inspired and possessed." The root of all poetry is love, not wit.

[23] Feuillerat's edition, pp. 5 and 32. Greville makes the same point in *A Treatise of Monarchy,* stanzas 475-6, ed. Grosart, I, 171. Remember also that Milton attributes to the devils in Hell an interest in poetry.

still doth after Venus move . . . because of Love / Boldness is handmaid"; that

> since men love, they therefore are more bold,
> And made to dare even death for their beloved;
> . . . All things submit to Love. . . .
> Celestials, animals, all corporeal things,
> Wise men and strong, slave-rich, and free-born kings
> Are love's contributories. . . .[24]

We can understand why Zenocrate is introduced into Marlowe's drama at the beginning of Tamburlaine's career: she provides the warrior a motive for his brave exploits. We find him saying that her beauty adds "more courage to my conquering mind." He boasts of the extensive conquests he will make "To gratify sweet Zenocrate." [25] Later, her beauty furnishes inspiration for his battle against Bajazet. To fortify his mind for this critical test, he meditates on her beauty, exalts it above the heavens, and concludes:

> Stir not *Zenocrate* vntill thou see
> Me martch victoriously with all my men,
> Triumphing ouer him and these his kings,
> Which I will bring as Vassals to thy feete. (*Tamb.* 1224-27.)

That she may continue to inspire him and his men with boldness, he preserves a picture after her death:

> Thou shalt be set vpon my royall tent.
> And when I meet an armie in the field,
> Those looks will shed such influence in my campe.
> As if Bellona, Goddesse of the war

---

[24] *Andromeda Liberata* (1614), Chapman's *Poems*, pp. 188-9. Mr. F. L. Schoell, *Études sur L'Humanisme Continental en Angleterre* (Paris, 1926), p. 15, shows that the lines here are an almost literal translation from Ficinus' *In Convivium Platonis de Amore Commentarium*, V. viii.

[25] *Tamb.* 2297 ff. Compare the anonymous play, *Caesar's Revenge*, I. vi. Caesar, struck by Cleopatra's "louely Tyranizing eyes," likens her to Helen of Troy, admits that his thoughts are "captiud to thy beauties conquering power," and declares that he will conquer Egypt and Africa for her.

Threw naked swords and sulphur bals of fire,
Vpon the heads of all our enemies. (*Tamb.* 3227-32.)

A second aspect of Renaissance theory regarding Beauty's effect is neatly stated in a couplet of Chapman's:

Beauty in heaven and earth this grace doth win,
It supples rigour, and it lessens sin.[26]

In accord with this theory we note that Zenocrate's beauty, earthly though it is, can modify the sternness of Tamburlaine's spirit. Under the spell of her beauty he spares her father's life. When in Part II of the drama Zenocrate's death has deprived him of Beauty's softening influence, he becomes increasingly savage.

III

Finally, Elizabethan theory enables us to comment on the nature of Tamburlaine's fury. We have already remarked that Renaissance writers were not Stoic in their theory of the passions. Instead of flatly repudiating inspiration, they adopted the Platonic distinction of two types of inspiration. This doctrine, well stated by Du Bartas, is that fury can arise from two widely different sources:

For euen as humane fury maks the man
Les then the man: So heauenly fury can
Make man pas man, and wander in holy mist,
Vpon the fyrie heauen to walk at list.[27]

Elizabethans regarded this as an important distinction. Barnabe Barnes elaborates upon it in his *A Divine Centurie*

---

[26] *Hero and Leander,* Third Sestyad, Chapman's *Poems,* p. 76. For other statements of this same theory, see Spenser, *Faerie Queene,* V. 8. 1; Bodenham, *Belvedere,* p. 44; and Nesca A. Robb, *Neoplatonism of the Italian Renaissance* (London, 1935), p. 218. The doctrine is Platonic.\

[27] *The Urania,* stanza 30. The translation here is that of King James, published in *The Essayes of a Prentise, in the Divine Art of Poesie* (Edinburgh, 1585). For Sylvester's later translation, see *Works of Sylvester,* ed. Grosart, II, 4.

of Spirituall Sonnets.[28]   And Chapman applies the dichotomy to poetic inspiration:

There being in Poesy a twofold rapture (or alienation of soul, as the above-said teacher terms it) one *insania,* a disease of the mind, and a mere madness, by which the infected is thrust beneath all degrees of humanity: *et ex homine, brutum quodammodo redditur:* (for which poor Poesy, in this diseased and impostorous age, is so barbarously vilified); the other is *divinus furor,* by which the sound and divinely healthful, *supra hominis naturam erigitur, et in Deum transit.* One a perfection directly infused from God; the other an infection obliquely and degenerately proceeding from man. Of the divine fury, my Lord, your Homer hath ever been both first and last instance.[29]

The Elizabethans did not, like some twentieth-century liberals, adopt the notion that all things "spiritual" are divine. Instead, they recognized that the human spirit sometimes burns with what Fulke Greville called "false flames spirituall but infernal."[30] An age which was devoted to Plato was well aware that the tyrant can amazingly resemble his direct opposite, the philosopher king; that indeed the tyrant is simply the tragic caricature of the philosopher.[31] Tamburlaine, it is true, asserts that his fury is inspired by

---

[28] He writes "To the Favourable and Christian Reader" (I quote from the reprint of London, 1815): "And if any man feele in himselfe, by the secret fire of immortal enthusiasme, the learned motions of strange and divine passions of spirite; let him refine and illuminate his numerous Muses with the most sacred splendour of the Holie Ghost: and then he shall, with divine Salust (the true learned Frenche poet,) finde, that as humane furie maketh a man lesse than a man, and the very same with wilde, unreasonable beastes; so divine rage and sacred instinct of a man maketh more than man, and leadeth him from his base terrestrial estate, to walke above the starres with angelles immortally."

[29] Epistle Dedicatory to his translation of the Odyssey, *Poems,* p. 238. The theory of the two types of ecstasy rests on a passage in Plato's *Phaedrus;* but Chapman has taken it from Ficinus' commentary on Plato's *Ion.* See Schoell, *Études,* pp. 1, 4-6. It is interesting to note that Burton, *Anat.* III. iv. 1. 1., applies the dichotomy to religion, saying that religion is of two kinds: false or true. He then points out that when false gods are worshipped or when God is falsely worshipped there results a furious disease of the soul, mere madness, *religiosa insania.*

[30] *Caelica,* CX, ed. Grosart, III, 143.

[31] See Plato's *Repub.,* Bk. IX.

heaven. It is Jove's spirit, he says, that living in him makes him "valiant, proud, ambitious."[32] But his enemies are not so sure Tamburlaine's inspiration is heaven-sent. The Governor of Babylon calls him "Vile monster . . . sent from hell to tyrannise on earth."[33] And the Souldan of Egypt thinks him a devil, since he is no man.[34] Ortygius, who raises the question "Whether from earth, or hell, or heauen he grow," is not sure whether Tamburlaine is a "God or Feend, or spirit of the earth, / Or Monster turned to a manly shape."[35]

If Elizabethans applied to the judgment of Tamburlaine's fury the current theory of the two types of inspiration which we have just cited, they must certainly have considered the conqueror's passion as arising from a human, not a divine, source. For as the drama proceeds, Tamburlaine becomes increasingly inhuman. His fury "nothing can quence but blood and Emperie."[36] Finally, when the madness causes him "to dare God out of heaven," as Greene put it, his inspiration is surely what Chapman called "an infection obliquely and degenerately proceeding from man."

In making this candid analysis of Tamburlaine's pretensions, we will find further support if we recall one of the central doctrines of the Elizabethans. It is stated, for example, in a sermon of Henry Smith, the popular Elizabethan divine. Magistrates, says Smith,

which use their power against God, which bear the Lawes against Gods Law, and be enemies to his servants . . . cannot so well be called *gods,* as Devils: such *gods* go to Hell.[37]

Or the pages of that popular Renaissance moralist, William

---

[32] *Tamb.* 3785 ff.
[33] *Tamb.* 4223.
[34] *Tamb.* 1414.
[35] *Tamb.* 826-34. Cf. 820-3.
[36] *Tamb.* 843-4.
[37] *Sermons,* p. 337 (edition of 1657). Smith's sermons were printed in many collected editions, beginning as early as 1591. Nashe eulogizes "Siluer-tongu'd *Smith*" in *Pierce Penilesse,* ed. McKerrow, I, 192-93.

Baldwin, will also furnish us commentary for judging Tamburlaine. Kings, Baldwin says, are given the name of gods because they have in charge the ministration of justice, but if they pervert this office, then they are not gods, but devils:

> What a fowle shame wer it for any now to take vpon them the name and office of God, and in their doinges to shew them selves divyls? God can not of Iustice, but plage such shameles presumption and hipocrisy, and that with shamefull death, diseases, or infamy.[38]

Regarded from the Elizabethan vantage point, Tamburlaine's idealism appears in quite another light than that in which modern criticism has interpreted it. The great Scythian's tragedy, when measured by the canons of Marlowe's day, is seen to be the result of uncontrolled, misdirected, and diseased passions. The spectator feels *pity* when he beholds Tamburlaine's aspiration turned wholly toward things of earth, carrying a noble man headlong into ambition and its attendant misery. And the spectator experiences *fear* and takes warning when he sees Tamburlaine's inspiration, grounded in human passions rather than in divine wisdom, bringing a fevered madness.

Certainly, however, there is no very good reason for identifying Marlowe with his stage-character Tamburlaine. Drayton tells us[39] that Marlowe had "that fine madnes. . . . Which rightly should possesse a Poets braine." Why, then, may we not suppose that the dramatist had in him the "divinely healthful" madness which Chapman says Homer possessed?

---

[38] *Mirror for Magistrates* (1559), "To the nobilitye and all other in office," ed. L. B. Campbell (Cambridge, 1938), p. 65.

[39] "To Henry Reynolds, of Poets and Poesie," *The Battaile of Agincourt, Elegies, etc.* (1627), p. 206.

CONCLUSION

TAMBURLAINE:
A SUMMARY INTERPRETATION

※ ※

Thus see we, how these vgly furious spirits
Of Warre, are cloth'd, colour'd, and disguis'd
With stiles of Vertue, Honour, Zeale, and Merits;
Whose owne complexion, well anatomis'd,
   A mixture is of pride, rage, auarice,
   Ambition, lust, and euery tragicke vice.[1]

I N *The Shadow of Night* (1594) Chapman issued a challenge to poets to give their skill to picturing the miseries
of tortured souls and the violent courses of certain Furies
who drown the world in blood "and stain the skies with
their spilt souls, made drunk with tyrannies." [2] I think we
may regard *Tamburlaine* as an early illustration of this
type of poetry. We remember that George Peele praised
Marlowe as a poet who was

> Fit to write passions for the souls below,
> If any wretched souls in passion speak.[3]

The prologue to *Tamburlaine* plainly proclaims a serious
intention. Rejecting the methods of popular rhymesters,
Marlowe invites us to attend the stately theme of War, presented in the "high astounding tearms" of the scourge
Tamburlaine.

We shall attempt in this chapter to view the tragedy as
the wisest of the Elizabethans might have viewed it. It
fulfills Sidney's prescription for a "high and excellent"

---

[1] *A Treatie of Warres*, stanza 20, ed. Grosart, *Works of Greville*, II, 110.
[2] This is my interpretation. See *Poems*, ed. cit., pp. 7-8; and my forthcom-
ing article in *Studies in Philology*, October, 1941, entitled "Chapman's *Shadow
of Night:* an Interpretation."
[3] In the prologue to "The Honour of the Garter," ed. Bullen, *Works of Peele*,
II, 320.

Tragedy, because it makes "Tyrants manifest their tiranni-
cal humors." It furnishes, as John Davies of Hereford
pointed out,[4] a mighty warning against ambition. Also, it
illustrates both the workings of Fortune, and the overruling
of Fortune by God's Providence.

Like the stories of Lydgate, Baldwin, and Higgins, Marlowe's story is a poetic account of the rise and fall of a single
great personage. Tamburlaine is a hero of no ordinary
fame. Histories had pointed him out as a singular example
of Fortune's favor; the title page of the drama correctly
calls his conquests "rare and woonderfull." His career
offers the spectacle of a lowly shepherd who became monarch of almost the whole world; who never suffered defeat;
who used the mightiest king of his day, the great Turk
Bajazet, as his footstool. Tamburlaine offers magnificent
example of Nature's pride—an heroic brigand, an accomplished tyrant, an inspired and ruthless destroyer. And
finally, to give point to the spectacle, he is a hero who
vaunts himself the Scourge of God.

Marlowe endows his hero with the gifts both spiritual
and physical which are appropriate to a Scourge of God.
He gives him the lineaments of a Hercules and an Orgoglio.
He credits him with a desire as tall as his stature. He
presents him

> In euery part proportioned like the man,
> Should make the world subdued to *Tamburlaine*.

"Thirsting with soueraignty, with loue of armes," this hero
is gifted with marvellous eloquence to instil in the hearts of
his followers the fever of his own ambition. In physical
type he is the choleric man—pale of complexion, exceedingly
fiery in spirit, prone to anger and bitter jesting. Giving
way to this humour, he is carried naturally into blasphemy

---

[4] See above, page 14.

and madness, which consume him in the fire of his own fury. An exalted dream of worldly glory furnishes his motive. Supporting it is the awful notion that he has a heaven-guided and heaven-guarded destiny.

I

Tamburlaine's rise, though rapid and wonderful, accords with the natural laws of success laid down by Machiavelli. The Persian monarchy is a "maimed Emperie." It is unable to protect its provinces from pirates, and it is threatened by mutinies within. Its braggadocio king, the witless and dainty Mycetes, is openly flouted. Tamburlaine and his fellow thieves have been enabled to start on their career of pillage because of the degeneracy of the times. Fortune offers the opportunity; and Tamburlaine, to use the phrase in which Du Bartas describes Nimrod's similar rise, simply snatches Fortune by the tresses. At the beginning he has a competitor in Cosroe, but Cosroe lacks the Lion-like and Fox-like *virtù* which Tamburlaine possesses.

If Fortune furnishes Tamburlaine opportunity, Beauty provides him boldness. Zenocrate, seized in the course of his brigandage, is a pretty piece of spoil. Tamburlaine, apparently smitten with love at first sight, begins to dream of making her empress of Asia, and ransacking the world's riches to place at her feet. Emboldened by her beauty, he spectacularly discards his shepherd's weeds for the garb of a warrior. Then his spirit stretches itself, like a lion stretching its paws; and "Affecting thoughts coequall with the cloudes," he announces that Zenocrate shall be kept captive, while he demonstrates to her that he can be a Lord and Emperor.

His treatment of Zenocrate furnishes interesting illustration of his character. Totally unconcerned for the fact that she is already betrothed, he tells her flatly she must grace his bed. Then, rebuffed by her disdain, he employs flattery which is brilliant and gorgeous. In lines that are as enchanting as any that Marlowe ever wrote, Tamburlaine magnificently declares:

> *Zenocrate*, louelier than the Loue of *Ioue*,
> Brighter than is the siluer Rhodope,
> Fairer than whitest snow of Scythian hils,
> Thy person is more woorth to *Tamburlaine*,
> Than the possession of the Persean Crowne,
> Which gratious starres haue promist at my birth,
> A hundreth Tartars shall attend on thee,
> Mounted on Steeds, swifter than *Pegasus*.
> Thy Garments shall be made of Medean silke,
> Enchast with precious iuelles of mine owne:
> More rich and valurous than *Zenocrates*.
> With milke-white Hartes vpon an Iuorie sled,
> Thou shalt be drawen amidst the frosen Pooles,
> And scale ysie mountaines lofty tops:
> Which with thy beautie will be soone resolu'd.
> My martiall prises with fiue hundred men,
> Wun on the fiftie headed *Vuolgas* waues,
> Shall all we offer to *Zenocrate*,
> And then my selfe to faire *Zenocrate*.

Provided thus with motive, we next have action—heroic and crafty action worthy of a man of *virtù*. Theridamas is approaching with a thousand horse, and Tamburlaine has only five hundred foot. Brilliantly he decides:

> Lay out our golden wedges to their view,
> That their reflexions may amaze the Perseans.
> ...Keep all your standings, and not stir a foote,
> My selfe will bide the danger of the brunt.

Then, using also the wedges of golden arguments, in "perswasions more patheticall" than speech of Hermes, he cracks Theridamas' loyalty and wins him as a follower. The speech begins with words of flattery and promise, then boasts his "charmed skin" and heaven-guarded destiny, finally returns again to the dream of sovereignty, the prospect that from their mean estate they may rise to be Consuls of the earth and, even more, "immortal like the Gods." Theridamas is enchanted by the argument. "But shall I prooue a Traitor to my king?" he asks. Tamburlaine gives the strategic reply: "No, but the trustie friend of *Tamburlaine.*"

Act II exhibits the folly of Mycetes, the folly of Cosroe, and the craft of Tamburlaine. For the moment Cosroe is allowed to bask in a dream of conquest with which Tamburlaine entertains him. Crowned by Tamburlaine after an easily won battle over Mycetes, he sets out, as he supposes, to sit upon his brother's throne. But Tamburlaine has "onely made him king to make vs sport." A touch of the fever, "Is it not braue to be a king, Techelles?" is enough to persuade his glory-thirsty followers to treachery against Cosroe. Explained in Machiavellian terms, Cosroe's fall is due to his mistake in calling on the help of a powerful rival. But an Elizabethan must have viewed it as an illustration of the wretched end of usurpers.

As Cosroe lies dying and upbraiding his erstwhile ally, Tamburlaine justifies his action in a speech that has become famous:

> Nature that fram'd vs of foure Elements,
> Warring within our breasts for regiment,
> Doth teach vs all to haue aspyring minds:
> Our soules, whose faculties can comprehend
> The wondrous Architecture of the world:
> And measure euery wandring plannets course,
> Still climing after knowledge infinite,
> And alwaies moouing as the restles Spheres,
> Wils vs to weare our selues and neuer rest,
> Vntill we reach the ripest fruit of all,
> That perfect blisse and sole felicitie,
> The sweet fruition of an earthly crowne.

The words epitomize Tamburlaine's naturalistic philosophy. Barbarian that he is, he knows no other felicity; for Nature is his only teacher. Undisturbed by Cosroe's dying curse, he takes the crown of Persia and puts it on.

Tamburlaine's meeting with Bajazet offers splendid opportunity for spectacle. Also, it illustrates how God employs one wicked man to subdue another. Bajazet, the mighty Turk is laying siege to Christian Constantinople. Tamburlaine is ambitious for further conquests. Bajazet boasts himself "The high and highest Monarke of the world." Tamburlaine proclaims himself "the Scourge and Wrath of God." Facing each other on the stage, the champions spit out threats, boasts, proud orations; then go to battle, leaving their respective queens to continue the reciprocal abuse in language fit for so great an occasion. Zenocrate, with pagan conscience like that of Helen or Criseyde, has inconstantly shifted her love to Tamburlaine. Now proudly wearing the conqueror's crown, she behaves in a manner befitting the mate of a warrior.

Tamburlaine is victor by the fortunes of war. Bajazet accepts his fate manfully, but disconsolately. There is for him the bitter thought that his enemies the Christians will rejoice in his overthrow; and that Mahomet has failed him. His humiliation furnishes spectacular illustration of the instability of worldly Fortune. By the moralist it can also be interpreted as Bajazet's deserved punishment for his cruelty and pride.

Act IV exhibits the spectacle of Tamburlaine triumphant; and it is a scene which reveals his fiendish mind and insatiable passion for conquest. Using for his footstool the mighty Bajazet, "Whose feet the kings of *Affrica* haue kist," the conqueror mounts to his throne. Then, established in his chair of state, he proclaims in language of cosmic symbolism the significance of this moment in his career. His rise, he says, has been like that of a planet, which having now reached the meridian line proposes to send up its beams in challenge to the sun. The seizure of Bajazet is but the first

blow in a campaign to disturb heaven: this act has struck
fire from heaven, and has made the welkin crack.   It
signalizes the beginning of greater heaven-jarring exploits:

> ere I martch to wealthy *Persea,*
> Or leaue Damascus and th' Egyptian fields,
> As was the fame of *Clymenes* brain-sicke sonne,
> That almost brent the Axeltree of heauen,
> So shall our swords, our lances and our shot
> Fill all the aire with fiery meteors.
> Then when the Sky shall waxe as red as blood,
> It shall be said, I made it red my selfe,
> To make me think of nought but blood and war.

The lines are Marlowe's advertisement that Tamburlaine's
career, which up until now has been like the rising of a star,
will henceforth begin to burn madly like a blazing meteor,
to the confusion of the whole world-order.

Tamburlaine, as he himself announces, is behaving like
a Scourge of God.   This moral fact is brought to our attention also by the Souldan of Egypt, who while gathering
an expedition to rescue his daughter Zenocrate, calls Tamburlaine

> Compact of Rapine, Pyracie, and spoile,
> The Scum of men, the hate and Scourge of God.

The Souldan also calls him "presumptuous Beast" and "Cali-
donian Boare"—for the significance of which appellations
we have a guide in Chapman's *Hymnus in Noctem.*   "Cale-
donian boars" is the title Chapman gives to "self-love's
paramours" who, bent on slaughter, ruin "the fruitful disposition of the earth." [5]

The bloodiness of Tamburlaine's triumphing is presented
imaginatively in scene 4 of Act IV.   The time, we are told,

---

[5] *Poems,* p. 5.

is the second day of the siege of Damascus. Bloody colors
are displayed by the tents. Tamburlaine and his followers
are drinking blood-red wine to the God of war. Though
there is no actual bloodshed on stage, the spirit of the scene
is that of a Thyestean banquet; for Tamburlaine invites Bajazet to butcher and eat his wife Zabina.

Secondly, the scene reveals that Tamburlaine's thirst for
conquest is now so great that no natural influence can allay
it. In reply to Zenocrate's plea for a truce with Damascus,
Tamburlaine insists he is just beginning a project to remake
the map of the world, and that Egypt and Arabia must be
his. Therefore, besides being a banquet of blood, it is also
a banquet of crowns. The crowns are shared symbolically
in the form of pastries, which Tamburlaine hands to his
disciples. Concluding the ceremony Tamburlaine outlines
the "holy" work which awaits them:

> when holy Fates
> Shall stablish me in strong *Egyptia,*
> We meane to traueile to th' Antartique Pole,
> Conquering the people vnderneath our feet,
> And be renowm'd, as neuer Emperours were.

Act V presents even more dramatic illustration of the
conqueror's bloody cruelty of heart. It is now the last day of
the siege of Damascus. The governor of the city hopes that
the sight of lovely virgins supplicating for mercy may be
"the means the ouerweighing heauens / Haue kept to quallifie these hot extremes" of Tamburlaine's wrath. Tamburlaine, like the true Machiavellian prince, makes show of pity,
yet is entirely ruthless. Clad in the devil's colors of black, he
jests with the white-clad virgins across the edge of his
sword, and in the name of his "honor" commands his
horsemen

> To chardge these Dames, and shew my seruant death.
> Sitting in scarlet on their armed speares.

As the virgins are led away he tells us that no wealth of Paradise or power of Beauty can alter his martial customs.

It shows Marlowe's remarkable dramatic instinct that from this ordering of the slaughter of the virgins Tamburlaine is made to turn immediately to a courtly soliloquy in praise of Beauty and of Zenocrate. He whom we have just beheld so empty of true compassion, now pretends that Zenocrate's "sorrows lay more siege vnto my soule, / Than all my Army to Damascus walles." Having just put beauty to the sword, he now takes time for "Beauties iust applause," for the selfish reason that

> euery warriour that is rapt in loue,
> Of fame, of valour, and of victory
> Must needs haue beauty beat on his conceites.

Then, from the exhibition of Tamburlaine's effeminate sorrows, we turn to the awfully actual sorrows of Bajazet and Zabina. The psychological misery of these unfortunate captives is extreme. They tell us they endure virtual Hell, because they suffer dismal torments without hope. They lose faith both in Fortune and in Providence; and in the spirit of this fatalism they dash out their brains against the bars which incage them. Their madness is the madness of despair; their tragedy arises partly from Fortune, partly from the weakness of their own Faith.

The spectacle of their torture, in accord with Elizabethan dramatic method, serves a moral purpose. Together with the sight of the slaughter of the virgins of Damascus, it causes Zenocrate to feel pity and fear. In the manner of a Chorus she utters the timely warning:

> Ah *Tamburlaine,* my loue, sweet *Tamburlaine,*
> That fights for Scepters and for slippery crowns,
> Behold the Turk and his great Emperesse.

Part I of the drama ends, however, without visible prospect of Tamburlaine's fall. His victorious return from battle against the Souldan seems to confirm the view that he can bind fast Fortune's wheel. Exalted with the glory of unchecked power, he boasts that he has made the heavens weep blood, and hell to overflow with the souls he has dispatched. In this furious mood, the sight of bloody Bajazet and Zabina raises no remorse. Their fate, he says, is a fit mirror in which may be seen his "honor, that consists in shedding blood."

Nevertheless, Zenocrate's beauty has temporary power to calm the fury of his sword. Momentarily, he proposes to hang his weapons on "Alcides poste" and bring Part I of his career to fitting conclusion by a marriage with the beauty who has emboldened him in his career of conquests.

II

Whatever
Vice is sustain'd withal, turns pestilent fever.[6]

The unity of the two parts of Tamburlaine has not always been recognized.[7] Romantic critics like to regard Part II as an afterthought, appended in haste to capitalize on the success of Part I.[8] But if the prologue is read through attentively to the end, it will be noted that the "generall welcomes" given Part I

Hath Made our Poet pen his second part,
Wher death cuts off the progres of his pomp,
And murdrous Fates throwes al his triumphs down.

[6] "An Invective against Ben Jonson," Chapman's *Poems,* p. 432.

[7] The unity of the Tamburlaine story seems to have been recognized, however, by the publishers. The three earliest editions (1590, 1593, 1597) contain the two parts with continuous signatures and bound together without separate title page for Part II.

[8] In any case, it cannot have been written long after Part I. Sir Edmund Chambers has discovered an allusion to the shooting of the Governor of Babylon in Part II, which indicates that it was being acted as early as November, 1587. See *London Times Lit. Supp.,* Aug. 28, 1930, p. 684.

The lines suggest that the poet's motives in writing Part II were not wholly commercial. There is the implication, at least, that Tamburlaine's history needs to be brought to its appropriate end, and that Fortune's wheel must now complete its circuit.

If the main problem of the first part was, What are the factors by which Tamburlaine can be brought to the highest worldly success? the problem of the second part is, How shall this proud atheist be brought to his deserved overthrow? To begin the second part, Marlowe entertains us with the suggestion that perhaps Tamburlaine may be overcome by a league of Christian and Mohammedan armies—representing, we may suppose, the forces of "religion" against the "atheism" of Tamburlaine. But the plan comes to disastrous failure through the perfidy of the Christians.

The episode of the Christians' perjury serves also as an *exemplum* of God's punishment of sin. The sin is so glaring it offends all religious faith—both Christian and Mohammedan. Like many a passage in Elizabethan books of moral philosophy, the episode seems to declare that Christians might well learn piety, humility, and sanity from the pagan Orcanes. Turk though he be, Orcanes has enough faith to believe that there is a God who punishes wickedness.

If Marlowe intends Sigismund as the mirror of the Christian of Elizabethan days, the picture is not at all complimentary; yet it is ultimately hopeful. Sigismund comes to his senses, is repentant for his sin, and has hope therefore of a second life through God's mercy. By contrast, the manner in which Tamburlaine meets the fact of defeat and death is conspicuously pagan. Sigismund's career serves as dramatic foil to Tamburlaine's, because, like Tamburlaine, Sigismund has attempted to take God's vengeance into his own hands. But whereas Sigismund, when checked, recognizes Divine Justice, Tamburlaine sees merely Fate.

Tamburlaine's history in Part II continues from Part I the

bloody story of new enterprises and fresh victories. His followers report to him amazing additions of territory they have conquered. Later, he has victory over four kings. Then, capturing Babylon, he is emperor of the whole Eastern world; and Callapine, who offers the only apparent threat to his power, is speedily routed. Thus Tamburlaine's military fortunes reach a very pinnacle of success, and seem to substantiate his early boast that he is the darling of the gods.

But this story of conquest is not the chief theme of Part II. The important episodes, as the title page of the 1606 Quarto points out for us, are three: 1) "his impassionate furie, for the death of his Lady and Loue, faire Zenocrate;" 2) "his forme of exhortation and discipline to his three Sonnes;" and 3) "the manner of his owne death." Let us look at each of these.

An early scene involving Tamburlaine, Zenocrate, and their three sons dramatizes the fact that Tamburlaine's whole desire for his sons is to have them succeed him in his Eumenidean office of fury and terror. Marlowe does not propose to have us ignorant of the "spiritual" legacy Tamburlaine is transmitting to his progeny. The father instructs his sons:

> Be al a scourge and terror to the world,
> Or els you are not sons of *Tamburlaine*.

The third son, Calyphas, who asks instead to "Let me accompany my gracious mother," is rebuked as "Bastardly boy, sprung from some coward's loins, / And not the issue of great Tamburlaine!" The father adds:

> For he shall weare the crowne of *Persea*,
> ... [Who] in the furrowes of his frowning browes,
> Harbors reuenge, war, death and cruelty.

It is a life for which the two sons, Celebinus and Amyras, declare themselves fully ready. They are willing to make their way to the title of kingship, though it be through pools of blood up to the chin.

The instruction is renewed in a second scene between father and sons following the death of their mother Zenocrate. This time there is a ceremony of dedication to the life of warfare, made and sealed between Tamburlaine and his two warlike sons by a covenant of blood.[9] Tamburlaine cuts his own arm, saying:

> Blood is the God of Wars rich liuery.

To this he adds the invitation to join him in the rite:

> Come boyes and with your fingers search my wound,
> In my blood wash all your hands at once,
> While I sit smiling to behold the sight.

Celebinus volunteers:

> Giue me a wound, father.

And Amyras joins in:

> And me another, my Lord.

Calyphas, the third son, who does not join in the blood covenant nor in the battle against the Turkish kings, is stabbed by his father as an act of "martiall iustice."

At the time of Tamburlaine's death there is a final scene between father and sons. Having pointed out to them the wide expanse of kingdoms of which he has made himself master, and having urged them to the conquest of what remains yet unsubdued, Tamburlaine says:

---

[9] The rite is ancient. Tertullian (*Apology*, IX) taunts pagan Rome with the fact that in his day "blood consecrated to Bellona, blood drawn from a punctured thigh, seals initiation into the rites of that goddess." Such a blood-covenant became, in the eyes of Renaissance Christians, the Devil's covenant—in contrast to the true blood-covenant made by Christ on the cross. Note how the rite is used in *Faustus* and in Barnabe Barnes, *The Diuils Charter* (1607).

> My flesh deuided in your precious shapes,
> Shal still retaine my spirit, though I die,
> And liue in all your seeds immortally.

The lines point to the Senecan theme of hereditary sin.

The second episode of import, Tamburlaine's fury at the death of Zenocrate, plainly exhibits how God can scourge the Scourging conqueror. The means of Tamburlaine's punishment are his own immoderate passions. We behold him "Rauing, impatient, desperate and mad," threatening to

> breake the frame of heauen,
> Batter the shining pallace of the Sun,
> And shiuer all the starry firmament:

because Death has taken Zenocrate from him. He has never before suffered loss to any power heavenly or earthly. Distracted to explain so unexpected an intrusion, Tamburlaine attributes it to the malice of the skies, or again, to the envy of amorous Jove. The holocaust of Larissa's towers is his appropriately vain attempt at retaliation. Like a Senecan madman he invokes fiery meteors, flying dragons, lightning, and Furies from Lethe and Styx.

After Zenocrate's death the conqueror becomes increasingly savage, taking all his joy in "the fire of this martiall flesh." The notion that he is the Scourge of God and Terror of the World becomes an obsession, and he tells us:

> I must apply myself to fit those tearmes,
> In war, in blood, in death, in crueltie.

Increasing madness shows itself in the violence of his language—"this effeminate brat" he calls his son Calyphas; and he threatens to make the captive kings bellow like "an heard of lusty Cymbrian bulls." While driving two of the kings in his chariot, he shouts:

> Holla, ye pampered Iades of *Asia*:
> What, can ye draw but twenty miles a day?

The spectacle, which is a conventional one for illustrating Ambition, offers Tamburlaine dramatic outlet for his fury.

The fits of madness which visit Tamburlaine in Part II reveal the psychological punishment which, according to Renaissance moral philosophy, automatically accompanies uncontrolled passion. Though his Fortune is so great that he goes unscarred by mortal steel, yet he cannot escape the laws of natural retributive punishment, prophesied by the king of Jerusalem in the lines:

> Thy victories are growne so violent,
> That shortly heauen, fild with the meteors
> Of blood and fire thy tyrannies haue made,
> Will poure down blood and fire on thy head:
> Whose scalding drops wil pierce thy seething braines,
> And with our bloods, reuenge our bloods on thee.

With the capture of Babylon, Tamburlaine's violent fury reaches the point of blasphemy—what Burton, quoting Melanchthon, called "monstrosam melancholiam." Fulfilling the pattern of a Scourge of God, Tamburlaine boasts himself proudly against God and burns the Scriptures. Then, within a few minutes, he finds himself strangely distempered. His physician reports that his lively spirits are parched—that is, his humours have suffered adustion. The king of Soria's prophecy that Tamburlaine's "cruel heart" would "Drie vp with anger and consume with heat" is fulfilled. God is now casting his Scourge into the fire.

Tamburlaine's "seething braines" hysterically urge impossible battles, and challenge the chimera of Death. The proposal to "set black streamers in the firmament" fitly climaxes a career of ambitious Titanism—and it points the moral significance of the utterance to remember from *Faustus* that God has reserved the firmament for the life-proclaiming streamers of Christ's red blood. Tamburlaine would reverse the whole moral order of the universe by planting in the firmament his own death-proclaiming banners of black.

There is dramatic irony in the fact that while Death thus "throwes al his triumphs down" Tamburlaine calls for a map and recounts his record of conquest. As it stirs in him again the dream of "golden Mines" and "rocks of Pearle," there breaks in also, like the tolling of a knell, the recurrent "And shall I die . . . ?"

At last accepting with Stoic fatalism the fact of death, Tamburlaine invests his sons with their legacy—his Scourge, his crown, his spirit, and his Machiavellian wisdom.

Certainly these ten acts of *Tamburlaine* offer one of the most grandly moral spectacles in the whole realm of English drama.

INDEX

INDEX

Abel, 151.
Absalom, 100.
Acontius, Jacobus, 29.
Adam, 40, 79n., 230.
Agamemnon, 164n.
Agathocles, 176, 212.
Aggas, Edward, 40n.
Agrippa, Cornelius, 33-34.
Agrippa, Marcus, 119.
Agydas, 153, 167.
Alexander the Great, 141n., 164-65, 172, 202, 211, 227, 231-32.
Alexander VI, Pope, 42n., 176n.
Alexander, Sir William, 14, 193, 205.
Allen, D. C., 40n., 137n.
Allen, J. W., 39n.
Amiot, Jacques, 228.
Amurath II, 157-58.
Anatomy of Melancholy, see Burton, Robert.
Anderson, Ruth L., 95n.
Antichrist, 43, 155, 166n., 176, 216.
Aquinas, see Thomas, St.
Ariosto, 168.
Aristotle, 16, 26, 28-29, 35n., 38-39, 54-57, 96n., 115, 117n., 215n.
Arminianism, 24, 73n., 82.
Ascham, Roger, 48.
Ashton, Peter, 109, 122n., 133.
Athanasius, St., 57.
Attila, 110, 129-31, 219.
Augustine, St., 27, 62, 64, 90, 114.

Babylon, 13, 112, 172, 254.
Bacon, Francis, 28n.
Baines, Richard, 9, 50n., 70.
Bainton, R. H., 29n., 40n., 57n.
Bajazet, 2n., 14, 138-40, 146-48, 161n., 248, 250-51.
Bakeless, John, 5-7, 16-17, 132n., 206n.
Baldwin, William, *Mirror for Magistrates,* 17, 122n., 239; *A Treatise of Morall Phylosophye,* 27, 114, 163.

Bale, John, 99, 172n.
Bang, W., 122n.
Barckley, Sir Richard, 12.
Barnes, Barnabe, 176n., 236-37, 255n.
Baro, Peter, 24.
Baughan, D. E., 48.
Beard, Thomas, 21, 42, 86, 92, 100.
Beau, J., 50n., 55n.
Beck, Hans, 47n.
Belleforest, François de, 168n.
Belus, 165n., 172.
Bergen, Henry, 165n.
Bessarion, 28n.
Beza, Theodore, 25.
Bhattacherje, M., 234n.
Blake, William, 9n.
Boas, F. S., 1, 6, 119n., 144.
Boccaccio, 16n., 79n., 87, 99.
Bodenham, John, 172n., 230, 236n.
Bodin, Jean, 41n., 174n.
Boehme, Jacob, 39n.
Boethius, 73n., 84, 90.
Bonfinius, Antonius, 156-59.
Born, L. K., 141n.
Bowes, Thomas, 13n., 27, 38, 43, 114.
Boyer, C. V., 215.
Bradbrook, Muriel C., 10n., 70n.
Brandl, Alois, 197n., 208-09, 215n.
Breen, Quirinus, 25n., 47.
Breton, Nicholas, 41n., 111n.
Brie, Friedrich, 31n., 43n.
Bright, Timothy, 220-21.
Brooke, C. F. T., 52n., 179.
Brown, Archibald, 101n.
Brown, Beatrice D., 166n.
Buchanan, George, 24, 101.
Buckley, G. T., 31n., 50n., 51, 65n.
Bullen, A. H., 178, 180, 243n.
Burd, L. A., 215n.
Burton, Robert, 23n., 42n., 43n., 44-46, 111n., 152, 202, 219, 221, 237n.
Bush, Douglas, 25, 29.
Byron, George Gordon, Lord, 9n.

261